SOVIET PERESTROIKA, 1985–1993
RUSSIA'S ROAD TO DEMOCRACY

EDITED BY
JOHN F.N. BRADLEY

EAST EUROPEAN MONOGRAPHS, BOULDER
DISTRIBUTED BY COLUMBIA UNIVERSITY PRESS, NEW YORK

1995

EAST EUROPEAN MONOGRAPHS, NO. CDXXXV

Table of Contents:

Historical Introduction..1
  John Bradley
Gorbachev: The Politics of Perestroika...17
  Michel Tatu
The 19th CPSU Programme...31
Perestroika and The Armed Forces..37
  Jean-Christophe Romer
Perestroika and The Nationalities..45
  Helene Carrere d'Encausse
France and Perestroika..61
  Anne de Tinguy
Perestroika and European Strategy...79
  Dominique David
Perestroika and Economic Reforms..87
  Jacques Sapir
Perestroika and Constitutionalism..95
  Dimitry Georges Lavroff
Perestroika and Central Asia...115
  Catherine Slater
Perestroika and Democratization..129
  Vladimir Pastukhov
Perestroika and Russia...139
  Gerhard Simon
Perestroika and Czechoslovakia...151
  Alexandr Ort
Perestroika and Germany...163
  Wilfried von Bredow
Perestroika and Soviet Foreign Policy..169
  Michal Klima
The August Coup D'etat: End of Perestroika....................................183
  Nicholas Bradley
Perestroika and The Warsaw Pact..197
  Zdenek Matejka

Authors:

John Bradley is professor of international politics at VSE, Prague

Michel Tatu is columnist with Le Monde, Paris

Jean-Christophe Romer is professor of defence studies at the university of Strasbourg I

Helene Carrere d'Encausse is member of the French Academy and member of the European Parliament

Anne de Tinguy is a researcher at the Fondation de sciences politiques, Paris

Dominique David is a special assistant to the director, Institut de Relations Internationales, Paris

Jacques Sapir is associate professor of economics at the Hautes Ecoles d'Etudes economiques et sociales, Paris

Catherine Slater is a writer and international lawyer, London

Vladimir Pastukhov is a senior researcher of comparative politics, Academy of Sciences, Moscow

Gerhard Simon is professor of Soviet history at the Bundesinstitut fur internationale Studien, Cologne

Alexandr Ort is professor of international law at VSE, Prague

Michal Klima is assistant professor at VSE, Prague

Nicholas Bradley is a freelance writer and university researcher

Zdenek Matejka is a diplomat and the last secretary general of WPT

Historical Introduction

I.

The Slavs were one of the last European tribal societies to establish their own states and while the racial origins of the 'Bulgarian Slavs' are uncertain, they were certainly the first to create formal state structures, aided and abetted by the Byzantine Greeks. The other Slavs, Western and Eastern, followed only slowly the Bulgarian example. However, strictly speaking their principalities were in the main established for them by Frankish, Scandinave or Norman outsiders. The Slav populations themselves continued to live throughout the late eighth and ninth centuries, when the processus had taken place, in what is termed 'tribal democracy'. Despite pressures in the west, chiefly from the neighboring Germanic tribes and in the east from the Persians and Khazars, who had already become settled and formed stable states long before them, the Slavs preferred to live over many unrecorded centuries in the 'primitive anarchy' of the vast forests, which the romantic historians of the 19th century likened to 'people's democracy'. For ages they practiced the most undeveloped form of agriculture, namely the 'slash/burn' exploitation of forests. Consequently they were regularly forced to move on, when the soil of their clearings became exhausted. Although this form of agricultural exploitation was supplemented by hunting and honey production, it never rose above the level of self-sufficiency. Thus, they did not establish, even among themselves, a bartering system of trading, which activity was again left to outsiders. In addition Slavic communities, the miry in Russian, or **plemia**, meaning a group of families, were never large enough to make the interchange of goods worthwhile. Thus, undoubtedly geographic isolation, economic 'underdevelopment' (Gorbachev's zastoy?) and above all the absence of trading enterprise were at the root of the general lagging behind of the Slavs in Eastern Europe and particularly on the Russian plains, right up to the borders of Asia. Trade routes from Scandinavia to Byzantium and the Middle East which crossed these neglected 'forest territories', remained under the control of foreigners: Varengians, Khazars, Jews, and Arabs. Another factor contributing to 'political' underdevelopment of the Slavs were the patriarchal or matriarchal tribal customs widespread particularly among the Russians.

These tended to diffuse power among male or female family groups and precluded the rise of strong native leaders. As far as the trading foreigners were concerned the Slavs and their civilisation appeared to them as 'uninteresting' or 'exotic'. They seemed to them as an inexhaustible source of slaves, wax, honey and furs needed for their trade. They simply happened to live along the trade-routes with the real centers of civilization in the Levant and southeastern Europe.

Inevitably, as trading developed and prospered, a strong leader with political ambitions did emerge in the East. Without surprise he was of Norse-Scandinavian descent (Hroerekr-in Russian Riurik). Prior to 882 A. D. this self-styled Prince Oleg (Helgi) Riurik had gained control of the major fortified trading posts-towns stretching from the bay of Riga, through to lake Ladoga and the river Volkhov, down to Smolensk and Kiev (Koenugard). In 882 he also added his dominion the Slav tribes along the 'Greek route' annexing them to his trading empire. Henceforth the Rus, as it was called, had a basic state organisation of a unique sort. A prince-leader together with a group of professional warriors (the Druzhina) ran an international economic enterprise and ruled in a loose fashion over the primitive Slav tribes and to a certain degree protected them against Eastern invasion. In winters the Riuriks busied themselves collecting tribute from the Slav population; as soon as weather allowed them it was trading again. Only after the adoption of Christianity this itenerant government becomes a truly 'real modern state' in contemporary terms. Christianity paradoxically forced on the Slavs a settled existence. In addition it separated them from the Mongol nomads and the Khazar empire. Moreover, as an ideology Christianity gave them links with the Greeks, who set up for them a state-church network with local administration, promulgated certain moral rules, infused in them a sense of nationalism and provided them with a mission going far beyond trade.

This dual development of state and society in Kievan Russia was more or less complete in the late 10th century. Prince Vladimir, who subsequently was called the Great, and was also proclaimed a saint by the Orthodox Church in recognition of his role in adopting Orthodox Christianity from the Byzantine Greeks, was thus the founder of a real Russian state. Nowadays it is still debated whether this peculiar amalgam of 'Slav tribal democracy', consisting of the 'veche,' (people's assembly), organized around fortified places and the princely trader-leader supported by his elite **Druzhina** amounted to a real state. However, it was a definite advance on tribal anarchy which solved problems with genicide. Thus, the Varengians enforced peace among the Slav tribesmen, meted out justice, while at the same time, collecting tribute for their exercise of power from the people. The bonds between ruler and the territorial kingdom were tenuous and ill-defined. For a long time after Vladimir's establishment of a 'modern state' his successors continued to use brute force against the princes and the people alike to maintain themselves in power.

Notwithstanding the Riurik dynasty's recourse to 'iron and blood,' its rule gave the Rus at least a semblance of statedom, in form comparable to the other contemporary states, be they feudal in Europe, or oriental tyrannies in the Middle East and elsewhere. Yet, because of this looseness and imprecision Vladimir had failed to create a dynastic state to serve and protect the Slavonic people. From the inception it was a hybrid structure incorporating certain features of Latin feudalism, Greek theocracy and Persian despotism. In his hurry he shortcircuited social, constitutional, economic and political development, which elsewhere in Europe had taken centuries. Instead he used naked violence to incorporate both princes and tribes into this quite unique state. The same means were used to 'convert' princes and peoples to the new transcendental ideology. Everyone was forced to be baptized whether he liked it or not. Symbolically the old wooden gods were thrown into the Dniepr and that seemed all. In return for these 'revolutionary' changes the Slavic tribes were promised security and prosperity. Notwithstanding, the Christian prince, Vladimir, and his successors continued to rule as despotically as before baptism, literally possessing their subjects together with their territory. Moreover, this form of government was enforced on everyone, noble or common, with great brutality. Unfortunately for the Slavs, who submitted only reluctantly to the will of the Riurik princes, the promises of protection against invasions of the nomadic eastern hordes, nor of a greater share in prosperity were kept. Neither was the dynastic problem of succession resolved sapping the state's power continually. Thus, from its very formation the Russian state was in need of re-structuring.

Historically speaking each time an overwhelming challenge arose from inside or outside of Russia, the kniaz, tsar, imperator, supreme leader (**vozhd**) or simple revolutionary leader would try to modernize this curious hybrid state to cope with such challenges. Thus, many **perestroikas** were launched by rulers to avoid perishing with outmoded state structures or improve social and economic prosperity. Needless to say many perestroikas went wrong and several examples from history will be discussed further. However, at inception Vladimir's modernisation failed to include primogeniture as a rule for succession. Given his brutal determination, a pre-requisite for any **perestroika**, he could have forced this 'efficient power transmission principle' on his family prior to his death, but did not. As a consequence of this lack of foresight his successors could only ascend the throne of Kiev after much family bloodletting. The new patrimonial Russian state had a vital flaw inscribed in it from the very beginning.

After Vladimir's death in 1015, the Kievan state which reflected the disordered Russian reality was neither a centralized Byzantine theocracy, nor a loose feudal Frankish kingdom, nor an oriental tyranny, even less the 'primitive tribal democracy' about which the Slavs were to romanticize for several centuries. However, the peculiar result was an ecclectic marriage of contemporary political, economic, security and societal elements prevalent in the East as well as in the North, some even in the West. Further features were to be added to this curious patrimonial entity during the centuries of Tartar rule. This made Russian state truly unique, a state where total proprietorial power (state=dvor) was exercised by a sovereign-gosudar without laws or institutional barriers -- only slightly mitigated by the moral precepts of Orthodox Christianity. The Riuriks farmed out tribute-tax collection to the Druzhina-nobles, clergy, and even foreigners other than the

Varengians. Immediately after 1015, factional (succession) conflicts broke out leading to a gradual, but inevitable, decline of the 'grand princedom' of Kiev. With succession unregulated each and every prince had a chance to become supreme leader, hence the prolonged internecine fighting; brother killing brothers, uncles, nephews, and grandchildren, if need be. In addition the Kievan Rus was devastated from the early 13th century onwards by eastern nomadic hordes. In 1240 its capital, Kiev, was totally destroyed by the Tartars-Mongols. Greek trade also declined because of western, mainly Venitian, intervention in the Eastern Mediterranean. Moreover, western parts of Kievan Russia were gradually overrun by the Hungarians, Lithuanians and Poles. As a result of the weakening of Kievan centre the northwestern parts of the princedom, Pskov and Novgorod, became practically independent, while in the East Moscow, under Tartar rule, began its long march towards becoming a new political center.

The Great Russians of Muscovy were forced to rebuild their state from the scratch. As in the Kievan past it was a princedom without natural borders facing the same allpowerful Eastern enemies. Ultimately the same patrimonial state as of old emerged, though the succession lesson of the Kievan Rus had been learned: the rules of succession were based on primogeniture. However, the task of re-building slow and was rude. To start with Moscow as the new center of power had to liberate itself from the Mongol rule and this liberation alone took some 200 years. At the same time it had to establish its own administration throughout the Slavic territory and only then try to raise the new state to the level of development of its contemporary neighbors.

After 1480, once the Mongols had been decisively beaten, the Moscow-based state began to take great strides towards catching up with the rest of the Christian world. This continuous process meant that the ruler of Muscovy had to modernize his kingdom in order to keep its eastern enemies at bay and to catch up with other Christian princes. However, most immediately, the **Russian kniaz** was forced to meet the challenges of its western neighbors by imitation rather then re-structuring. Like them in order to achieve internal political stability, develop the still primitive economy, and bring about general prosperity a permanent policy of expansion had to be pursued. Since Russia itself lacked fertile soils, mineral resources, and was largely landlocked all these factors had to be sought where they could be found: in the south and west. Thus, apart from systematic expansion modernizations were partial and ecclectic in response to particular problems arising from time to time. Certain ideas for modernisation came from the west, others were adopted from the occupiers, Tartars. In the 16th century when the Russian army was finally equipped with artillery bought from the west, it brought to an end the security threat which the Tartars continued to constitute. Yet, the inefficient Tartar tax system was kept by the Russians, as it was thought the most effective for the conditions in Russia. Nonetheless, the new-old system failed to raise enough revenue even to pay for the 'restructured' army. Here lies the key to another Russian paradox, which henceforth would reappear throughout its history: even security modernisation cannot not be paid for by the rulers, if not with foreign aid.

As a result, on the one hand, Russia could not pay for a fundamental or sustained modernization herself. On the other hand conquest, expansion or massive foreign loans could only pay for the most basic restructuring. Since the fifteenth century this systemetic fact has not changed. However, in the 15th century the hybrid patrimonial system, enriched with certain techniques of Tartar tyranny, seemed flourishing enough to enable at least the ruler to enrich himself. Consequently the more 'ambitious' rulers took the wealth they desired from their subjects only to gratify their own personal whims or greed, without creating anything in return. Within the system they were omnipotent and no rules nor social contracts existed to prevent them from acting as they did. They either repaid the despoiled subjects with conquered land or had them killed to cancel such 'debts'. Another example of the gratuitedness of the patrimonialm system is the Russian army. Borrowing from the West the ruler was able to create a professional army (streltsy) equipped with western artillery in order to destroy Tartar power. Yet, when the outdated udelny system failed to produce enough taxes to pay for this modern standing army, 'professional' warriors were forced to fight in profitless foreign wars or conduct widespread campaigns of terror against their own population. Modernisation had always had only limited objectives and never served to create wealth, but rather indulge personal ambitions of rulers, on the whole obsessed with the security in the East or increasingly in the West. The patrimonial state could never deliver the necessary wealth to the prince, not to mention the citizens, as a result of successful modernisations.

Historically speaking princes-leaders alone decided, if and when such partial restructuring (**perestroikas**) should take place. After all, at least in theory, sovereigns 'owned' the state, and not the subjects who were only free to move about. In time princes found excuses for abolishing even this freedom. Certain tsars had claimed that such restrictions on the freedom of movement were necessary to provide optimal conditions for the Orthodox Church to carry out its evangalising mission. Others sought to improve the "anarchic conditions" in the country resulting from the freedom of movement of princes and peasants alike. More recently the excuse used was central economic planification to prevent the population from moving within and without the imperial territory. Nonetheless, to carry out even these partial perestroikas successfully a single ruler-leader comparable in method and determination to Vladimir's had to emerge. In such conditions the people, the nation or society have either remained indifferent towards such efforts or activily opposed them. Invariably the 'reforming' ruler forced on them with "iron and blood" his arbitrary will taking away their money in taxes and provided little in return. Paradoxically romantic historians in the 19th century described these brutal and arbitrary acts and the seemingly inexhaustible patience of the Russian Slavs tolerating them as a form of 'peculiar Slav' democracy. Western sociologists and political scientists labelled these ways of government as oriental despotism, popular fatalism, social stagnation and economic under-development.

Thus, throughout its history Russian tsars (or their revolutionary successors) had always felt free to launch restructuring of the country as a result of their own decisions and according to their personal ideas, reached invariably under duress, external or internal. This was particularly true after lost wars. But perestroikas could follow a sudden realization of inferiory of their system compared to the political systems of their eastern, southern and western neighbors. Thus they would launch successful or unsuccessful reforms whether they were desirable, necessary, practicable, or not. In whatever case they would claim that such perestroikas were indispensable, and without them the very state would perish. After all the interests and destinies of the people, nation, society and sovereigns or revolutionary leaders were identical. Invariably such aberations were given a 'rational' meaning by messianic ideologies, be they nationalistic or communist. These ideologies inspired a mystical sense of national mission in the mass of the population and helped to surmount vicissitudes brought about by such upheavals- modernizations. However, such perestroikas were never launched to serve the need of the people.

II.

An example of a more fundamental modernization, comparable to modern **perestroikas**, took place in the 16th century in the reign of Tsar (no longer Great Prince) Ivan IV (1533-84), later called the Terrible. It had all the features of past modernizations though it was much more profound than any previous one. Ivan, ascending the throne at the age of three, became surprisingly a strong sovereign, although the vicissitudes of his early childhood deeply influenced his character and made a lasting impression in his mind. These early experiences determined his power methods once on the throne. During his adolescence he surrounded himself with Orthodox clerics and became convinced that he was chosen by God to rule Russia and make her great. In the same way as his ancestors he continued their policies of expansion under the guise of the reunification of Russian territories under his central control. Moreover, he wanted to acomplish the reforms started by his grandfather, Ivan III. At the same time he had to face the same external threats to security as his predecessors and decided to resolve them once for all. To achieve this successfully he had to employ peaceful reform at home, and gather his people around in national consensus against the Mongol threat. But to wage war to implement his security decision and domestic modernization proved incompatible.

In 1549, in an unprecedented gesture of good intentions, Ivan called together a sobor (general assembly) in order to 'reform the Russias through consultation and discussion with the people', whose representatives attended this nationwide jamboree on the tsar's expressed orders. Thus, Ivan III's **Sudebnik**, a new judicial code, was approved by the sobor. Justice advanced considerably. Politically the sobor helped to strengthen Ivan's central power and weaken the power of appanage princes, a prerequisite to waging wars. It was also used to stamp out corruption in the state service. At the same time an elective administration was also established all over Russia, which collected taxes for the center, i.e. the sovereign. The Tsar redistributed land around Moscow and in Central Russia among his personal servants and granted new estates to lesser nobles disadvantaging the established historical nobles, the boyars. Henceforth, armies were raised by the sovereign himself and not by the boyars. The Church supplied such armies with arms and horses, another innovation. In 1551 a synod fundamentally restructured the Orthodox Church to make it fit its new role. But this ecclesiastical perestroika went much farther. It regulated every aspect of Church's life. It even went into details, such as the shape of ecclesiastic beards and the methods of painting of icons. Above all the Church became the servant of the nascent centralised state, which turned out to be the real purpose of Ivan's ecclesiastical reforms, but as a result the Church was weakened economically. It could no longer acquire additional land or property without the tsar's consent. However, according to the Tsar's claims all these reforms were necessary and aimed at creating a 'modern state within which a free and happy society would prosper'.

Whether all the reforms would have been realized according to the Tsar's wishes, remains another of the many unaswerable historical questions. Before any of them could be put to test of Ivan decided first to implement his decision to achieve permanent security in the East and began to wage war. To start with he even thought that the war would help the reforms along, since his armies were remarkably successful. In 1552 the modernized army of streltsy, with the aid of German siege engineers, took Kazan, the Tartar's last remaining stronghold threatening his capital. Four years later his armies inflicted another defeat on the Tartars and Ivan was able to annex Astrakhan, the last stronghold on the Volga river. However, the war dragged on and the exhausted country had to give up reforms. Unfortunately for Russia Ivan failed to conquer the Crimea and thus break the Tartars' power for good. In addition, in 1560 he became involved in additional wars, particularly in Livonia (present-day Latvia and Estonia). These endless and unprofitable wars had weakened Russia considerably and played havoc with his domestic perestroika.

By then the tsar was at odds with everyone, the boyars, the peasants and the clergy. They were all grumbling against the wars. However, Ivan became convinced that the grumbling was directed at him and his dynasty. Because of continuing wars he began to suspect everyone of high treason. He could not understand why they all complained so loudly since his reforms were bringing them 'happiness' and Russia desired security. In his paranoia he began to doubt whether any of the reforms had been implemented? He also became convinced that the sobor was not a practical tool for instituting reform aimed at happiness. Nonetheless, he continued to convoke it so that "the people might ratify his decisions", which, therefore, could not be wrong (1566, 1575). He shrewdly observed that once permitted to assemble the Russian boyars, ecclesiastics, "bourgeois" (burghers) and peasants were not interested in reforms and debating finances, land tenure or restructuring local administration. Instead they seem to have lapsed into "the ancient primitive democracy" of Kievan Russia. To his consternation he had created a huge talkingshop in which Russians talked to no purpose. By then he became subject to irrational rages. In a fit of temper, he even abdicated. In turn the sobor representatives were amazed. They unanimously begged the tsar to remain on the throne. Nonetheless they continued their chaotic discussions despite the evident crisis. Ivan observed that only the state administration and the army, both personal instruments of his, were able to endure and keep out of this 'democratic' chaos. However paradoxical it may be the two institutions were at the root of the Russian crisis. According to everyone else the very military success against the Tartars and subsequent wars in the West were responsible for the lasting domestic troubles, and not the sobor. But Ivan refused this interpretation. Instead he felt obliged to abandon his reforms allegedly leading to popular happiness. Moreover, his victory over the Tartars had the unforeseen consequence of opening the floodgates of emigration eastward. Since in the south and in the east the 'fear of the terrible Tartars' had been permanently removed, Central Russia began to empty itself of nobles and peasants alike, who preferred to look for their individual happiness elsewhere. The most fundamental crisis of Ivan's reign was therefore self-created.

By then it became evident that Ivan was mentally deranged. Nonetheless he was determined to use his newly invented power instruments, a modernised army and a modern state to accomplish the terrible perestroika in his own mad way. Whether he had intended to create a "modern centralized, nation-state" all along is open to debate. Nevertheless, once he decided on creating a happy and secure Russia he took advantage of the circumstances to make sure that he remained at the head of the allpowerful state. Henceforth he had no other option but to impose his will on Russia to redress the catastrophic situation he brought about. Thus, he wielded power more absolutely and tyranically than any of his predecessors, who had lacked the means of enforcement. He, therefore, established an organization of terror, the **oprichnina**, to carry out the restructuring by naked force. The boyars, previously weakened by wholesale land seizure, were now "liquidated" by mass assassination. If resistance to Ivan's will was even suspected, they and their families were massacred preventively. Their estates and city property were taken over by the **oprichniki** who were Ivan's personal servants. The army was deployed in the east to contain the flight of the peasants. In the end even the Orthodox clergy was 'subdued'. Many cities were punished with **oprichnina** terror and rebellious Novgorod was destroyed. This first attempt at fundamental perestroika went wrong and resulted instead in horror and senseless devastation.

All the same, Ivan IV became, whether in his lucid or mad moments, the first tsar-autocrat of all the Russias appointed by God, to offer happiness to the Russians. For God's benefit he even revived the theory of Moscow as Third Rome. For the benefit of his unhappy subjects he invented mass murder as a means of ruling them. Paradoxically, the wealth derived from the confiscated estates of the boyars was insufficient to finance his westward expansion and wars. Therefore Ivan's security requirements were never achieved despite the terrible sacrifices. Only his personal 'apparat' of terror was built up and bequeathed to his successor. The **oprichniki**, were omnipotent servants, who not only decided the questions of life and death. They also raised and collected taxes directly, without any intermediaries (voyvody), albeit only in the territories under **oprichnina** control. According to the tsar everybody living in those territories was happy, particularly the dead. The rest of Russia was abandoned to 'lawlessness and chaos'. The army, after failing to defeat decisively foreign enemies, became a repressive body of internal enemies isolating the Russians from the world in the east, west and the south. A century in advance of the West, Ivan became the first absolute monarch of a centralized nation-state administered by a terrorist meritocracy, with a peasantry tightly bound to the land. He not only had the power of life and death over his subjects, but absolute power over every aspect of national life, including trade and manufacturing. In his lifetime the handpicked terrorists-**oprichniki** enforced this 'modernized system' of government in a largely medieval Russia most efficiently, just because it was the tsar's will. Upon his death, after Ivan's succession had failed, the system disintegrated leaving behind as an epitaph the tales of woes and the sobriquet "Terrible". However, as consequence of this self-willed, terroristic modernization was followed by a long period of SMUTA-CHAOS (primitive democracy?), which only came to an end as another dynasty replaced the Riuriks.

The second example of a major restructuring in Russia took place two centuries later. It was decided upon by another strong sovereign, Peter I, called "the Great" by a Senate **ukaz,** issued during his lifetime. Just like Ivan IV, Peter I had also had a disturbed childhood. In reaction to his unhappy experiences he became an autocrat by his own decision. Like Ivan he was also obsessed with military power and security problems. As before the excuse for launching a fundamental perestroika were the largely imaginary Turkish and Swedish security threats to Russia. In Peter's mind they became real, hence an absolute necessity for Russia's westward expansion and drive towards the warm seas. However, unlike Ivan the Terrible, Peter kept himself open to contemporary ideas, gladly mixed with foreigners and travelled extensively abroad. Comparing western countries to Russia he realized that his ramshackle empire was lagging behind Europe in economic, cultural, social, political, scientific, and technological development. This **zastoy** was a subsidiary reason Peter's perestroika. Like Ivan, Peter decided on fundamental reforms, early in his rein, after he had successfully gained access to the Black Sea with the capture of Azov. There and then he determined that his victorious army and navy would be modernized by westerners, 'as no one in Russia could do it for him'. But his methods of implementation were Ivan's. The mutinous, old army consisting of the riflemen-streltsy, was simply massacred and replaced by nationwide recruited Russian soldiers officered by foreigners. Unwittingly Peter invented the most up-to-date method of military recruitment based on national service and used even in the 20th century all over the world. Quite logically, once the seas were reached a naval force had to be built. Again foreigners were hired, chiefly the Dutch to carry out the task, since Russians built only river boats. Cannon and guns production in Russian arsenals was modernised. By the end of his reign Peter had modern armed forces comparable to European (Swedish, Polish) armies, capable of offensive operations in Europe and above all in Asia.

This was, however, the only achievement of Peter's modernisation. At his death in 1718, after all these expenses in money and blood, Russia had outlets in the Baltic and Black Seas, but was economically bled white and in social turmoil. Just like Ivan, Peter was also convinced from the very inception of his military perestroika that Russian society, too, had to be re-structured in a most profound fashion. According to him the historical nobility, the boayrs, had outlived their usefulness to the state. They were allowed to keep their estates, but were systematically eliminated from positions of power and replaced by serving nobles, the dvoryanins, a meritocratic state elite, appointed by the tsar, now called emperor (imperator). A new political order was peacefully installed, supervised by the emperor and his new political executive, the secret police. Originally he had set up a secret political police to ensure state security, especially his own safety. However, in time state security also covered such political crimes as criticism of the emperor and 'subversive' literature. In the end this new secret department became a cruel watchdog of everything that happened in Russia. Indeed such departments also existed in Western absolutist monarchies, but they never had such extensive powers and never tracked down subversion in taverns or rumourmongers in cities. In addition Peter established a school system to overcome illiteracy and 'civilise the Russians'. To rid himself of religious 'obscurantism' he transformed the Orthodox Church into another department of state. In time all the aspects of national life were supposed to be under his personal supervision including foreign trade and culture. This huge, allpowerful bureaucracy supposedly enabled Russia to catch up with the European powers. It was also supposed to make the country as prosperous as the West. Ivan's dream of a happy Russia was equivalent to Peter's dream of prosperous Russia.

Inevitably Peter's both military and domestic perestroikas ended in failure. While the re-organised Russian armed forces turned to expansion and conquest, they also became a most serious drain of scarce resources. To carry out Peter's domestic perestroika successfully Russia needed peace and not war. The new tax system proved as inefficient as the old one and most of the administrative reforms remained on paper. Initially state officials were paid by the state, and did not 'live of the land' as of old. But soon, because of the needs of war, Peter had to revert to the ancient **kormlenie**; state servants had to earn a living by their wits, through corruption. Economic activity (agriculture, manufacture and trade) was also restructured to fit with Peter's observations of his travels in Europe. But again no permanent improvement came of it in neither branch, because state monopoly tended to strifle private enterprise. The state itself lacked investments because of the continuous wars and private investments were not forthcoming. The peasants were the greatest losers of Peter's modernisation-perestroika: they become legal serfs as compared to Ivan's peasants with unenforceable restrictions on their movements. All the same even in this case the 'modern petrine' state had no real means to enforce legalised serfdom. Peter's new capital, St. Petersburg, exemplified best the monarch's dreams going wrong. It was built to show Europe how fast his Russian empire was catching up. Forced labour was used as neither noble nor peasant wanted to move to and work in such an insalutory place. Nobles were compelled to build palaces with threats and thousands of peasant lives paid for the completion of the megalomanic project. Peter did become the most absolutist monarch in the contemporary world.

Though the signs of failure of Peter's ambitious perestroika began to appear during his lifetime, his determination and ruthlessness kept the process going right to his death. As in Ivan's days the terrorist secret police made sure of it. However, compared to Ivan's **oprichniki** secret police activity was almost trivial. It cloberred most severely lots of drunks who dared to abuse the emperor and his reforms in taverns or in streets. It specialized in 'eliminating' ennobled opposition without legal procedure, on denunciation. However, even these judicial murders were carried out against individuals on a much smaller scale than under **oprichnina**. However, the atmosphere of fear created by Peter's secret policemen made sure that re-structuring went on to the bitter end. The reformed administration simply could not work, as it was grossly underfunded. Numerous taxes it invented remained uncollected and war expenditure invariably exceeded state revenues. As in Ivan's days the system of terror alone survived Peter. Paradoxically Peter deprived himself of a legitimate successor by killing him in a fit of rage. On his death the Petrine system collapsed and his 'totalitarian empire on paper' dissolved in confused succession struggles. It transformed itself into 'police controlled' dynastic chaos.

Russia had to wait for almost two hundred years for the next attempt at fundamental re-structuring. With Peter's female successors the police empire continued to decline, though its formal structures remained intact. His weak grandson, Peter III, finally liberated the serving nobles (dvoryane) from Peter's 'state serfdom' by grating them such dangerous ideological concessions as freedom of movement at home and abroad. Despite his liberalisation he was assassinated in a barbaric way by the same liberated nobles, probably at the behest of his wife, Catherine II, who later also became the Great. To start with this great empress flirted with reforms, but ended her days a even more absolute monarch than Peter. Her only positive contribution to the language of politics were the 'Potemkin villages'. Her official lover, Prince Potemkin, responsible for the implementation of her paper reforms, built these sham structures all along the routes of inspection to prove to her how prosperous Russia was under her reforming guidance. In reality her reforms only improved the financing of the state bureaucracy. The secret police was allocated additional resources to carry out repression more effectively, since the 'liberated' nobles were getting out of hand. Catherine's half-crazed son, Paul, was strangled by them, with the knowledge of his son and successor, Alexander I. Like his grandmother, this 'enlightened' monarch also tried liberal reforms--for a time the secret police was dissolved--but again ended up, because of wars, as a tough **samoderzhavets**-outdated absolutist ruler without a constitution. At the time when Europe was replacing absolute monarchies with constitutional regimes, very gradually moving towards liberal democratic systems, Russia continued to strengthen its unique 'absolutist' system. Some of Alexander's successors tinkered with the unfinished police system, but all dreaded liberalism. Thus, Nicholas I re-established officially the secret political police and carried out literary censorship in person. His successor, Alexander II, after a lost war, tried again to reform Russia, but after abolishing serfdom thus 'liberating' the peasants, the reforming spirit petered out. Subsequently he proved unable to reconcile the new social forces unleashed by his limited re-structuring process with his new Russia. In the end he was assassinated by intellectual revolutionaries who easily outmanoeevered his inadequate security forces. As in the past the Russian state could not pay for itself and had insufficient means to assure even the sovereign's personal security. Peter's dream of a police state regulated by the sovereign in person was never achieved because of the huge costs involved. Significantly Alexander's overdue abolition of serfdom, coming years after the rest of Europe had done so, had the same economic effects: it launched an industrial revolution. However, no one understood this process. Curiously such economic modernisation would have provided his predecessors with the wealth they needed to make the police state really effective, but for the Romanovs it came too late.

Neither Alexander III and Nicholas II grasped the point that an efficient police state required greater financial resources and improved communication techniques. Instead they both tried to make their inefficient police state capable of protecting at least their lives and those of their family against the newfangled adversaries, intellectual revolutionaries. Moreover, they both thought they could combatted with draconian laws. In face of failure they tended to overreact, especially after assassination attempts on themselves. Thus the secret police had all the administrative powers, it needed, but again no more financial resources. 'Temporary exceptional laws' , passed in 1881, brought **everything** under its control, including ice cream licences. Exile was institutionalised and by 1898 some 300,000 deportees populated Siberia. Labour camps made their appearance and by the end of the century some 60,000 prisoners languished in them. Discrimination was legalised and without a police certificate of good conduct no one could be admitted to universities, civil service and even to the most humble jobs sponsored by the state. The 'temporary' law remained in force, with a short interruption in 1905-1907, until the end of the Romanovs' reign in 1917. However, at the time when private property was real power in Russia, the grossly underfunded **Okhrana**, as the secret political police was then known, proved incapable of safeguarding the state and not to mention the imperial family. Archdukes and prime ministers, and particularly interior ministers, continued to be assassinated by terrorists by the right and left wings of the intelligentsia. In addition, in 1905, Nicholas faced with a spontaneous revolt, provoked by his security forces, was forced to promise his people a liberal constitution (a kind of democratic **perestroika**). For two years he witnessed the incompetence of the liberal intelligentsia in running the imperfect system that emerged after the 1905 'revolution'. Though Nicholas' disolution of it seemed justified, it was a real pity that this liberal experiment was so shortlived and was not given a chance to prove itself. By then, after a series of 'revolutionary' measures aimed at developing and sustaining industrial production Russia was genuinely 'economically catching up with Europe'. The standard of living was rising, although literacy and housing were still grossly inadequate. Nonetheless Russia was modernising herself and growing richer in the process. Modern means of communication increased the power of the state immeasurably and armed forces were to be ready for modern wars in 1917. But instead of letting Russia benefit from this spontaneous development Nicholas brought back the 'temporary exceptional laws' and became involved in the 1st World War. By 1917 not only were his armies shattered, but such anarchy and chaos reigned in the rear that no security forces could control them given the scale of disorders. Then a simple bread riot swept the Romanovs out of power. However, this time the state had broken down together with the dynasty. 'Power was in the street to be picked up by any determined and ruthless leader'.

Among the mass of intellectual revolutionaries it was only the cruel, cynical and terroristic-minded Ulyanov-Lenin who proved capable of seizing power and keeping it. The rest just talked about liberal democracy, but did nothing practical. For tactical reasons Lenin also spoke of liberty and social democracy. But he held on to power despite the bloodiest civil war and the most senseless destruction that the world has ever seen. Whatever remained of the inadequate imperial structures was totally destroyed by Lenin's new 'oprichniki'-bolsheviki, not for freedom's sake, but for reasons of expediency. At this stage, Lenin was not interested in a fundamental re-structuring, despite his ideological claims based on inadequate notions as class hatred and social justice. One month after his coup de force he began to re-structure the only effective and tested instruments of imperial power: the secret police and the Army. To manipulate these instruments according to his implacable will he entrusted them to the new ideologically motivated elite, the communist party. Thus, he lay the foundations of the most modern police state, bureaucratic totalitariasm-communism. At the time when the rest of Europe and the world was slowly 'democratising' their political systems, Russia was missing the boat by building up an obsolete system of its own.

By 1924, when Lenin died, the economy lay in ruin and entire classes, particularly the crosssectional elite, the intelligentsia, were shattered. He had no time to destroy the peasantry, but left behind to his successors sufficient means to effect it. Two centuries after Peter he made the secret police (CheKa, NKVD, GPU, KGB etc), the sword of the revolution, finally omnipotent. Wholesale nationalisations of the means of production and mass requisitions practically eliminated private property. The new elite abolished all 'class' privileges as well as liberties making the new re-structured state all-powerful for its own sake. Lenin's successor, Dzhugashvili-Stalin, then completed 'the building of communism' in Russia, by collectivising agriculture, instituting a centrally planned economy with industry and trade fulfilling orders handed down to them from the bureacratic centre, monopolising culture and enforcing the communist ideology on an indifferent population struggling to survive in the midst of these apocaliptic changes. By 1939 Stalin had achieved all that Lenin only dreamt of. Technological progress, improved communications and wholesale expropriations gave him the means and wealth to realize all that Peter wanted to. He crowned his efforts with Ivan-like purges whose scales had no precedent even in Russia's bloody past. The poor were turned against the rich and given the means to destroy each other; the young against the old, one nationality against another, the uneducated against the intellectual and so on. In this way Stalin perfected a new model of communism, the modern totalitarian system. In the process he killed off also the enthusiastic communist helpers, including the NKVD executors. The resulting party-state had the monopoly of everything and used naked terror to enforce its power. Terror and renewed nationalism enabled Stalin to survive even a greater upheaval than the civil war, World War II. The totalitarian despot presided over this unnatural infernal machine for another decade before he died in 1953. The 'machine' went on ticking over for some forty years after his death, albeit with increasing difficulty.

III.

On Stalin's death, his successors, Khrushchev, Brezhnev, Andropov and Chernenko discarded terror as an instrument of power. In fact they gave up the use of it against each other, or the CP factions they either represented or combatted. Henceforth, terror was directed against their 'political enemies'. None felt any need for a fundamental re-structuring of the Stalinist system. They all wanted only minor adjustments within the CP and the state structures including the economy. However, such tinkering, even when extended to the state apparatus in general and the security police in particular, proved useless. The totalitarian edifice could not work without 'terror', its true dynamism. In addition, when Khrushchev's CP re-structuring was thought to have gone too far by his fellow leaders, they ejected him from power in a palace coup. According to them Khrushchev had tried to weaken the communist party and separate it from the state, which to them was no re-structuring, but a betrayal of communism. After 1964, for the next twenty years, Kosygin and Brezhnev attempted their own cautious re-structuring in vain. Not surprisingly the CP had known its most stable period of existence, but the state 'apparat', including the economy, remained as cumbersome as before and showed no improvement in its functioning. In fact they continued with the welltried Stalinist methods of running the state , economy and society, including culture: the enforcement of the CP's arbitrary decisions from the centre. However, in contrast to Stalin's days the bureaucratic apparat found it impossible to keep the country isolated from outside and immune to foreign influence. For twenty years, while Stalin's cold war lasted, while the armament industries kept the economy turning and while one bad harvest followed a good one, it was possible for Brezhnev could continue the Stalinist ritual of governing without major dislocations. Inevitably, as with the 'armament perestroikas' of Ivan and Peter, guns, (missiles) and armies or navies flourished, while bread and butter (consumer goods) became scarce. After Brezhnev's death, during the short successions of Andropov and Chernenko, signs of a deeper, structural, crisis were discerned, particularly by the future CP leader, Mikhail Sergeyevich Gorbachev. Significantly in 1984 he had prepared reports on the state of affairs in the USSR for the CP leadership.

Since all knew that the USSR was heading towards a deep crisis, on his accession to power, in March 1985, Gorbachev was forced into a major restructuring-perestroika. However, he was badly equipped for dealing with such complicated structural problems facing him. Compared to Ivan IV, Peter I, Lenin or Stalin he was not a strong personality, ruthless and determined enough to impose his decisions even on the CP, whose contested leader he became. He soon proved incapable to stick to the tough decisions once taken. Thus, he was only a skilfull manipulator of CP apparatchiks with a penchant for worldwide publicity, not a sufficient basis for success. Soon it became clear that he was capable of dealing successfully only with international problems, but not with the internal crisis. To start with Gorbachev thought that a few deeper and unusual economic or intra-party reforms could save the communist system and safeguard his own position as supreme leader. By launching this two-fold drive to reform the CP and the economy he was able to outmaneouvre the CP gerontologues and replace them with his own men. But that was all. In the fundamantal perestroika of the CP system he employed two new elements employed, glasnost-transparance, and demokratizatsia-democratisation, which were supposed to re-dynamize communism. To his mind all depended on his ability to controll the process once launched. Henceforth this volume will analyze the various aspects and phases of perestroika from March 1985 to 1993 and its actual outcome.

In foreign affairs Gorbachev was immediately successful. The democracies of the West were ready for a reduction of tensions, controlled disarmament and a modus vivendi with the USSR. He had more trouble with lining up in favour of his foreign policy aims the once abject satellites. A series of arms control agreements reduced the cold war to normalcy. Internal perestroika depended vitally on such peaceful international development. Now it was up to Gorbachev to prove himself as a leader.

To Gorbachev's surprise both the state and CP apparats opposed perestroika tooth and nail. Haltingingly, he forced new forms of intra-party democracy onto them, such as multiple candidacies for elections to offices at higher levels. However, to transform the totalitarian party into a democratic one soon appeared impossible. The bureaucratic state apparat was only gradually and painfully modified, chiefly through glasnost exposures of its corruption and malpractices. But the armed forces and the KGB were left largely untouched, only their leading cadres were slowly purged. Though much greater progress was made with the political system, it was not a democracy. Still Gorbachev persuaded the CP that it should try and practise democracy as it was. During these years the democratic ritual of election was gradually adopted by all the Soviets and the franchise was 'dangerously' extended. Instead of rubber stamping CP decisions the Soviets, at all level, began to discuss them and enact them in legislative acts only afterwards. This was not very revolutionary, but even such timid progress in democratization was significant. The CP apparat found it increasingly difficult to control this democratic political process.

However, soon the economy escaped CP control altogether. Limited privatisations of manufacture, agriculture and trade with foreign joint ventures in industry became 'warning signs of economic democracy'. Culture and the communication media still under

CP tight control were applying glastnost rather hesitantly. After the nuclear Chernobyl accident glasnost was taken up more seriously. After widespread corruption had been revealed **glasnost** and DEMOKRATIZATSIA, advanced hand in hand out of bounds of CP control. What radicalised Gorbachev's domestic perestroika most was his raprochement with the United States ending of the cold war. As soon as the cold war conditions vanished and the dogma of 'international class hatred' with them, the perestroika process became spontaneous, out of Gorbachev's control. In 1989 the turning point was Gorbachev's decision to permit broader suffrage (though not yet quite democratic) in republican and regional elections to facilitate takeovers from the CPs the republics and regions. After much hesitation Gorbachev also wanted to boost up the lagging economy.

However, the communist economy was beyond repair and Gorbachev had to deal with nationalist and inter-ethnic troubles. By then it seemed probable that the Soviet Union would collapse under the impact of such internal pressures. The coup de grace was an external shock: the satellite system dissolved itself proclaiming independence. The Baltic states followed suit aspiring to complete independence. Thoughout 1990, under increasing pressure from all sides, Gorbachev tried to reverse disintegration by negotiation. However, the CP conservatives began to resist him actively and their efforts culminated in an attempted coup d'Etat in August 1991. The attempt failed ignominiously and after two years of indecision the totalitarian system collapsed of its own and the USSR with it. The CP was banned in the aftermath of the failed coup, the Union broke up and by 1992 Gorbachev was out of power. The way was open for a free market economy and unlimited political democracy under new leaders. At long last the armed forces and the secret police were neutralised and their perestroikas enacted. 'Dissident' apparatchiks with a clearer vision of the future assumed power. Not unexpectedly the Slavs, now divided into Russia, Ukraine and Byelarus, reached the end of their march from communism to democracy in political, economic and social disarray. The historical and societal factors unleashed by Gorbachev's two-pronged perestroika resulted into something unique: anarcho-democracy and anarcho-capitalism or both? However, in 1993 the new system is only beginning...

Gorbachev: The Politics of Perestroika

Michel Tatu

Right up to March 1985 Mikhail Sergeevich Gorbachev had been an examplary apparatchik. He was born on 2 March 1931 in the Stavropol region and he made his career there as well: from the leadership of Komsomol in Stavropol city to the first secretary of this agricultural region. Inexonarably he ascended the pyramid of the party apparat until 1978, when Brezhnev-Suslov called him to Moscow. He assumed the responsibility for agriculture in the central secretariat which led to the pinnacle of Soviet power: after a brief period as candidate he was made full-member of the Politbyro in 1980. By 1985 he was responsible for all sorts of matters and an obvious candidate for the supreme leadership among the gerontocrats. Once secretary-general the relatively young Gorbachev was able to compare party ideology with Soviet reality and asked himself the most fundamental question: what should he do with all the power he had inherited from his predecessors?

Subsequently he asked himself many additional questions: how should he exercise this immense power, and to what end? Since March 1985 we have answers to these questions and are able to compare his words and deeds. The present analysis was written in early 1991, four years since the start of perestroika, and almost six years since Gorbachev assumed power. After these eventful years - far more momentous than could be expected back in 1987 - what is the situation in the USSR?

First we are faced with a paradox: three years ago, up to half way through 1989, the Soviet Union was pioneering perestroyka within the "socialist system". It had forged ahead of its satellites and was taking huge strides in implementing reforms, while the "dinosaurs" of the Stalin-Brenev era, such as Honecker,Zhivkov, Ceausescu and alia were dragging their feet. To-day the torch of progress is in other countries' possession; the USSR has been overtaken by its disciples.

A striking feature of the different evolution of the old satellites and the Soviet Union is the speed with which reforms are carried out in the former, while the country where perestroyka was first introduced is taking a long time in reforming its system. Such apparachiks as Egon Krenz in East Germany, Urbanek in Czechoslovakia and Grosz in Hungary were obviously unable to cling to power because of past misdeeds. They had to withdraw after a few weeks, but, seen from a Soviet point of view, these leaders of the "new look socialist revolution" showed a high degree of realism. They were fully aware of the need to discard, together with their national "dinosaurs", most of the Stalinist legacy: the party monopoly of power, Lenin's myth of "democratic centralism"; in many cases Marxism itself, has been thrown to the wind in the space of a few days, at worst a few weeks. This course was also followed by the few apparatchiks still in power today, such as Jaruzelski in Poland.   Nothing of the sort occurred in the Soviet Union. A multi-party system is emerging gradually, but alongside a remarkably rigid set of Stalinist institutions. In February 1990 the international press hailed as a great achievement the fact that the validity of article 6 of the Soviet constitution guaranteeing "the leading role of the communist party" was tested in the Supreme Soviet and found wanting. Yet few people bothered to notice that several years of glasnost had been necessary to bring about the examination of the article. In any case the article was fairly recent and was written into the constitution by Brenev in 1976.   Neither Lenin, nor Stalin felt any need of it, when they instituted a totalitarian system. So presumably many such "victories" will be needed before the promised "rule of law" is the norm.

In every other respect the USSR remains behind the old satellite countries: the implementation of the main components of the economic reform have been either postponed, or are still being debated and amended out of recognition. The draft legislation on land ownership avoids the fateful "private property" phrase and its first draft, acclaimed late in February as "re-establishing peasant ownership", only considers the handing over of leases - inheritance including- not full ownership by the peasants. The principle of a market economy had made some progress, but only in words: there is no question of {making the ruble convertible nor freeing prices in the foreseable future, which in the prevailing circumstances could mean never.

Of course, several basic laws of the "rule of law" have been finally passed. A law on the press makes it possible for a newspaper or even a television broadcasting station to be started by people other than party members or associated organiations. However, the question of technical equipment, offices and running costs is left unanswered. In the meantime what is left of the Party- State keeps its own property. Immediately after its election the progressive Moscow City Council lost 37 buildings through a decree hastily voted by the old authorities. Similarly Gorbachev's decree, which "liberalied" television, made sure that Gosteleradio, the old state organiation, was not to lose any of its regional stations.

It is clear that things, unthinkable to day will become a reality to morrow, just as political pluralism developed in society well before it was officially recognied. Yet any progress in democratiation or economic reform suffers from the syndrome of "too little and too late". Too late especially to bring about solutions of those problems which have all been getting worse.   What are the causes for such long delays? Obviously there are political hurdles to overcome. However, the main body of resistance to reforms in depth, is situated in an area other than the "old guard" in the apparat, often blamed for it. First and foremost, society as a whole is involved in the country's reluctance to change. In reality neither the undoubted popular appeal of radical reformers, nor the numbers of demonstrators {for the reforms should be taken at face value. The man in the street wants nothing better than to send all the old leaders packing, whether at the top or the bottom of the r3gime, at the center of the Soviet Union or in the regions. After the decades of oppression, he has lost faith in Marxism, thinks little of Lenin and slips easily back into his old creed, nationalistic, religious and cultural. This by no means implies that he is willing to accept the consequences of all the genuine political and economic reforms. As the post-war experience showed in the West and now in Eastern Europe, all reforms lead to the western model of parliamentary democracy and market economy. In the USSR, two factors stand in the way, unlike in Eastern European countries. One is the legacy of seventy years of communism, in turn war communism, then the Stalinist r3gime, ending with "stagnation", a legacy of levelling of society and loss of the sense of responsibility. The forty years of communism in the satellite countries were not sufficient to root out old reflexes. Their populations still remember the preceding 'capitalist' era. This national epoch has often been pictured by the old generation in glowing terms, as a reaction to the sombre recent past or present. In economic development, especially, a Chinese peasant knows more about private enterprise than the most educated Moscow official, which explains why economic reforms were more successful in China, than at least during the first ten years of the revolutionary regime.

In the USSR, except in the Baltic countries, which have also come under communism more recently, all of the past experience is {forgotten. The situation is all the more disastrous because the starting point of development was much lower than in the West, which represents another obstacle to change.

Russia had her entrepreneurial class, and a very dynamic one, early in the century, but only for a decade or two. Russian economy really took off round 1910, to be brutally cut short by the war in 1914 and the revolution in 1917. Even in this short period of expansion, capitalism was only one element in a diversified society, whose main components were an enormous peasantry and a small ruling, but declining, aristocracy . The ruling class was itself divided between idle and obscurantist landlords and more enlightened towndwellers, both of whom unanimously despised the emerging new class of "merchants" (kuptsy), as they were then still called, instead of "industrialists" (promyshlenniki). The old populist ideal of egalitarianism, always strong in the intelligentsia, flewked the picture of Russian society still further. Money making, individual wealth and private enterprise held never much appeal to the Russians. This constitutes the main difference between them and most of the Eastern European nations. Undoubtedly, since Peter the Great, there has always been a movement opposed to the Slavophiles,"Westernisers". Their very name shows that they stood for the opposite of the Slavophiles, who favoured Russian traditions and untainted Russianness itself. In fact both movements suffered from an inferiority complex towards the West and its riches, but each drew different conclusions. The Westernisers wanted to imitate their Western model blindly, if need be force it on Russia. The Slavophiles believed in a special mission for Russia, devizing a specific model, neither fully fledged capitalism nor Western parliamentiary democracy. The Western type of democracy, acclaimed as an ideal by Eatern European countries, is seen in a different light in Russia. It has an entirely negative value, providing an empty framework in which individuals can develop freely, but falling short of providing values which would satisfy the generous aspirations of the Slavophiles. The basic principle of the rule of law, "Everything is allowed which is not forbidden by law" hurts the susceptibilities, not only of totalitarian die hards who claimed the opposite for decades, but also of Russian moralists who cannot accept that the state be neutral. Solhenitsyn, for example, who is one of the chief spokesmen of this trend of thought, holds that morality is more important than law. Truth in its almost mystical sense ("Istina", more than the down to earth "Pravda") is what the country lacks, not so much Freedom. It seems to him that the Stalinist regime's worst characteristic was institutionalied lies, violent repression of society, rather than absence of democracy or political pluralism.

At present the Slavophile trend is gaining ground, since it seems to be the only way to salvage something of the Stalin-Brenev heritage (patriotism tainted with chauvinism and xenophobia, cultural values unsullied by profit motives), adding to it more respectable values stemming from the old Marxist thought (religion, ecology). In short, these thinkers are able to re-establish links with the era prior to communism, without forcing a complete and heartrending break with the more recent past.

The proof of this assertion is in the fact that old "Stalinists" and new "patriots" club together, as well as old bolshevik atheists closing ranks with new religiously minded conservatives. Many of the former are quite willing to throw overboard their old "Marxist-Leninist" creed clearly bankrupt, to join the latter in upholding old reactionary values. These, though presented as instruments of the class struggle, were always present in communist ideology, that is to say, respect of law and order, hatred of "democrats" and all radicals, not to mention Jews, free masons or foreigners of all kind. The excesses of Pamiat, an ultra-nationalist association, only reveal the top of the iceberg.

This organiation is certainly the backbone of the most determined opposition to perestroyka. An egalitarian outlook is the source of the well publicied hostility that cooperatives, early forms of private enterprise, are meeting with. The average Russian prefers denunciation or intrigue to bring back to his level a man who has grown richer rather than imitate him and raise his own standards of living. Another reason is that morality is widely seen as more important than law. No amount of coertion from the authorities nor legislative measures have any impact on this popular belief.

In any event one of the draft laws passed on cooperatives put several limitations on them, one of which was abstaining from "speculation". Besides the fact that the term is rather imprecise. The legislators overlooked the effect these restrictions on the newly created cooperatives, giving them a {marginal character and laying them open to public criticism. So long as they represent only 1% or 2% of the economic activity of the country, as is the case now, they will remain exceptions in a sea of shortages and derive unfair advantage from the situation. On the other hand, if their share of the market grows to 40 or 50% , they will have a stimulating influence on it and will compete with the nationalied sector. However, this is just that the authorities hold against them. They play on popular feelings , and allow for "ideal" cooperatives only, which are unworkable in practice. This is a vicious circle and it will remain unbroken, until the legislators, even those in favour of reforms, find the courage to ignore their own propaganda values and morality, when drafting new laws.

Another impediment to changes such as were seen in Eastern Europe is the problem of nationalities. As the last colonial empire on earth, the Soviet Union cannot be democratied, even partially, without having to face identical demands from the many nations which it comprises: a call for real independance from the peoples subjugated in the past. No Eastern European country, not even Romania with its Hungarian minority, finds itself in the same position. It is one of Mikhail Gorbachev's most blatant miscalculations that he failed to foresee this unavoidable consequence of glasnost.

The problem was made more acute, if not created, by political reforms, as well as the economic crisis. Before deviing the best way to share the national income, there has to be wealth to share. In the event shortages and resentments are {such that people see in the OTHER, member of a minority, either living near by or deported on Stalin's orders, the cause of their difficulties: a parasite or black marketeer, in short a scapegoat who attracts, sometimes with the authorities' blessing, violent antagonism.

To all this must be added the impact of events in Eastern Europe. On the one hand, many people are saddened by the loss of empire. They are the old generation raised in the days of the "Great Patriotic War" and hatred of Germany; Army personnel used to view Eastern and Central Europe as a buffer one and an exercie ground. And they all refuse to accept the humiliation the upheaval brought them. On the other hand, how could the Baltic populations fail to react to the collapse of neighboring communist states, how could Moldavians - in reality Romanians belonging to the Soviet Union - remain unaffected by the disappearance of Ceaucescu who had served as a convenient scarcrow so far? Especially, since they had in both cases fallen victims to the shameful agreements, nowadays disavowed, entered into by Stalin and Hitler, just like the other "fraternal countries" of liberated Eastern Europe.

Thus, the danger from nationalism facing the central leader, Gorbachev, is many-sided. In the Southern Republics (Caucasus and Central Asia) nationalism erupted violently, causing bloodshed in Armenia and Dushanbe through Karabakh and Baku. However, from a political point of view, the solution is easy because the Russian central power and its army are the only forces capable of restoring law and order and ending pogroms, thereby acquiring legitimacy. Even foreign powers prefer law and order, be it of the Soviet variety, to violent disorders and massacres.

It is quite another matter with the Baltic challenge to Soviet power. It is a non violent movement, heralding the unavoidable break up of the empire as a whole. The only way left to Gorbachev to avoid the immediate secession of Lithuania and of the other Baltic republics, is to send troops in. This time with no pretence of restoring public order, and at the cost of halting political and economical reforms, at home and abroad for a long time. The "Brezhnev doctrine" of limited sovereignty was abolished as far as the "external" empire is concerned, but it could not be re-established on the border of the "internal empire", namely in the Baltic countries. It causes considerable damage to the political image of the Soviet leader and the atmosphere of detente in Europe, especially to the "common European home" which has become slightly more credible in recent months.

One has to remember the new sense of national identity enjoyed by the major republics, to start with Russia, which after electing Boris Yeltsin as President and setting up an independent communist party, under Polozkov, a conservative, has become an alternative center of power. By the same token, the Ukraine and Byelorussia, followed by most of the Union's republics, proclaiming themselves sovereign, even "neutral". They are, of course, mere verbal assertions, but they make the "Federal Pact" dear to Gorbachev seem looser and looser. For the time being the latter can only bide his time in dealing with this problem and many others, but he is losing ground. Things have reached a point when nobody can hope to have his orders obeyed, and "graduated plans " have lost all credibility. Therefore, it is impossible to envisage ,for example, the application of a law on secession, as it provides for five years' interval between the holding of a referendum in a given republic and ratification of its result by the Congress of Deputies in Moscow. Neither would payment of "financial reparations" to the federation be enforceable on the republics about to leave, as it would also apply to those which were annexed in the most brutal manner by Stalin.

Only in the event of a complete turn around by the Moscow authorities could imminent territorial losses be avoided for the empire. In long term, however, there may be a ray of hope, with the creation of an updated federation, of a voluntary nature, centered round the Slavic republics of Russia, the Ukraine and Bielorussia. But to entice a few at least of the non-Slavic republics, such a federation should enjoy even looser ties than the United States of America, which have in common cultural affinities and a successful economic system totally lacking in the USSR. It seems probable also that nothing of the kind can be set up before the collapse of the old regime, as it is obviously too inflexible to be amended. Most nationalists hold that they have to secede before any step can be taken to reactivate an associative union.

It is important to stress that the problems to be solved in Soviet society act as background to purely political questions. Nowadays Soviet life does not revolve round the all powerful party and its Holy of Holies, the Politburo, whose only function was to crush society and any manifestation of real life. The latter had come to the fore even under the rule of "stagnation", as facts speak for themselves sooner or later. It is now society's turn to take the limelight, whatever the wishes of individuals may be. Even so, politics is still at the center of the debate, as it has retained many past characteristics. The chief of these is being dominated by a supposedly charismatic leader, who holds more and more key functions, while being less and less able to control the situation. This contradiction is at the core of all the difficulties facing the USSR in the autumn of 1990.

In reality Gorbachev, the apparatchik, has changed less rapidly than the country at large, so that his repeated warnings to his opponents, accused of "fighting for personal power", are in fact directed at himself. The man who had first refused the job as Head of State held by his predecessors (in the past a purely honorary one) finally accepted it. Moreover, he had himself elected to the job three times in three years, and each time with increased powers. Besides, at least once a year since 1987, a crisis more serious than the preceding one gave grounds for wondering whether the Secretary General's position was not under threat, whether the "die hards" of the apparat were not about to seie control again. Each time Mikhail Gorbachev "bounced back", taking a firm grip of the situation and adding to his already vast power.

Already late in 1988 a crisis ended in the Party Secretariat being divided into "commissions". Ligachev, his main opponent, was partially shelved. Early in 1990 the setting up of a presidential regime curbed the government's power together with {that of its head, Nikolay Ryzhkov, who is a potential rival. Then came a serious alert in the following spring when a group of conservatives rebelled and Russian communists rose against their leader, only to be followed by the 28th congress of the federal party deciding, much to everyone's surprise, to drop Egor Ligachev, to clean up the Central Committee and to weaken the Poliburo for good. If the party came out of the crisis with ruffled feathers, none of this affected its head, who not only was confirmed in his position, but was the only person to hold a dual mandate, gaining as the head of state what he lost as party leader. How did he achieve this? In the traditional way, that is getting hold of trump cards rather than changing the rules of the game. To start with, like several predecessors of his, he tried to modernie the system without tampering with its structures, to motivate the party while increasing his influence and prerogatives. But like them he had to manoeuver and strengthen his personal power over the apparat and the central leadership he had inherited, so he isolated and later eliminated his opponents within the Politburo, without breaching the statutory regulations of "democratic centralism", of collegiate leadership and cooption. We know from past experience that this is a task all the more difficult as the leader is more ambitious: Khrushchev foundered finally, while Brezhnev succeeded, after six or seven years at least, and mainly because his only ambition was to usher in the heyday of Nomenklarura. The only people who managed to make the party serve their own ambition were Stalin and later, Mao Tse tung in China - only for a time though in the latter case. To achieve their end, both had to break up not only the {apparat, but the party itself, and build a new one over the ashes of the old party.

It would be a cynical view of perestroika to give to Gorbachev the same motives as those of Stalin or Mao. The main difference being that, while the two dictators chose to destroy the party in the name of revolutionary purity and totalitarian extremism, he does it in the name of democratiation. Another difference is that, while this task encountered the same obstacles and met with the same reflexes of "fighting for survival" in a doomed apparat, it has also put in motion a social process which got out of control and forced on Gorbachev all manners of choices and decisions at an ever increasing rate, which he could not easily deal with, as he was still tied to collegiate leadership. At the top anyhow the methods he used were of the most classical kind. Following in his predecessors' footsteps, Gorbachev was able to use the enormous prerogatives of his position of secretary general (a monopoly of taking initiatives, free access to the media, ability to hold the levers of command of all the organiations under his control, whether legally or otherwise) and the "legitimist" reflex of most of the conservatives. When all is said and done, the system defended by the "old guard" of the Central Committee is that of democratic centralism, which deprives them of any say in the face of the Secretary General and "collegiate" leadership of the Politburo. So long as this body has not proposed to the "Parliament of the Party" the name of another leader and a new political program, the Central Committee must be content with ratifying whatever {comes to it from above for approval. This is for instance what it did at the end of its plenum in February 1990, when it voted almost unanimously a "political platform" which had been criticied by a majority of speakers. This is the course followed by the Congress in July of the same year when it voted for Gorbachev as head of the Party, though he was cordially detested by a majority of the delegates, only because the old Politburo had no other credible candidate to replace him.

Another method has proved worth using: when the political situation makes it impossible to purge in the right way the institutions, the latter can be effectively weakened, both in status and competence. As was seen above the Party Secretariat often embarrassed Gorbachev, while Ligachev ruled supreme there, in 1987 and 1988. Hard luck for it- it was practically abolished late in 1988. Likewise for the Politburo, a body where, by all accounts, it is even more difficult to oust a member than to have a new one admitted. The unfortunate Politburo, from early 1990 lost many of its prerogatives, and met infrequently, only to be completely overhauled by the Party Congress a few months later. Of course, all this rests on a basic notion which is respectable: shifting power from the Party to the State, as a preliminary to rationaliing institutions. However, this is not the only aim or explanation, since the government in this case should have been given pride of place, while it has lost gradually its prerogatives to the president, as it could not be radically purged in its membership.

Overall Gorbachev has managed to shed his opponents faster than any of his predecessors, including Stalin, though he is not {given a free hand to do it. An example of his stepping back was the June 1989 Party Conference. This was the first time that an open debate was taking place in the USSR - well before the meeting of the Congress of Deputies the following spring, which was to be the first parliamentary debate. The Conference roused wide inerest in the country and public opinion was thrilled by it. In the event it ended with a draw: the resolutions that were passed were no more than "orientations" for the next Party Congress, the statutes were not amended and the Central Committee was not renewed. It is tempting to draw a parallel with the conference of the fraternal Hungarian party (still the socialist workers' party, therefore communist) held at the same time, in May 1989. These proceedings turned into a congress, which ousted Janos Kadar for ever and replaced all members of the Central Committee, making far reaching reforms possible, and giving Hungary a leading position among Eastern European countries for growing democracy. In Moscow, with hindsight, it has to be admitted that then a golden opportunity was missed.

In effect the radical changes occurred only two years later at the 28th Congress, which means unfortunately two years too late. It took five years to liquidate Ligachev, even longer to do the same with Ryzhkov, which is acceptable in comparison with past achievements, but far too long in a context of revolutionary unrest spreading dangerously all over the country. Thus, the time taken by Gorbachev in his struggle for power cannot be used in dealing with more urgent tasks. Hence these years which normally would represent a formidable feat of political skill, amount to a {long list of missed opportunities. Here are but a few. First the economic reform. Undoubtedly the task was immense, in view of Russian mentalities, and had never been attempted. If the process of "building socialism" has proved to be a failure everywhere, there is no guaranteed method for the "building of capitalism", especially on the ruins left behind by a regime whose main characteristic was a complete refusal of commonsense solutions. Yet the experience of Germany in 1948 and 1990, as well as that of some other countries of Central Europe to a lesser extent, should provide two basic rules of conduct: 1. the most painful changes have to be brought about at the very start and as quickly as possible, for example the end of price fixing, convertibility of currency; 2. to do so it is necessary to take advantage of a favorable political climate, and incorporate the changes in a consensual movement.

Gorbachev could avail himself of this climate of consensus in 1987, in 1988 undoubtedly, and probably up to the summer of 1989. However, whether he was prevented from acting by an excessively conservative apparat, especially at government level, or whether, and may be concurrently, his grasp of economic problems was not sufficient, he allowed the opportunity to slip by. After announcing, at a plenum in the summer of 1987, a "radical reform" of the economy, he drew back as if overawed by the magnitude of the task, letting Ryzhkov, the Prime Minister, take half measures, which only resulted in making problems worse. Towards the end of 1989, everyone noticed a sharp deterioration of an already shaky economic situation. In the spring of 1990, the new presidential regime was presented as the necessary condition for implementing the much delayed reform. But once again, nothing happened; the first meetings of the new Presidential Council ended in fresh postponements of decisions to be made in the autumn. Since the population, under the impact of food shortages, no longer trusts either

Gorbachev or any other authority, it seems most unlikely that any measures taken can bring an improvement.

Another missed opportunity was the redefining of relations between republics and drafting a new "federation pact". From 1986, start of the first nationalist clashes in Kazakhstan, and probably up to the summer of 1989, Mikhail Gorbachev was well able to give the country the new constitution he had promised from the beginning of perestroika. (In March 1986 the 27th Congress elected a constitutional commission under his chairmanship). The new constitution could only be an improvement compared to the old one, and promised to be well received by most of the republics. Only in 1989 did separatist movements gain ground, particularly in the Baltic countries.

Yet again Gorbachev failed to take his chance. Already his hesitation in the Karabakh affair, his refusal to come down in favor of autodetermination for the local population, deprived him of support among the Armenians, later the Aeris, which ended with the whole Caucasus entering a stage of latent secession. Then it became clear with the Lithuanian CP declaration of independence in December 1989, and that of the republic itself in March 1990, that the autonomy movement was getting the upper hand. Henceforth the most docile republics will only accept deals which have been negotiated with their participation, not only with the Union whose credibility is fast crumbling, but with individual republics, approached directly. Especially since the Russian federation, under Yeltsin, declared its willingness to enter into direct negotiations with other republics. The newly elected "President Gorbachev" saw his extended power shrink rapidly, to such an extent that some Soviet observers compare him to Perez de Cuellar, the UNO General Secretary, whose only mission is to act as go-between among sovereign states. Unless it is more the case of a Lebanese presidential leadership, with internecine quarrels between races and militias making it impossible to govern.

These two main "blunders" account for the drop in popularity of the father of perestroyka in Russian public opinion. No doubt Gorbachev from the start was more popular abroad than at home, but the split became worse after the summer of 1989. While Eastern Europe was liberating itself (with Gorbachev taking much credit for it in the West, merely because he stood by), in the USSR itself perestroyka entered a phase of stagnation, when a marked improvement in political pluralism and parliamentary life were not sufficient to counterbalance a worsening of the economic and nationality crisis.

To make matters worse for the Soviet leader, it was becoming increasingly more obvious that he did not have the legitimacy required under the new circumstances. He was elected secretary general of the party in the old fashion, then was appointed as head of state by successive parliaments, but he never went through the test of universal suffrage. In March 1989, another {missed opportunity, since he could have been elected easily in a constituency, he preferred to to follow his Politburo and enter parliament in the worst possible manner. He joined a list of hundred people chosen by the party Central Committee, to be elected all together. A year later, while it has been accepted that the President must be elected by universal suffrage, he decided that, in view of the "emergency", the rule will not be applied this time. Mikhail Gorbachev was elected by members of the Congress only, with no credible competitor as counter-candidate, for five years. In other words, he became the leader without democratic rules. On the one hand, he ensured that the apparat could not harm him by discarding the old regulations of cooption; as President of the USSR, he can only be sacked by the Congress plenum, no longer by the "Presidium of the Supreme Soviet", which was a tool of the Politburo. Yet as party leader, he can no longer be dismissed by the Central Committee alone, as happened to Khrushchev in 1964; a new Congress has to be convened for this. But on the other hand, he managed to avoid for a long time an unavoidable component of all democratic regimes: universal suffrage. There lies his main difference, and inferiority complex, vis-a-vis Boris Yeltsin, the electorate's darling, who was twice elected by popular vote (nearly 80% of the votes in Moscow and Sverdlovsk) and draws much benefit from this discrepancy. Or even vis-a-vis Ion Iliescu, a man who, in different circumstances, but in good time, was elected by a wide majority as leader of an amended party-state in Romania.   This is the reason why the balance sheet of Gorbachev's rule is not so impressive as it was in 1987 when the book was completed. This was the most promising period of perestroika, not only because since then problems have become so pressing as to seem insoluble, but also because some weaknesses have appeared in the leader's character. He tends to ignore the hard realities of economic life, thinking problems can be solved with a few directives and instructions from the center. He finds it difficult to make decisions in difficult circumstances, which can be seen from the number of advisers he gathers around himself. These "advisers", more or less radical in their ideas, and disappointed at seeing their advice ignored, are eager to communicate their solutions to the media. While a real statesman has few advisers, who keep the lowest possible profile.   To this must be added an equally well known tendency to being authoritarian, which may be due in part to Raissa's strong influence, as well as a taste for the trappings of power. To prove it is the law passed in the spring of 1990 making punishable attacks on "president's prestige", at his express demand. Another example is his unbending attitude to Sakharov (there was a shameful clash at the Congress of Deputies between the President and the Academician, only two days before the latter's death, which was viewed by public opinion as the reason for the death of the famous dissident). Another evidence can be found in the threats against Starkov, , who was guilty of disrespect towards the President. The editor of Arguments and Facts, a highly popular weekly, is the only member of the press whose head Gorbachev would like to see roll, for the simple {reason that he published an opinion poll unfavorable to the secretary general. There are also some late revelations: Boris Yeltsin' memoirs show that Gorbachev went blind with rage when he was criticied during a sitting of the Politburo in 1987, that he left the assembly for several minutes before coming back without a word of apology.

This is not to say that the achievements are not there. Even more than Khrushchev who is rightly rehabilitated, Mikhail Gorbachev will be remembered in history as the man who gave new life to a fossilied system, who allowed Eastern Europe to recover her freedom and the Germanys to be reunified, who put an end to costly foreign ventures and a vain military confrontation with the rest of the world. The only remaining question to answer is whether his achievements are not in the past nowadays, whether Gorbachev is the right man to preside over a crumbling empire and a system drifting into chaos. There probably is no recipe for miracles, nor saviour to remedy such compounded difficulties. However, there is no standing still either, as the USSR is engulfed in a revolutionary situation. It is a matter either of a leap forward to a genuine revolution, to introduce full democracy and a market economy, as did most Eastern European countries. Or it will be a leap backwards to the old dictatorship of the apparat and the army, as in China.

Up till now Gorbachev has refused the latter solution, but he has failed to choose the former and appears to apply the brakes rather than pushing forward with the necessary changes, and even worse, he clings to outmoded myths. Can he sincerely {believe that communism as we have seen it so far can be reformed, that first it has to come tumbling down altogether, before a normal society can be built according to his wishes? It would be good to know that his hesitation is only tactical, that his references to Lenin are temporary, that his aim is to take Russia into the international fold. However, there is no evidence that his main and ultimate aim is not personal power. Already from his five years in power one can be sure that if he has to choose between socialism and his remaining in power, he will certainly go for the latter. But if he has to choose between that and democracy, what will be his choice? It would be reassuring to know that this time it will not be personal power.

Let us haard a guess. Some time in 1991 or even later the situation has become so chaotic that a delegation of high ranking officers and top conservative officials meets the President to beg him to restore order. They have prepared a decree to declare a state of emergency in the republics most affected or even in the whole country. This emergency law was passed in the spring of 1990 and gave the President every power in the land: he can dissolve those parties or associations which are not to his liking, establish press censorship, requisition workers and even suspend legal institutions, such as parliaments and local government. To be sure, this has to be endorsed by the Supreme Soviet of the USSR, with a two thirds majority in favor. However, will this obstacle be enough in the face of the Army taking control of everything, putting pressure on reluctant deputies or even arresting them? More to the point, how will President Gorbachev react, when he is told that the decree is the only way to stop the Army acting independently, as well as keeping his power? Especially if he is reminded that his prestige abroad can ensure that the West will prove understanding and allow a return to naked power, since he is the only person capable of explaining to Bush, Mitterand, Thatcher and all and sundry that the putsch is not illegal, that it is only a regrettable parenthesis on the way to perestroika. These are questions whose answers are all too clear to be brushed aside lightly.

By August 1991 we obtained the answers to all the questions posed in my analysis. By then President Gorbachev refused to sanction a coup d'Etat, but failed to preempt it. As a consequence he lost his office and the Soviet Union disintegrated. The communist party was outlawed, the KGB re-organised, while the army gradually decomposed. Gorbachev failed to re-structure the USSR, but unwittingly led Russia to imperfect democracy.

The 19th CPSU Programme

The 19th CPSU Conference resolution called for legal protection of the individual and secure guarantees of people's rights and freedoms. Law reform in the economic sphere had already begun, under the slogan `Everything is permissible unless prohibited by law', with laws on Individual Labour Activity (1986), on State Enterprises (1987) and on Cooperatives (1988). These laws permitted private enterprise, imposed self management and financial accountability on State Enterprises and permitted Cooperatives to form and compete with State Enterprises. The first steps towards a `Socialist rule-of-law State' were taken by amending the constitution of the Soviet Union.

This was done by the Supreme Soviet on 1st December 1988. It was as a result of these amendments that the Committee of Constitutional Review was established, appointed by the newly formed Congress of Peoples Deputies. The Congress was also given responsibility for appointing the Procurator-General, the chief prosecutor, and other important state officials. These amendments were consistent with the doctrine of the division of powers; the Executive accountable to the Legislative and both bodies subject to a Constitution, enforced by a Constitutional Court. Of course this intention was in part contradicted by the Supreme Soviet's unwillingness to abolish the constitutional guarantee (Article 6) of the party's leading role, thus adding a fourth power, the CPSU, to the usual triumvirate of Executive, Legislative and Judiciary.(4) The first meeting of the Congress of Peoples' Deputies (June 1989) established a commission charged with drafting a new constitution for the Soviet Union consistent with the ideals and reforms of Perestroika and Glasnost. One of the members of the commission was Boris Yeltsin, whose draft constitution as President of the Russian Federation was finally accepted in the referendum held alongside the Russian elections of late 1993. The Yeltsin Constitution is based on the traditional model of a tripartite division of powers and includes a fully independent Constitutional Court.

The object of ensuring respect for the individual and providing secure guarantees of peoples' rights and freedoms was pursued in two ways; by law reform, creating new rights and abolishing old crimes, and by reforming the criminal justice system. Laws were passed on `On the Press and Other News Media' (1990) and `On Freedom of Conscience and Religious Organisations' (1990) allowing freedom of speech and information and freedom of worship. With regard to the difficulties to be faced in overcoming peoples' alienation from the legal system it should be noted that these `new' rights, such as freedom of speech, had always been `guaranteed' by the Soviet legal system ever since the first RSFSR Constitution of 1918, albeit subject to the responsibility of soviet citizens to exercise their rights `in accordance with the interests of the working people and with a view to strengthening the socialist system'. The duty of Soviet Citizens was redefined in Article 39 of the amended Constitution; ` Enjoyment by citizens of their rights and freedoms must not be to the detriment of the interests of society or the State or infringe the rights of other citizens'.

Significant steps were taken to repeal the political crimes contained in the RSFSR Criminal Code, but this was marred by a failure to repeal all political crimes. Article 70, `Agitation or propaganda carried on for the purpose of subverting or weakening Soviet power...', and Article 190-1, `Circulation of Known Falsehoods Derogatory to the Soviet State and Social System', were repealed but the other crimes, such as Article 7 of the USSR law `On Criminal Liability for Crimes Against the State', `Appeals for the Violent Overthrow or Alteration of the Soviet State and Social System', were amended but not repealed. The addition of the word `Violent' was a late amendment to the proposed article. Article 11-1 of the same law, `Insulting or Discrediting State Agencies and Social Organisations', was also retained.

Nonetheless, under Gorbachev the Soviet Union clearly demonstrated a new attitude to civil rights, freeing prominent dissidents, tolerating religious freedom (including the public celebration by the Russian Orthodox Church of the millennium of Christianity in Russia), establishing a Commission for Humanitarian Affairs and International Co-operation in 1988 and hosting, and being allowed to host, a Human Rights Conference under the Helsinki process in Moscow in 1991.

In reforming the Criminal Code attention was not just paid to political crimes. A number of leading Soviet jurists had criticised it as being overloaded with offences and ranking as one of the harshest criminal codes in the world. The blame for this was attributed to the end of the Khrushchev era and the Brezhnev era and the attempts made to control a faltering economy and a disintegrating society by creating more and more offences with ever harsher punishments. A well known example is the edict of May 6, 1963 `On Increasing Liability for Feeding Cattle and Poultry Bread and Other Grain Products'. The penalty for this offence was a fine or, in cases of systematic or large scale offending, up to three years in prison. The offence was created because the price of bread, which was controlled by the State, was lower than the price of animal fodder, which was not. Izvestia reported that there were more than 30,000 enforceable acts in effect in the Soviet Union (22.9.87).

Reform of the Criminal Code, in pursuit of the `Socialist rule of law State' and `socialist humanism' led to a reduction of the number of offences, a reduction of the number of offences punishable with imprisonment and the restriction of the death penalty to crimes of violence threatening life (Izvestia 2.10.92). The death sentence formerly applied to other offences including hard currency trafficking and large scale embezzlement.

At the same time a reform of the prison system was begun which liberalised some of the conditions under which Soviet prisoners were held such as convicts' diet, the punishments that could be used, payment for labour and communication and visits by next of kin. (5)

Another problem with the Criminal code was the fact that many of the offences were vaguely or subjectively drafted. An example is the law `On Increased Liability for Hooliganism' (1966) which imposed penalties of up to 1 year's correctional labour for `Hooliganism - that is, intentional actions violating public order in a coarse manner and expressing clear disrespect toward society'. `Malicious hooliganism - that is, the same actions, but distinguished in their content by exceptional cynicism or special impudence...' could be punished by up to 5 years in prison.

The vast number of potential offences and the fact that many were vaguely or subjectively drafted gave enormous power to the State officials charged with enforcing them. It lead to official decision making that was arbitrary when it was not corrupt.

Reforms to the Criminal Justice system were designed to encourage public confidence in the system and to free it from the legacy of the past. Given the deep rooted public perception of Judge and Procurator collaborating to secure convictions, with the Judge led by the Procurator and the Party giving instructions behind the scenes (6), an Anglo-Saxon model of criminal proceedings was adopted. The independence of the judiciary from the State, the introduction of trial by jury, full legal representation of the accused, the Presumption of Innocence, Habeas Corpus and the separation of the roles of the investigator and the prosecutor became the key objectives for reform.

How to ensure the independence of Judges was a matter of considerable debate. Apart from clearly separating the judge's role of reaching a verdict from the Procurator's role of presenting the evidence against the accused, it was felt that the status of Judges in society needed to be raised. In the past the position of Judge was of low status, akin to that of an administrative functionary of the State and if Judges were to be independent of the state, and beyond the reach of threats and corruption, their status needed to be raised. The law `On Disrespect for the Court' (1989) imposed penalties for contempt of court; up to one year in prison or a fine of 300 - 1000 rubles for `Exertion of any influence on Judges or People's Assessors, up to three years in prison or one to two years correctional labour if the offence involved `taking advantage of one's official position'. Further offences of `Insulting a Judge or a Peoples' Assessor regarding his actions in the administration of justice', `Intentional noncompliance with a judicial decision' and `Disrespect for the Court' were also created.

The issue of Judges' salaries was also addressed and salaries raised. However the issue is not without complication, as can be seen by the reaction to Yeltsin's Presidential

Decree (31/7/92) granting the highest professional ranking and a 30% increase in salary to the Judges of the RF Constitutional Court. The opposition to Yeltsin claimed that he was buying the support of the Judges of the Constitutional Court and provoked a scandal that can only have damaged the reputation for independence that the Court had established. (7) This is not to say that the court has not been able to assert its independence since; ruling Yeltsin's proposal (20/3/93) to sign a decree on special rule unconstitutional and hearing the Defendants' allegations against the Procurator General during the trial of the organisers of the August 1991 Coup. The latter decision led the newspaper Izvestia to celebrate " For the first time since the emergence of Soviet power in Russia, the court did not heed the opinion of the Procurator General but took an independent decision" (19/5/93).

To further protect the independence of Judges the USSR Constitution was amended (1.12.88) to extend their term of office from 5 years to 10 years and to require their immunity from prosecution. The power to elect Judges, all Soviet Judges were elected, was moved from the level of government equivalent to the level of the court to the level above; so that a Judge of a City Court would be elected by the Territorial Soviet rather than the City Soviet. To date Judges' complaints remain poor pay, overwork, inadequate working conditions and lack of personal protection.(8)

The following year further reforms were enacted when the USSR Supreme Soviet passed the law `Principles of the USSR and Union-Republic Legislation on the Judicial System' (1989). Under Article 11 jury trial was allowed for serious offences. As a number of Soviet Jurists pointed out at the time this was not a new step for Russia but a return to the reforms of Tsar Alexander II of 1864. Nonetheless, jury trial remains a relatively untried novelty in the Former Soviet Union today. Although Judges in the District Court, the lowest court, have always sat with two elected Peoples' Assessors there is very little experience of conducting jury trials; the Peoples' Assessors being more akin to Justices of the Peace than to members of a jury. Article 11 provided for a jury in the form of an enlarged panel of Peoples' Assessors but in Russia today the aim is to empanel juries from citizens selected for the purpose rather than elected as Peoples' Assessors for the full 5 year term. In 1994 the first jury trials have begun in selected judicial districts and jury trial is expected to become the norm for serious offences.

Article 14(2) of the same law affirmed the Presumption of Innocence while Article 14(1) gave the accused a right to defence, that right to be secured by Defence Counsel's participation from the moment of detention, arrest or indictment. The right of defence was of immense significance because under Stalin, Vishinskii had developed the notion that there was little need for the accused to be represented given the commitment of Investigator, Procurator and Judge to establishing the truth. As a result any accused person was unlikely to be represented until the moment of trial and there was no means of opposing any abuse of process committed by the investigator or the prosecutor. Article 14(1) gave effect to the Constitutional guarantee of a right to defence (Article 158) introduced in 1988. The right was backed up by Article 161 of the Constitution which requires 'Kollegyia' (Collectives) of Advocates to be available to render legal assistance to citizens and organisations. The 1989 law also provided for hearings to be held in public. The question of the investigation and prosecution of crime required a change in attitudes more than any structural reform. Firstly, there needed to be an independent judiciary and able and confident Defence Counsel willing to challenge any abuse of process. Speaking in 1989, Alexander Sukharev, then Procurator General of the USSR spoke of the need to improve the image of advocates and to persuade them "in spite of all the difficulties, to overcome their fear of being compromised and to become involved at an earlier stage of proceedings i.e. at the time of arrest".(9) In the past Judges too ran the risk of being 'compromised' if they did not cooperate with the investigator's and the prosecutor's ambition to secure a conviction.(10) Sukharev, interviewed in the Moscow News (11) gave the conviction rate in Soviet courts as 99.7%.

In discussing the Procurator's Office, it should be noted that the power and competence of the Soviet Procuracy was much wider than that of a State Prosecutor. Under the law 'Procuratorial Supervision in the USSR' (1955) the tasks of the Procuracy, in addition to the prosecution of criminal offences, included supervision of the legality of criminal investigations, supervision of the strict execution of laws by State bodies and officials, supervision of the legality and well-foundedness of judicial decisions, supervision of the legality of execution of judgements and supervision of the observance of legality in prisons. The law required Procurators to participate in administrative, civil and criminal hearings, to prosecute crimes and to bring or intervene in proceedings where necessary to protect the interests of the State or citizens. The Procuracy was required to protest any illegal action observed to higher authority and, in judicial matters to protest any 'illegal and ill-founded' judgement. It is this later power which gave Procurators so much power and influence in criminal cases.

Reformers proposed shifting two key areas of responsibility from the Procurators Office to an independent judiciary, appeals against illegal acts of State officials and supervision of the investigative process. The first was given effect by the law 'On the Procedure for Judicial Review of Illegal Administrative Actions' (1989) which allowed citizens access to the courts to complain about actions of State Officials. At present it is the Russian Procuracy that still supervises criminal investigations, authorising procedures such as arrest and entry and search of premises.

In the main, however, reformers relied on the establishment of an independent judiciary and legal glasnost to overcome the abuses of the past. By ensuring that all questions of rights were directed to the courts, that hearings were public and that the media was free to scrutinise the workings of the State and the legal system it was hoped that an independent judiciary, empowered to fight official lawlessness, would provide the necessary 'checks and balances' to State power to bring to an end the excesses of Soviet bureaucracy.

(4)   Article 6 was finally modified to recognise the role of other political parties in
        February 1990.
(5)   (See Press Briefing on activities of the RF Interior Ministry's Penitentiaries
        Directorate 17.11.92 - Official Kremlin International News Broadcast)
(6)   For examples of miscarriages of justice and a discussion of the causes of and
        solutions to 'Legal Nihilism' see - The Debate over Justice and Individual Rights,
        Chapter 4 of The Glasnost Papers: Voices on Reform from Moscow (1990) - Ed
        A Melville & G W Lapidus - Westview Press
(7)   Source: Kuranty, p4, 15/8/92
(8)   See for example reports of the first Convention of Judges of the Russian
        Federation held in October 1991
(9)   Source: Report of Law Society of England & Wales delegation to the Soviet
        Union April 1989
(10)   See The Glasnost Papers, p159
(11)   No 23, 11 - 18 June 1989, p13

Perestroika and the Armed Forces

Jean-Christophe Romer

Under Leonid Brezhnev's leadership the Soviet armed forces were the regime's 'clear favourites', both as far as individual arms were concerned, and weapons and armament in particular. Soon after his accession to power, Mikhail Gorbachev reexamined the question of the Soviet army's role in society and diplomacy. When he first met "his" officers, in July 1985 at Minsk, the new Secretary General of the Communist Party was rumored to have informed them that the time for favoritism, especially in the area of expenditure, was over. Instead he wanted to give priority to the production of consumer goods and raising the living standards of the population.

In the first half of the 1980s the army showed two strong characteristics: it took a lion's share of the national budget and was most secretive as regarded daily organization as well as matters of armaments. Thus,in 1987, when the new leaders decided to reveal to the public defense expenditures, the list was only partial and approximative, due to old habits of secret classification and blurred frontiers between defense and other public spending. However,in February 1989, N. Ryjkov, who was Prime Minister at the time, admitted that 75% of research expenses went to the military. A few weeks later, M. Gorbachev officially announced that the budget for defense amounted to 77,3 billion rubles. In fact according to some experts, in the East as the West, 30% of the GNP in the USSR was allocated to defense.

Yet M. Gorbachev was not merely concerned with budgetary reform and figures. The new leadership was intent on ending the USSR's dependence on military power for cutting a figure in the world, as had been the case for decades. This was the reason why M. Gorbachev, on February 16, 1987, declared that never before had internal policies been so decisive in shaping the international policy of the USSR. In short, the Soviet

Union had to emerge from its long series of crises in order to come to terms with internal development.

The new directives brought about a complete remodeling of the military establishment, in the area of armaments, numbers, military doctrine and thereby, a radical change in the mental attitudes of its officers. This upheaval could not take place without conflicts or opposition from various members of a social body well known for conservatism and so far enjoying preferential treatment.

It was not until January 1987 that the first signs of perestroyka being introduced into the army became visible. It concerned three areas where other social reforms launched by M. Gorbachev were at work: social conditions, depolitization in the army and the future of conscription.

With the introduction of glasnost, the Soviet press - including the military press - gave increasingly detailed information on all aspects of military life. Yet it was remarkable that this new transparency of the army, unlike what happened in the West, was limited to examples of mismanagement in living conditions, and on the other hand anything to do with equipment and deployment of military forces was kept in shrouds of secrecy.

One of the topics most frequently mentioned in the press was that of poor housing for army personnel and their families. At the last congress of the CP, in July 1990, Marshal Jazov, who was then Defense Minister, claimed that some 200,000 officers and their families had no adequate housing. He stressed also that the numbers would increase with the forces stationed in satellite countries being repatriated. The situation often brought extreme hardship on these families and explains why, in the negotiations between the USSR and Germany after the fall of the Berlin Wall, the Bonn government allocated special funds to the Russians for building accomodation for officers returning from what used to be East Germany. The West Germans were showing good will towards the USSR after its defeat, but they also, and may be primarily, wanted to prevent the Russians using their difficulties in providing accomodation as an excuse for delaying the departure of the "Western Forces Group" from Germany.

Apart from this main subject of interest for the press, military or otherwise, it became apparent that the officer corps was not as closely knit and privileged as was thought. Though the officers of crack regiments were given many privileges by the regime, it was quite different for less prestigious regiments and/or those stationed far from important decision centers. This applied to building battalions (Stroibat) whose men were frequently given the most thankless tasks and whose officers were hardly better off. A climate of violence pervaded these lacklustre units, but it could be found in other units also, as evidenced by the denunciations of the victims' families as well as more muted accusations of the military press. Acts of violence within the military were three fold: naked violence, raw treatment given to new arrivals (dedovshchina) and clashes between various ethnic groups (groupovshchina) mostly between Slavs and non-Slavs. In 1991, military tribunals counted 3.000 victims a year on average, 25% of which were suicides.

Thus perestroyka destroyed the official myth of a homogeneous army, capable of shaping the new "homo sovieticus". Tensions inside the military machine, which had for a long time been underestimated in the West came to the fore during the August 1991 putsch. It is most probable that the failure of the putsch was due in part to divisions inside the Soviet army, since while a section of the military hierarchy was indeed behind the creation of the "National Committee for Martial Law", another caused its failure by refusing to obey orders, which were in any case rather confusing.

The army had not only to face a problem of identity in Soviet society, it also ,since 1987, had to answer the question of its specificity in the establishment: should it remain the military arm of the CP or should it be depoliticized? There were three different views corresponding to three main trends inside the institution. The first one championed the principle of the "army-military arm of the communist party" This position which was upheld by the more conservative elements had to be revized after March 1990. This was the time when a constitutional reform changed Article 6 of the 1977 Constitution and brought to an end the leading role of the CP in Soviet political and social life. Indeed, unlike what happened in other countries of the surviving Warsaw Pact, the article did not simply disappear in the USSR, it was altered to turn the CP into one of the political forces of the country together with other parties.

So, to allow a semblance of legality, the conservatives fought for the principle of a politicized army, but one in which all political parties could express themselves. Does it mean that orthodox communists had endorsed the idea of pluralism in public life? Certainly not since at the time - and it was still the case in 1992 - though a manner of pluralism existed in the USSR, no political party had acquired proper structures of its own, therefore the CP retained a leading position in the Red Army.

Inversely, the reformers, especially numerous among the younger high ranking officers, were in favor of depoliticizing the army. A clash of opinion did occur at the time of the 18th -and last - Congress of the CP. A Colonel of the Air Force revealed the fact that the army delegates to the Congress were not representatives of the majority. Paradoxically the allegation was made in a journal of the political leadership of the army. The delegates in question were accused of stating that officers were in favor of retaining a political army while, according to an opinion poll taken in the Colonel's unit, 80% of the people answering took the opposite stand. The putsch and its political consequences were going to bring the debate to an end through a ban of the PC and abolishing the political leadership in the army.

The third debate that was started by perestroyka was still topical in 1992: should the principle of conscription be operative or should the Soviet Army gradually become a professional one? The debate started in 1988 and until 1990 favored retaining conscription: the Soviet Army can only be a people's army. Yet some technical constraints - the smaller numbers needed to accomodate technical changes - and also the new situation arising from the experience of the Gulf War, gradually led the hierarchy to tend cautiously towards a "professional" army, as a tentative step before openly abandoning conscription.

After the putsch and the disintegration of the USSR, all the independent republics which used to make up the USSR created their national armies, and set their sights on professionalism for the year 2000. In the meantime, essentially for reasons of economy, their armed forces rest on conscription and/or volunteering.

Early in 1922, as far as the Russian army was concerned, under the leadership of B. Yeltsin, the official policy was to introduce a combination of conscription and volunteering, while reducing the time of military service from two years to eighteen months and tweve months eventually. The need for increased professionalism among conscripts and volunteers alike was also stressed. This is regarded as a period of transition leading, within ten years, to a professional army.

In other words, as the August 1991 putsch proved, the military establishment has been given a hard time by the political leaders. Yet, and it may prove to be the greatest paradox of this development, the army seems to have remained loyal to the people in power, as it had always been when it represented the "military arm of the CP". Its internal differences in reality only reflect the opposition of two possible interpretations of loyalty to the authorities. It could either be loyalty to the Lenin-Stalin legacy as represented by the bureaucratic image acquired under Brezhnev, or loyalty to the man who had assumed the leadership of the CP in 1985.

The opposition between the two kinds of loyalty was exacerbated at the time of the putsch in August 1991. The National Committee for Martial Law embodied then a new kind of legitimacy acquired by well tried methods. Opposite, for the first time in the history of the USSR, stood another form of legitimacy equally ...legitimate. Indeed Boris Yeltsin, as the president elected by universal suffrage in June 1991, stood against the putsch leaders from the first day, on August 19. Yet there is no doubt that it was not so much its respect for universal suffrage which drove the army to disobey orders - insofar as these orders were firm, coherent and chanelled through the "usual" chain of command - as the image of a man who represented the new born Russian nation and was obviously in charge of events.

How else can we explain the situation in which one of the putsch leaders, Marshal Jazov, Defense Minister, gave his "blessing" to General Shaposhnikov, Commander-in-Chief of the Air Force, and his successor-to-be, who had decided against the putsch and disregarded his ministers' orders. In other words, the army, after an unprecedented ordeal, had to choose its allegiance. It can be said that the Army proved to be both the instigator of the putsch and the instrument of its failure.

However, the trials and tribulations that the army went through were not limited to issues of internal policies, they extended to international affairs, and the leaders had to agree to political decisions that could only be perceived as rebuffs and humiliations.

The USSR had experienced since the late 70s various crises - Euromissiles, Afghanistan, Poland - and the first task facing M. Gorbachev was to extricate his country from difficulties which were undermining its credibility in one half of the world and isolating it diplomatically in the other half. In the area of international politics also, M. Gorbachev tried, in 1987, to effect restructuration (perestroyka) and introduce his "new thinking". One of his major concerns was to restore the credibility of the USSR worldwide, first of all by taking several measures to help it emerge from various crises without too much damage to its reputation. The most pressing problem was that of Afghanistan and to put an end to this, he signed in April 1988, an agreement on complete withdrawal of all Soviet armed forces from Afghan territory - the notorious "limited expeditionary corps", within a year. On February 15, 1989, in accordance with a timetable that was scrupulously observed, the withdrawal was completed.

The same tendency was also visible in other parts of the world, as for example in Southern Africa where the USSR dropped its commitments altogether, making it possible for Angola, Namibia and even indirectly South Africa, to return to "normal". Likewise the Soviet regime distanced itself from its Vietnamese ally, encouraging it, through financial enticements especially, to withdraw its troops from Cambodia, and deciding to close down the base at Cam Ranh, without obvious advantages in return.

Though Soviet disengagement in various third world countries was comparatively painless for the army, the withdrawal from Afghanistan was a sad experience for thousands of officers who had served there during the ten year long war, especially as the USSR had not been defeated in military terms by the "Afghan bandits".

In an effort to bring old conflicts to an end, relations with Poland and Hungary became easier after 1987, though there tensions had been less open. From then on, their leaders were allowed to carry out significant reforms. Even if it was out of the question to give up the "special relationship with the USSR", some Soviet conservatives expressed alarm at the "liberties" that were taken with orthodox Marxism-Leninism. Obviously, after the summer of 1989, the question of the satellite countries was one arousing the most bitterness in military circles.

Throughout the period following the Iron Curtain being half dismantled in Hungary and Poland giving herself a non-communist government, until the fall of the Berlin Wall, many in the USSR felt appaled at the loss of the buffer zone set up in 1945 at great cost. However, it was not until the late spring of 1990 that Soviet officers started voicing their discontent openly and denouncing the defeatist attitude of the leadership. This is when political power went increasingly to the conservatives, who tried to seize control in August 1991, after making their mark in January 1991 through the repression in Lithuania and Latvia and the slowing down of disarmament talks.

The declaration of January 16, 1986, announcing the total disappearance of nuclear weapons by the year 2000, was typical of the declamatory utterances that the Soviet regime made at regular intervals in the field of disarmament. Yet in the context of his policy of restructuration, M. Gorbachev seems to have meant what he said. After years of stalling, it was necessary to advance qualitatively rather than quantitatively. Gradually a new doctrine of disarmament emerged which made the Soviets accept,one after the other, most of the principles that had been systematically rejected so far: one sided reductions, on the spot checks, physical destruction of some categories of material, including the most up to date.

The first example of the new Soviet attitudes was undoubtedly the Washington Treaty, signed on December 8, 1987, in which the destruction of a whole category of weapons was envisaged as well as sending on the spot inspectors, a thing unheard of in the history of disarmament. In purely strategic terms, the treaty was beneficial to the parties involved in the sense that it would prevent a conflict in Europe spreading to the sanctuaries of the two superpowers. On this score, it could only be welcome to the army. On the other hand, since it dealt not only with destroying modern weapons in higher numbers than the American ones, but also with checks on the spot to make sure that the agreement was observed, the military were far from pleased. However, willy nilly the treaty was applied and the last SS 20 was destroyed in May 1991.

Negotiations on conventional weapons were also delicate for the military. In the Vienna talks on reduction of conventional forces in Europe, the Soviet envoys did accept - a point that had been discussed in the specialized press since 1987 - the principle of assymetrical reductions, admitting officially for the first time what had long been known in the West: that the conventional Warsaw Pact forces were vastly superior. This notion of assymetrical reductions had been strongly, though not overtly, resisted by the hierarchy, which for example disapproved vehemently the one sided reduction of 500.000 men, some 10% of the Soviet Army, announced by M. Gorbachev on December 8, 1988, to the United Nations Assembly. This decision was instrumental in the resignation - forced or genuine - of the Chief of the General Staff, Marshal Akhromeyev. Yet it was seen as a proof of the willingness of the Soviet authorities to engage in a real process of reducing their armed forces, making it possible for the Vienna negotiations, in March 1989, to start in auspicious circumstances.

Still, a general feeling of uneasiness was manifest in the autumn and winter 1990-91, and largely responsible for the growing influence of the conservatives. There was a marked stiffening of Soviet attitudes in disarmament talks everywhere. For instance, in the weeks preceding the signature of the Paris agreements (November 1990) military equipments were either transfered beyond the Urals - that is to say outside the area from the Atlantic to the Urals concerned by the treaty - or they were allocated to the Navy, which was not included in the treaty. In the advanced stage of desintegration and uncertainty affecting Soviet political power, it is difficult to know whether such decisions were made by the army, with the assent of a section of the political establishment, as it was opposed to a rapprochement between East and West, or whether, in order to pacify the army uneasy at the extent of concessions made by the USSR in the negotiations, the political leadership was forced to agree to the transfers.

In any event, the late 1990 and early 1991 saw a marked cooling off of relations between the two sides, coinciding with the stance adopted by the Soviet authorities in the Gulf crisis and ensuing war which caused much heartache in the army. The army found it difficult to accept the decision to withdraw support from Irak and also, perhaps above all, the fact that Moscow gave the West information about a quantity of Soviet equipment that had been sent to Irak. While trying to play down the value of the Soviet equipment that had found its way into Iraqui hands, the most conservative elements in the army did their best to use the crisis for their own ends and reactivate the debate on military strategy.

If the strategic debate was started in the late 70s under the influence of Marshal Ogarkov, there is no doubt that it took a different turn after M. Gorbachev came to power. From 1987, in an effort to reduce tensions - as well as military expenditure - the new Soviet leadership advocated a purely defensive strategy. Gorbachev rejected outright nuclear power and the argument of dissuasion and instead promoted the notion of " reasonable defensive sufficiency".

The first inkling of this new outlook came in May 1987 in the announcement of the "defensive doctrine of the Warsaw Pact countries". It was first received in the West as another example of Soviet posturing, but when actions followed, particularly the news given on December 7, 1988, of the reduction of forces by 500.000 men, the declaration became more credible. But times had changed and a decision taken at the top was no longer sufficient to close the debate. Indeed the notion of defensive strategy had to be well defined to avoid confusion due to the numerous and almost contrary interpretations given to it. They ranged from one close to the classical Sokolovsky approach, therefore aggressive, to a genuinely defensive concept, in which forces would be limited by agreement, to such an extent that any offensive venture became impossible.

In November 1990, the journal of the General Staff published a document on military doctrine. This semi official publication seemed to close the debate by giving the final version of the new Soviet strategic doctrine. Yet the document, which attempted to combine all the arguments put forward since 1987, gave an ambiguous interpretation of the new doctrine. In short, it was bound to irritate both the advocates of an offensive stance and those who favored the really defensive approach. It stated for instance that, in the event of an armed conflict, the first reaction of the Soviet army would be entirely defensive, there would be no attempt to gain victory, especially through nuclear weapons. However, it went on: " the next reaction would be determined in the light of the enemy's military decisions."

In reality, the "official" doctrine did not remain applicable for long, since throughout 1991, with events in Irak, a purely defensive doctrine had to be closely reappraised. As early as January 1991, a general of the Reserve Army, I. Vorobev, suggested that the November document should be amended and instead of the defensive concept that of "adequate response" be introduced. From then on, the idea was adopted, under various guises, by the entire Soviet military establishment. However, it seemed certain, even then, that the notion of defensive strategy was a thing of the past, as a result of the strategy that led to the coalition against Irak in the Gulf. A characteristic of the new way of thinking was that it followed an independent course in the midst of the internal changes occurring in the USSR. Before and after the August putsch, there were some officers who argued for the "adequate" strategy, while others wanted one capable of responding to any kind of military action, even to an offensive action, and others still prefered a "flexible, balanced and bold" response.

After the USSR broke up on December 8, 1991, the matter of military doctrine ceased being of public interest, at least temporarily, as the various republics, especially Russia, had other more immediate concerns. Yet for historical reasons, as well as reasons of international politics, the debate should be reopened in the spring of 1992, at the point where it was interrupted.

In 1992 the Red Army known as the Soviet Army ceased to exist in effect. The attempt at setting up "United Armed Forces of the CIE", making the army the last and only federal body, could not satisfy anyone in fact. Early on, at the second CIE summit meeting which took place at Minsk on December 30 and 31, 1991, three republics, and not the lesser ones, announced that they were determined to create their own armed forces, and three others that, in accordance with the agreement signed on December 31, they would use eventually their "legal right" to an independent army. What part did Russia, as it will always be, in whatever circumstances, the major power in what used to be the USSR, play in this failure to create a common army for the Union?

Though he publicly declared himself opposed to a Russian national army, in the first three months after setting up the CIE, as soon as Boris Yeltsin assumed the functions of Defense Minister, and decided to have a Russian Army, he was de facto sealing the fate of the idea of federal forces. Was Russia compelled by events to make the decision, in the face of the Ukrainian attitude? Or was Yeltsin from the start certain that Russia had to have a national army, since many officers - Russian nationalists - wanted it this way? It is still difficult to know. However, as early as February 1992, the die was cast. The only question left now is what kind of relations can prevail between the various armies after signing the various bilateral and plurilateral treaties they have entered.

***

Selected Bibliography

Gelman H., Gorbachev's First Five Years in the Soviet Leadership (Santa Monica 1990)
Gorbachev M., Perestroika: New Ideas for our Country and the World (New York 1987)
Romer J.C., Approches Polemologiques (Paris 1991)
Kokochin A. et al., Problems of ensuring stability with radical cuts in armed forces and conventional armaments in Europe (Moscow 1989)

Perestroika and the Nationalities

Helene Carrere d'Encausse

Fortunately for Mikhail Gorbachev he was appointed head of the Communist Party-supreme leader of the USSR- on 11 March 1985, eleven months before the next Party Congress. For it was not sufficient for the leader to get to the top power position, he also had to establish himself by eliminating his potential rivals, who in past years had built up empires within the system. The power struggle, far from coming to an end when the top position had been reached, was only just beginning.

In the USSR, the struggle took place inside the Communist Party (described as the "ruling group" in the 1977 Constitution) whose members hold all the important jobs in the state. To redistribute responsibilities, traditionally there was nothing better than a Party Congress, which occurrs every five years and offers a chance to bring in a completely new set of leaders. From Stalin to Brezhnev all Soviet autocrats had used the device, having recourse to various manoeuvers to sweep out of power all their opponents and instead appoint their own men. Gorbachev benefited from the unique opportunity of being able to convene the Congress eleven months after coming to power, while Khrushchev, for example, had to wait three years to ease the Stalinists out and embark on a new course. Like Khrushchev, Gorbachev intended to change things; he would have to get rid of the men Brezhnev put in and end the situation of stagnation that Brezhnev had left behind. At the time, his favorite word was Uskorenie, acceleration. He was a person in a hurry, and wanted changes to take place quickly so that efficiency could be improved. It was only fair that Fate should help him by giving him an opportunity to hurry things along.

The opening date of the 27th Congress of the Communist Party, the first of the Gorbachev years, was symbolic. It was the same as that of the 20th Congress, another turning point, when Nikita Khrushchev, on February 25, 1956, embarked on his task of destalinization. After the 20th Congress, the USSR acquired a completely different appearance from the one it had under Stalin. Was Gorbachev able to carry out such a revolution?

Indeed his report on the state of the USSR, its failures and doubts, was radically opposed to the usual complacent picture of non existent achievements, that Soviet citizens so far had been supposed to take at face value. This new approach, giving a more accurate account of reality, was also more in tune with changing mentalities. During the preceding few years, Soviet borders had no longer been sealed hermetically, more men were allowed to go abroad, modern means of communication provided ordinary citizens with an altered image of their country, all this had to be taken into account. Gorbachev's speech did not really surprise anyone, but his conclusions were not universally acclaimed as evident. Even more than the contents of Gorbachev's adress, what was really revolutionary in 1986 was the change over from an individual knowledge of reality to collective knowledge, which is the condition sine qua non of the constitution of an authentic civilian society.

Of course the USSR is also and primarily a pluri-ethnic society, and Gorbachev, curiously, at the time of the 20th Congress, had nothing to offer to remedy its frustration and tensions. As soon as he referred to the Empire, which was the subject of a large section of his speech, Gorbachev reverted to the old apparatchik phraseology: "The Soviet people is a social and international community of a new kind" in which "oppressions and inequalities have been wiped out" to be replaced with "friendship between peoples, respect for national cultures and national dignity for everyone". Here Gorbachev, to describe the Empire, used the same phrases and incantations as all Soviet leaders since 1922. The USSR is in a bad way indeed, but the Empire is thriving, though experiencing a few minor problems or deficiencies. As he drew a balance sheet of Soviet history, Gorbachev firmly included Lenin's imperial legacy as an unprecedented success pointing forward to further achievements. The state designed to accomodate peoples of various origins had succeeded fully in its process of integration. Seeing in this the only cause for satisfaction after all the hardships of Soviet rule, Gorbachev meant to make the Empire a pillar of his reconstruction of the whole tottering structure.

Yet the section of the speech dealing with the Empire, in which ideological stereotypes repeated ad nauseam fall into outmoded patterns, indirectly reveals Gorbachev's centralist solution to the national crisis. Concerning economic difficulties and corruption in high circles, Gorbachev angrily pointed out what was happening in outlying areas. He accused some of the republics of being "parasites", only interested in their own gains, convinced that the only raison d'etre of the Soviet Union is to subsidize them without getting anything in return. The right course is exactly the opposite; each republic is duty bound to share in the development of a single economic complex in which the common good takes precedence over the special interests of each individual nation.

Apart from a few contradictions, Gorbachev's meaning was clear: the USSR must be a single economic entity. To attain this, national cultures and the policy of choosing leaders in the local population have to take second place. The two points on which the Soviet regime made a show of respecting national identities (giving a chance to all national cultures to express themselves and recruiting local elites were Stalin's directives, though the reality might have been different), came under Gorbachev's harsh scrutiny, as he exposed various wrongdoings in the more distant provinces. He admitted that every culture is important, but this should not obscure the fact that all the various parts of the Empire should be brought together, to be integrated in a common ideology and adapted to the socialist ideal of internationalism. There was no room for narrow national values, instead national characteristics should find a protection in the all embracing socialist state.

Gorbachev showed the danger of narrow nationalistic values (mesnichestvo) at another level, that of administrative cadres where the very organs of the economy and political organization were concerned. He showed how political elites in the republics of the USSR tended to live among themselves, applying a policy of "national nepotism" which made them give preference to their own nationals in the matter of promotions rather than more competent Russians. In general, Gorbachev remarked, this attitude leads to discrimination against those who do not belong to the majority in a given republic, and therefore cannot play their rightful part in the command hierarchy, either proportionate to their qualification or the size of their ethnic group. In short Gorbachev blamed the republics and large ethnic regions in the Soviet Union for their policy of "national preference", necessarily resulting in nepotism and corruption, as a particular group was favored to the detriment of the common economic good and racial relations.

This odd demonstration is interesting because of its contradictions. On the one hand, in 1986, Gorbachev painted an idyllic picture of the problem of nationalities, which stands out in his speech as the one bright spot of the entire Soviet history, and promised to be the foundation for recovery. On the other, he rebuffed all national claims and criticized local leaders in the far flung regions for taking advantage of the years of stagnation under Brezhnev and building their own empires. He did not go as far as Brezhnev who, in the latter part of his rule, had warned the republics that "it was time they paid their debt to Russia". Yet a certain irritation towards national demands and the refusal of local leaders to cooperate in the development of the Union was visible under the customary phrases of congratulation.

It would appear that mentioning the Soviet people as already in existence and at the same time calling some of the local leaders parasites is contradictory, but it is so only on the surface. Gorbachev in his speech, explained that the steps taken by the Soviet people were decisive advances on the way to internationalism; the faults that he exposed were the consequences of relics of the past and of years of political stagnation which changed the course of Soviet society.

In spite of his sharp criticism, this vision of the achievements of his predecessors in this matter seems quite optimistic, In summing up the situation in front of the Congress, Gorbachev pinpointed the question of nationalities as the one bright spot in an overall depressing picture. His critical conclusions spurred him on to find remedies and use perestroyka as a base for reconstruction. His denounciation of corruption in some of the republics was an argument to mobilize people in an unprecedented effort to revitalize the economy, These parasitic and inefficient republics would have to redeem themselves through hard work for the common cause. All the evils of national discrimination, nepotism and corruption gave him the justification he needed for a purge of local leaders, and for appointing a new set of people chosen for their qualifications and potential. In other words Gorbachev was enabled to strike a deadly blow at the fortresses of power that Brezhnev had allowed to establish themselves and which stood in the way of reform. Moreover, Gorbachev's attack of the principle of local appointments of cadres paved the way for installing his own men in all regions of the USSR. As he regretted there being so few "minority elements" (mainly Russian and Ukrainian) in the top echelons of responsibility in the republics, it became easy to reorganize the leadership in a new direction, more in keeping with the ideal of internationalism, another key word in his address.

The nail that Gorbachev had driven was pushed home by Ligachev, who stood out as second in command at the time of the Congress. He openly advocated an "exchange of leaders between republics, in a double movement from the center to the periphery and vice versa". This exchange meant in effect that the Moscow leaders could appoint their own men throughout the Empire, in keeping with old Soviet traditions designed to prevent stable national networks of authority able to represent society as a whole in all legitimacy. From the early 20s, central leaders gave themselves two objectives: the formation of an elite which would be able to develop the country, to be picked from all the various ethnic groupings so as to avoid an imbalance between master nations and subjects which could only generate resentment and rebellions; taking care at the same time not to allow local strata of authority to perpetuate themselves instead of giving preference to a higher Soviet elite, the vanguard of the future Soviet people. Stalin's compromise between national culture and proletarian culture found its accomplishment there. Individual nations could retain their own cultures as a temporary arrangement, but the Soviet elite was the embodiment of the proletarian culture they would all share one day. Once Krushchev and again Brezhnev had made concessions to nationalities which were eager to have their own elites, but they both recoiled from the consequences of an eventual alliance of the local population and their leaders against the center. At the 26th Congress, one year before he died, Brezhnev warned of the danger of the growing self-confidence of national elites, with Russian elements   left defenceless on the periphery.

In 1986, dealing with the problem of nationalities, Gorbachev was obviously in sympathy with the Party and with the feeling of frustration that was beginning to show among Russians. In this matter, the program that was endorsed by the 27th Congress was very similar to the previous one, except that it used the concept of "unified Soviet people" (edinyi sovetskii narod) which so far had not been mentioned on such a document, even though it had been widely used since 1977 by Party spokesmen. When a draft of the program was released, a public debate was launched in Pravda, with strong emphasis on Russia's role in Soviet history, the impetus given to the development of all the regions of the Union by the Russians, the need for a common Russian language as a civilizing influence to be spoken everywhere, and finally for a clear definition of objectives: a common state for an unified people. Undoubtedly Pravda's policy was to stress areas of frustration for Russians and the consequences to be drawn from the belief in the Soviet people as a reality. However, it indicates a trend in the Party's apparat, which at the time was still in control of the whole system. It is enough to remember that, unlike his three immediate predecessors, Gorbachev did not try to acquire any title other than Secretary General of the Party, letting men like Mikoyan or Ryjkov represent state power or the Government. The political line adopted at the 27th Congress was to be applied throughout the territory of the USSR.

In December 1986, clashes occurred at Alma-Ata between Kazakh demonstrators and police forces. These riots, the first under Gorbachev, did not seem to ruffle the Secretary General's certainties, nor that of the Party leadership. A few weeks later, on January 27, 1987, Gorbachev in a speech to the plenum of the Central Committee, only touched on the nationality troubles, though he referred to them more openly than was the case under past rulers. This is the first example of glasnost in an area where ready-made phrases used to gloss over reality. Yet even if Gorbachev recognized that difficulties may appear in a pluri-ethnic federation, he did not contemplate a change of policy on the question of nationalities. The reasons for confrontations were those he had mentioned in an unspecific way at the Congress: local discrimination, racial insularity, sometimes going as far as "national arrogance", all these phenomena were relics of the past which had survived under Brezhnev, in the years of stagnation. He concurred with his predecessors that remedies were to be found in adhering to strict internationalism and appointing leaders along these lines, that is to say all discrimination against Russian-speaking people had to cease at local level. There was nothing new in all that.

Yet Gorbachev was aware of increasingly bad relations among the personnel of the outlying regions. Reports from specialists appeared in the Press reflecting troubles encountered by the central authorities in applying their policies; suddenly the notion of ethnic conflict made an appearance. This explains why at the 70th anniversary of the October revolution Gorbachev dwelt on this topical question at some length. He seemed particularly helpless in adressing himself to the problem.

Once again, Gorbachev repeated that the Soviet system had solved the nationality problem, but he admitted that relations between nations were far from simple and required great attention on the part of the Party. Yet, for the first time since he came to power, he included the question in his policy of perestroyka and democratization, not as a pious wish, but as an element to consider in redefining general guidelines. This was a new departure.

There was no room for complacency though, since Gorbachev still insisted that friendship between the peoples of the Union, an enduring myth in Soviet history, was an achievement not to be endangered by new experiments; he still believed that there lay all the power and glory of the USSR. He condemned outright anything that could destabilize it. Yet a hopeful sign was that old taboos could be ignored and glasnost cast a new light on reality. When Gorbachev, in November 1987, publicly consented to examine problems arising from a pluri-ethnic Union, he more or less recognized them as more serious than previously admitted; he also accepted the notion that they should be discussed in the open like everything else.

In fact, he was letting himself be carried on the tide of events. Since the summer of 1986, glasnost was getting out of hand and the original limits that had been set were no longer observed, especially on the periphery. Gorbachev, when he acknowledged that debates were legitimate, seemed to endorse the opinion of their instigators. It looked as if he would, like Krushchev in 1956, change from rigid orthodoxy to a greater awareness of national interests. Though in the past this did not prove long-lived, it was likely to have far-reaching consequences.

There were many contradictions in Gorbachev's speeches on the question of nationalities problems, but when it came to the establishment, everything became much clearer. He had no anxiety about the basis on which the Soviet Union rested, as well as its apparat, this was the reason why he did not pay much attention to the republics and their national pride. Under his rule, the provisions of national representation that had been in force since 1956 were ignored.

In his selection of new men for the leadership, especially to the Politburo and the Secretariat, Gorbachev leant towards centralization. Two examples are enough to prove it: the incumbents of the highest echelons in the system became largely Russian and, above all, they were completely ignorant of the periphery. The first point stands out in the last Politburo under Brzhnev as contrasted with the one appointed in 1985-1986. Sheer figures do not give a fair idea of racial imbalance. In 1982, the Politburo had three non-Russian members, out of 13 entitled to vote. It was the same in 1987. Yet national representativity was different. Brezhnev's colleagues were appointed because they were the top leaders in their republics, with one exception. Shcherbitski, a Ukrainian, Kunaev, a Kazakh, just as much as the candidate members Aliev, a Azerbaidzani, Shevardnaze, a Georgian, Rashidov, an Uzbek and Kiselev, a Byelorussian, were First Secretaries of the Communist Party and they attended Politburo sessions just as much in order to defend their republics' interests, as to define common policies that would have to be imposed on their countrymen. Two years after Gorbachev's accession to power, things were quite different. Though Shcherbitski remained in the Politburo to represent the Ukrainian party, the two other national representatives were not in positions of power in their own republics. Shevardnaze, who up to 1985 had been First Secretary of the Georgian CP, was appointed Foreign Minister and therefore became one of the full members of the Politburo; his local party was no longer represented in this category. The same applies to Sliunkov, a Byelorussian, who entered the Politburo to replace his fellow countryman (Kiselev, ex First Secretary of the Byelorussian party) and who was appointed Secretary of the Central Committee in 1987, and from then on had a seat on the Politburo. As for the six candidate members of the Politburo, they were all Russians. Not only did national dignitaries no longer represent the regions they came from, but even more ominously, large parts of the periphery ceased to figure in the top echelons of the Party. Under Brezhnev, full and candidate members spoke in the name of the Muslim republics of Central Asia and Caucasus, Georgia, and the two Slav states, Ukraine and Byelorussia. There were some who were not represented (Balts and Armenians), but the more numerous peoples were. In 1987, all the Muslim republics and the Caucasus no longer figured on the Politburo, but their place was not taken by those who had previously been ignored. The Russian preference was reinforced by the overwhelming presence of the Slavs. Though in the Central Committee one member, Nikolai Sliunkov, was not Russian, all the same he was a Slav.

It should be remembered that there were times when the Secretariat was open to non-Russian minorities. In 1960, there were three of them, among whom a Muslim, Muhitdinov, who previously had been Secretary General of the CP of Uzbekistan. The sudden disappearance of the southern part of the USSR from the leadership, the part that was least homogeneous culturally, with the highest birth-rate and lowest standard of living, with preference given to the Slavic populations bound together by culture, religion social customs and level of development was to pose a serious problem from then on. Decisions made in the days of perestroyka were influenced by this comparatively close knit Slavic community of peoples.

To make matters worse, the Russians who held all positions of power had no experience of the non-Russian parts of the Union. This was also a new phenomenon. In past years Soviet leaders had to serve in the various republics before being sent to Moscow, and they had learnt quite a lot about conditions at the periphery during their period in the wilderness. With Mikhail Gorbachev, things took a new turn. Among his close associates, only two men had served in non-Russian parts: Victor Chebrikov, Chairman of the KGB in 1987, who had worked in the Ukraine for a while, and General Jazov, Defense Minister, who was in charge of the Central Asia Military District for a short time. Of course commanding a military region is no great incentive for mixing with the local population, quite the opposite in fact, while working for the KGB does not make for popularity. It is not very likely that Ukrainians or Central Asians regarded these representatives of law and order as spokesmen for their national claims. Apart from these two top leaders, no Politburo member or Secretary ever came to visit the far reaches of the Union.

This situation was unprecedented in the post-Stalinist era and had two main consequences. The nationalities feeling ignored, if not despised, by the Center, became convinced that, as soon as a conflict would break out, difficulties would have to be settled by force on the spot. Since they had no way to make their voice heard in Moscow, what could they do? But in Gorbachev's entourage the effects of the leadership's Russification or Slavization were equally harmful. Lack of experience made the leadership insensitive to growing tensions in peripheric areas. Later on, these tensions were ignored as due to general causes such as corruption, hooliganism, shortage of administrative personnel. Each explosion of violence was consistently underestimated and new crises wrongly assessed. Gorbachev and his men saw little difference between racial troubles and riots caused by food shortages. They had no inkling of the potential dangers of the nationalities question.

Largely responsible for these shortcomings in dealing with a Federation of Republics requiring a common process in decision making, was one man, Gorbachev. The very qualities which made him attractive to the outside world, his modern outlook, his intellectual attainments, higher than those of his predecessors, his "European" look, made him vulnerable in the sense that as a Russian, born far away from the center of the Empire, but sent to Moscow early on as a student, he had no experience of living and working outside Russian-speaking or European territories. He stood for industrial USSR, facing underdeveloped parts of the Union; the face looking to the West against the USSR of the past and traditions; of Christian USSR against the Muslim one. When he traveled through France as a young man, Gorbachev must have learnt a lot about it, but he had no such experience of his own country. He had no contact with men who came from the distant parts of the Empire and who could have advised him when the need arose. Stalin was well acquainted with the Caucasus and its inhabitants; Krushchev with the Ukraine; Brezhnev, the Ukraine, Moldavia and Kazakhstan; Andropov, Karelia. Even the most insignificant of the Secretary Generals, the short-lived Chernenko, had once held a leading position in Moldavia. They all learnt from the experience and made contacts. Gorbachev knew nothing outside Russia. He relied on a Georgian in foreign affairs, but after his appointment, this man who had been a KGB leader for a long time and knew Georgia and its inhabitants intimately, was cut off from them and could not help in this matter. The list of Gorbachev's advisers shows that most of them were Russians. Though Aganbegian, an economist, was Armenian, he was a Moscow Armenian, completely assimilated, who returned to his motherland only after a massacre and an earthquake had hit it. No wonder that Gorbachev was regarded as primarily Russian by the other nationalities.

The divorce started as early as 1985. Gorbachev as a faithful follower of Lenin, had a Leninist conception of the USSR. What mattered most was neither Nation nor Federation, but the Union to be built. Like Lenin, he knew nothing outside Russia; like him, he did not think it mattered, since central power would be able to deal with all the problems that might arise. Stalin's catch word of Kadry vse rechaiet (cadres can solve anything) was replaced by Gorbachev with one that Lenin applied in real life: Vlast vse rechaiet (central power can solve anything). Central power is not bound by national frontiers nor territorial ones. Gorbachev labored under the illusion that his authority and impeccable Leninist vision would carry the day, but the dangerous climate of rising national aspirations made his task impossible. The purge of corrupt personnel which had to be carried out before reconstruction could start, raised suspicions at local level and accelerated the process of desintegration of the Union, which the new Secretary General had unwittingly launched. At the beginning of the 1990s Lenin's rhetorical question

'Khto z kogo'? (Who beats whom) was answered in the USSR and in the parts of Europe which had been colonized by the Soviets for nearly fifty years. The answer came loud and clear: a sense of national identity caused communism to disappear from the face of the earth to join other utopias of the past in the bin.

The main theater for communism's defeat was the USSR, where various nationalities intent on regaining their power of decision making, dealt it mortal blows. This is not surprising as communism was first victorious in Russia, and the USSR which succeeded her, had done everything possible to impose the ideology on other nations; only its weakening in the mother country could bring about a general crisis. The very solidarity that Moscow leaders had established between numerous peoples of different origins eventually turned against the system and brought it down. Only a general uprising of the peoples making up the Soviet Union, depriving Gorbachev of any hope of it becoming once again a great power, could allow other nations to become independent, while he frantically tried to safeguard his central possessions.

Thus the movement of rebellion which had started in the USSR, spread outside, only to return into various regions of the Union like a boomerang, making the Empire more fragile still. Failure breeds failures, according to an English saying. The point was proved by the collapse of communism everywhere.

Men of varying importance presided over the collapse. At the heart of events, overseeing the total bankrupcy of the system, Mikhail Gorbachev stood like a giant. He wisely chose not to resist the movement, when he realized that his predecessors had prepared the ground for an inevitable breakdown of the whole structure.

The mental process which guided Gorbachev in this is worth examining. In a few months, he gave up his initial belief that the USSR could be reorganized, and struck by the extent of the disaster, embarked on his policy of democratization. He did not use force to try to preserve for a while a structure that was doomed, as his training must have encouraged him to do. He threw all his resources into the task of closing the balance sheet of seventy years of communism and replacing utopia with an attempt at modernization.

The only quality he lacked in this clearsighted and courageous enterprise, was an awareness of nationalities. In this he was a disciple of Lenin, who saw the Nation purely in strategic terms and as historically doomed. The price Gorbachev had to pay, for keeping to an ideological stance so unlike his usual pragmatism, was heavy. He had to look on helplessly, when the country lurched from one national crisis to another, seeing all his plans ruined, as he was unable to restore order.

Facing a statesman of outstanding merit, but having no resources to deal with mounting troubles, there were no national leaders of comparable stature, an unusual occurrence in history. No genuine statesman had emerged in the course of these crucial years, from the various nationalities making up the Union, and from the political movements that had developed on the periphery. In other countries, of course, Mazowiecki or Havel showed their mettle after becoming national leaders, while they could only display limited qualities of courage and inventiveness in the struggle for power.

Nonetheless, it was quite obvious that no charismatic figure had emerged from the years of national struggle in the USSR. Early in the century, when national awareness started to develop in the Russian Empire, there had been a flowering of prestigious intellectuals and politicians everywhere. Irakli Tseretelli in Georgia, for example, Sultan Galiev for the Muslims, many others had played a leading part at the time. In Lithuania, independence was achieved against all odds, under the influence of an unknown, unprepossessing music teacher, who wisely handled the movement for independence, but did not gain a great aura in so doing. There is not much chance of Landsbergis becoming a mythical figure some day, unlike Walesa for instance. Yet his achievements at national level are remarkable.

In spite of this absence of heroes able to rally whole populations, all nationalities erupted until drastic changes affected the European political landscape. What was at work then was a passionate wish on the part of the various peoples to resurrect their past, society as a whole was concerned, not mere individuals. Gorbachev's objective of modernization paled into insignificance, for all its urgency, compared to the glory of gaining national independence. Gorbachev had to pay dearly for failing to understand that he could not mobilize his fellow citizens under the banner of modernizing the USSR in order to restore its greatness. He will probably be remembered only for the fact that he did not try to crush these national outbursts, with a few exceptions here and there, though he did not grasp their implications until it was too late and he had been rendered impotent.

The aftermath of the collapse of the Soviet Empire may give rise to a multiplicity of Nation-states which will each strike out for itself. As the crisis of identity reaches its full intensity, in what used to be the Soviet Union, each individual nation is probably tempted by a full divorce with no room for retaining any connection, even on a new basis. Yet in the long run, this attitude will have to be modified under the influence of geography and history. The vast territorial expanse making up the Russian Empire, later to become Soviet Empire, was a melting pot for many peoples of widely differing origins, with cultural and economic interaction occurring in the process.

It is a different proposition for an empire giving independence to far away possessions, overseas, from which settlers and administrators can be withdrawn. In Eastern and Central Europe, in spite of material difficulties, the USSR may also recall troops and advisers detailed there, in the end may be all connection will be severed. In the USSR proper or Russia, it is a daunting prospect to draw boundaries between each entity. They have changed so often in the past, with whole populations being transfered, that no one knows where they are exactly. The same applies to territories outside Russia. Where is the border separating Uzbekistan from Tadjikistan ? where is the border between the Ukraine and a Tatar region now claimed by the descendants of Stalin's exiles? Where is that between Lithuania which looks both to Scandinavia and Slavic Byelorussia? There is no end to the conflicting claims made by the new national units in the area. Economic constraints are equally compelling. Some measure of interdependence can be discarded, having been artificially imposed from the center, such as specialization in production or road network. Yet after gaining independence each nation has to earn a living and this cannot be done in a state of isolation. Lithuania learnt it the hard way, when it suffered a blocus, however imperfect this might have been.

In order to defuse existing conflicts, avoid new ones and solve problems of interdependence, there are two options: mass transfers of populations and altered boundaries or a compromise. The first one is usually enforced after a hot conflict, in blood and tears. Poland is remarkable for its internal cohesiveness nowadays, but it is easy to forget that until 1939 it was a hotbed of national unrest and that Jews, Ukrainians and Byelorussians complained bitterly in those days of their humiliating condition as second class citizens. The problem was solved, as it were, by Germany carrying out genocide and by Stalin when he annexed Western Ukraine... Not everyone would choose such solutions for the countries of the ex USSR.

Compromise would give a chance to establish pluri-ethnic nation-states in which various communities could live side by side. It is clear that a balance between communities would be best achieved by appartenance to larger units, in which local differences would be less apparent. This is why, above the call for independence, national parties and fronts always take care to mention in their programs the need for a common framework for the various new states. It might be an association between the three Slavic states as equal partners. Many Russians would agree to that; the Ukrainian RUKH is not resolutely against it, neither is the Byelorussian Popular Front. If this were to happen, a Union of 220 million men and more, with huge territories and resources allowing for guaranteed prosperity in future would be established, but where would its boundaries be? It would be unlikely to end at the Urals. Most Russian groups would want it to go as far as the Pacific Ocean and probably cover Northern Kazahstan, as it has a large Russian population and is rich in mineral deposits.

Would it be possible for a collection of Muslim states under the probable authority of Uzbekistan to coexist with Greater Russia or a Federation of Slavic states? Or an Union of Muslim states? Even if some emerging political parties in Central Asia, the ERK for example, can be heard to suggest such a thing, no one in Russia would feel confortable having a neighbor with a fast rising population pressing on the borders, and especially those who bemoan the high cost of the periphery, would find it advisable to reach a compromise with the distant regions, rather than treating it as a potential enemy. There are many in Central Asia who accuse the USSR of ruining them through specialization, preventing internal development and condemning this area to stagnation and worse. The population increase among Muslims, as well as their new found political self-confidence should prevent the Russians from withdrawing into an European and Slavic citadel. But what about the Caucasian nations? should they be left to their internecine struggles with

Christian Georgians and Armenians facing an uncertain future at the hands of the Muslim populations surrounding them.

What is left of the USSR is facing a grave dilemma. There is no doubt that the Empire is finished, and that individual peoples have to choose their destinies. No one at the center is able, nor willing probably, to deny the right to self determination to the nations demanding it. Yet at the same time,if countless tragedies are to be averted, Russia as the successor of the USSR, must set up a community of equals from the various parts of the old Empire. A new Treaty of Union is under way, and a lively debate on its contents is going on. But it will take a long time to complete, and it is significant that an opinion poll taken during the 28th Congress of the CPSU showed that delegates rated 70% in favor of retaining a Federation, 11% for a Confederation, and 14% for a mixture of both. This shows the enormous gap dividing the conservative CP and the rest of the population in a country in turmoil.

The days of an Empire based on a common ideology (the Russian Christian Monarchy or Communism) forcibly imposed, and using the fallacy of historical development and progress as a pretext for domination over all outlying areas, these days are gone for ever. The USSR was the last example of this phenomenon, which gave it considerable power, but also prevented it from embarking on real modernization. After the fall of the Empire, each individual nation has to decide on the best way to achieve this elusive modernization.

It is clear that the nation-state will be the framework needed, either as a separate entity or in alliance with others, now there could be no going back to any form of Empire at the far end of Europe. This development had seemed likely in the aftermath of the Monarchy's collapse, but it was merely postponed by the revolution for almost a century. Now the situation must be faced squarely, nationalism is there to stay, and it will probably grow stronger with independence. Old quarrels will flare up again, border disputes will occur between neighbors, as they do already in the ex satellite countries.

Should nationalism be seen as an unfortunate development for the European regions which used to be under a communist regime? Was advance towards democracy the only possible way forward and are democracy and nationalism absolutely incompatible? This view is based on contemporary wisdom in developed countries which acquired independence a long time back and built up democratic institutions slowly, but it does not take into account the fact that the nation-state is the natural breeding ground for a modern society. The European nation, even in Eastern Europe, is not a tribe; a passionate wish for a stronger central state does not imply a return to the tribal system. National awareness, that is to say a feeling of belonging to a large community bound together by geography and a common history, in a framework of institutions freely accepted, is a feature of civilization; it marks a progress from primitive society, not the other way round.

The nation is based on common memories. Therefore necessarily, with old memories coming to the surface again after a long time, the peoples emerging from bondage discover past conflicts and resentment vis-a-vis their neighbors. This process of remembering is far from simple and though a nation has to go through it painfully to achieve national unity, it takes time to sort out the really important events. The cost to be paid for recovering national identity is that old tensions will erupt again. Nationalism often proves aggressive and violent, but this is the result of a long period of oppression and humiliations, sometimes complete obliteration of individual peoples.

Much later, can a generous and confident kind of nationalism appear, when time has proved that it could work. We would imitate Lenin, if we forgot that these peoples cannot have access to modernization and democracy without going through a stage of aggressive nationalism. A theory cannot replace the lengthy process of social development. Everyone is aware of this fact in the USSR and, after an initial period when nationalism was underestimated, all politicians take it into account in planning for the future.

Does it mean that the disintegration of the USSR which resulted from this outburst of nationalism is seen by all and sundry as irreversible, that nothing can happen to stop or slow down a complete collapse?

The present situation in the USSR is odd. As a military power, the Soviet Union still enjoys almost unlimited resources. In spite of the disarmament agreements that were signed, the military machine is practically untouched. The army is huge, with sophisticated equipment, substantial strategic capability, but can it be used to stop the country falling apart? It is a fact that if the Empire comes to an end, within a short space of time, nuclear strategic power will collapse also. It is difficult to imagine the people in authority - leaders of the political apparatus, the Army and the KGB - taking a back stand in such an event, when they still have the means to intervene.

Yet experience has shown that, apart from a few isolated incidents, at Tbilissi or in Azerbaidzan, Soviet leaders chose not to assert their authority. Was it a conscious choice or realization of the fatal sickness affecting the very military power at the heart of the ex Empire?

The latter explanation is the more plausible. Military leaders may vigorously condemn the Empire's dissolution, but they express different opinions as to ways of remedying the situation. Many of them voice distrust of a pluri-ethnic army in which racial tensions are rife. Could such an unreliable instrument be used to restore order in the far reaches of Soviet territory. Besides, as an institution, the army is no longer tolerated by society, as military authorities know full well. They suspect that it would be inacceptable to send armed forces to restore order on the periphery. This was the case during the intervention in Azerbaidzan, which was seen as violation of national territory. The presidential decree of July 26, 1990, demanding that national milices be disbanded unless force be used against them, leaves room for skepticism. There may be some police operations here and there, but can they be carried out in the Caucasus as well as Central Asia? The various arms stockpiles hidden all over are impossible to retrieve in their entirety, as no organization could be relied on to do so.

The tasks that a demoralized Army cannot accomplish are also beyond the grasp of the KGB, which makes it almost certain that the rush to independence will continue unchecked. The situation of the USSR in 1990 is similar to that of Russia in 1917. In both instances, central power is almost intact, but it is struck with paralysis and cannot resist enemy forces. The main difference lies in the fact that in 1917, society and the various nations were disrupted by the effects of the war, and they were unaware of the evils of a totalitarian regime, so that they became an easy prey to the bolsheviks who confiscated their revolution by force. It is another matter in this late part of the 20th century, when the bitter experience of past tragedies have made people wiser, and national leaders, both in Russia and on the periphery, make sure that the sources of totalitarian oppression are well understood. There may be hope in this realization for nationalism to merge with democracy one day.

Right up to 11 March 1990, when Lithuania proclaimed independence, the Soviet Union consisted of fifteen republics. Negotiations on the Treaty of Union had reached the point where 9+1 were to be associated, with the 7 other republics ready for any kind of arrangement.

In August, after endless discussions and many adjustments, there was some measure of agreement. A loose document, allowing much leeway to the republics was about to be endorsed. Probably not unanimously, since Ukraine at least would wait until the elections due at the end of the year. As for Russia, it meant to gain more advantages, and on the eve of the signing ceremony, Yeltsin confidently told an assembly of journalists that, together with Nazarbaev, President of Kazakhstan, he would try to have the draft altered substantially, to reduce central power further. In the end, the only republics ready to sign on August 20th were, apart from Russia and Kazakhstan, who made reservations, Uzbekistan, Tadjikistan and Kirghizia, all of five republics. The others (minus Ukraine) promised to sign in September, but the Union did not attract much enthusiasm.

However, Gorbachev was desperately trying to achieve some form of Union, even if it meant watering down the original treaty. All hope of achieving this was shattered on August, 19th, when the putsch destroyed what was left of the USSR.

All analyses of the putsch, of which quite a number have appeared in the USSR, mention the fact that one of the main aims of the conspiracy was to prevent the Union Treaty being signed. The plotters thought that any attempt at stopping further erosion of the Soviet system, and of its structures, was doomed to fail if its original framework, the USSR, was not preserved. The document ready to be signed, on August 20th, was a hotch potch which did not satisfy any of the potential signatories and it was violently attacked, on August 19, by Lukianov, President of the Supreme Soviet. He was later to be described as the brain behind the putsch, and he pointed out at the time that the treaty had not taken into account the criticism made by the Supreme Soviet of the USSR, and allowed the republics to suspend the application of Union laws on their territories, which would act as a detonator for endless conflicts, particularly of a legal character.

The Ministerial Cabinet of the USSR, meeting on a restricted basis two days earlier, had expressed the same reservations. The difficulties encountered by the central authorities, resulting in countless alterations of the original draft of the treaty, the rapid rise of Russia after Boris Yeltsin was elected and its posing as a rival of the Union, even the symbolic gesture of installing Yeltsin's office in the Kremlin and floating the two flags together at the heart of what represented Soviet power since 1918, everything pointed to an uncertain future for the Union.

After the putsch failed, there came an acceleration of the process that Gorbachev had long tried to curb. Those who had opted out, were further encouraged to strike out for themselves. Latvia, after passing a law declaring de facto independence on May, 4, 1990, made it statutory on August 21. Moldavia endorsed the process of gradual secession. In Estonia and Lithuania, a ban on the Communist Party was evidence of a total break with the last relic of central power. Zviad Gamsakurdia, President of Georgia called on the international community to recognize the republics' independence, before a successful putsch could challenge it. For the same reason, the Ukrainian government insisted on considering once again the old motion of setting up national armed forces and putting under Ukrainian command all Soviet troops stationed on the territory. In Armenia, the September 21 referendum, with a participation of 94,3%, gave 99,31% in favor of immediate independence. All the republics, after the putsch, wanted to reinforce their capacity of resistance to the Center, to a sick Union they increasingly want to discard, since it could bring them nothing but trouble.

After the aborted putsch, was there a chance of reviving the treaty? Gorbachev thought so at first, when he returned from Foros, the holiday resort where he was held in detention for a few hours. In reality he had to lower his sights considerably, under the impact of his close advisers being implicated in the putsch, and raising doubts on the part he played (was he an accomplice or did he prove too soft?) as well as the immense prestige acquired by those who had resisted the putsch, foremost among whom Yeltsin.

The new Soviet Parliament, appointed after the putsch, was given the task to deal with the question of the Union at its first meeting. What a strange gathering this was, representing a state that did not really exist. On September 2, 1991, the Congress of the people's deputies of the USSR, sitting at an extraordinary session, drew its conclusions from the aborted putsch and admitted that the state machinery had ceased to exist. Nursultan Nazarbaev, president of Kazakhstan, one of the key national figures in the days following the putsch, became the spokesman for a drastic political revolution. Realizing that the Constitution was no longer applicable, he suggested establishing transitional political structures before the Treaty of Union could take effect and fix the territorial limits of the new system. In the meantime, the Congress, unwilling to commit suicide, appointed a new assembly, empowered to put the finishing touches to the Treaty of Union and in the first place to set up provisional power structures, among which a Council of State. In this constitutional reform, the main feature was the new role played by the republics. Their presidents sit on the Council as equals of the President of the USSR, and central power is reduced to insignificance.

***

Select Bibliography

Carrere d'Encausse Helene, La gloire des nations (Paris 1992)
Gorbachev M., Perestroika, New Thinking for our Country and the World (New York 1987)
Nove A., Glasnost in Action (London 1989)
Tatu M., Gorbachev. A Political Biography (New York 1991)
Bialer S., Politics, Society and Nationality inside Gorbachev's Russia (Boulder 1989)
Conquest R., The Last Empire: Nationality and the Soviet Future (Stanford 1986)

France And Perestroika

Anne de Tinguy

Within a few years of its launching Soviet perestroïka had disrupted relations of the Soviet Union with the Western world considerably. France was no exception. However, French-Soviet relations were of a different nature from relations between the USSR and the other Western countries. They alternated more sharply, above all between extremes. It took a long time, in spite of the "Gorbachev effect", for a thaw to set in and wipe out the difficulties encountered at the beginning of the 1980s. From 1989, France reacted very positively to the political reforms carried out in the Soviet Union, especially to the collapse of the Empire due to the 'velvet revolutions' in Eastern Europe. In the troubled period that follwed 1989 France became for the Soviet Union a dependable ally. But the relationship between the two countries did not return to the privileged status it had enjoyed during the 1960s; it was henceforth on a "normal"footing[1].

I - Strained relationship during F. Mitterrand first seven-year term
"Drying out cure" (1981-84)
France was never so stand-offish towards the Soviet Union than during the first years of F. Mitterrand's presidency. When the latter came to power in 1981, France's status of privileged partner with the Soviet Union which had started under General de Gaulle was over; instead, relations between East and West were very strained. Soviet intervention in Afghanistan, the proclamation of martial law in Poland in 1981, the Euromissile deployment campaign and other confrontations put an end to the relative ease of détente that had marked the 1970s. In France, all such developments provoked strong reactions from the new men in power. François Mitterrand declared that "normal" relations between Paris and Moscow were out of the question so long as the Soviets occupied Afghanistan. He vehemently denounced the "threat stemming from the inacceptable

---

[1] Expression of Foreign minister, R. Dumas, interview in <u>France-URSS Magazine</u>, july 1989

deployment of the Soviet SS-20 missiles in Europe". In addition the President backed up openly the NATO December 1979's twofold decision to deploy Pershing II and Cruise missiles as response. Afterwards, since socialist Paris supported an effective deployment of new American missiles in Europe relations became strained. And when Moscow demanded that in calculating the balance between Western 'Euromissiles' and its SS-20 consideration be given to French and British nuclear forces, tension between the two countries could only increase still further[2].

A general reappraisal of relations with the USSR, decided by the French president, resulted in a postponement of contacts at the highest level[3]. Whereas almost every year summits had taken place between 1970 and 1980, F. Mitterrand did not go to Moscow for three years (until June 1984) after his election as President. He was the first President, since General de Gaulle came to power in 1958, to put off for such a long time his meeting with the Soviet leaders. On April 5, 1983, the expulsion of 47 Soviet diplomats and government officials, who were accused of spying (an unprecedented measure in the history of French-Soviet relations, in view of the numbers of spies involved) and a persistent denounciation of non-respect of human rights in the Soviet Union, testified to France's firm attitude. This unbending position was especially galling for Moscow since, at the same time, France moved closer to Washington. The Kremlin strongly denounced F. Mitterrand's Atlantic choices and accused him of reneging on General de Gaulle's policy of independence. But it had to be admitted that Mitterrand's readjustments would probably endure, because they were closely linked with the internal situation in France. Previously President Giscard d'Estaing needed the Gaullist support, hence he continued de Gaulle's friendly attitutdes towards the USSR. In addition he had to be able, should the need arise, to use these relations as leverage vis-à-vis the Communists, who were still an important political force. Hence the necessity to ensure continuity in foreign policy and to maintain a dialogue with the Soviets. President F. Mitterrand had to seek neither the Gaullists' support since they were in opposition anyhow, nor was he obliged to think of the possibility of neutralizing the   French Communists, who after 1981 were in government and whose influence in French political life had considerably shrunk. But unlike V. Giscard d'Estaing, he had to get Washington's support, because of the American leaders' concern at the presence of Communists in a NATO member country's Cabinet. Moreover, F. Mitterrand had to show the French people that his freedom of decision was not affected by the presence of the communists in government[4].

---

[2]   Michel Tatu Eux et nous, Paris, 1985, p.135-146
[3]   Contact is not completely cut : several ministers (Agriculture, External Trade, Research and Industry...) went to Moscow at the beginning of the first Mitterrand seven-year term. But it is on another level.
[4]   A. de Tinguy "Heurs et malheurs des relations franco-soviétiques, 1981-86" Le Courrier des Pays de l'Est n313, déc. 1986 p.23-42, M. Tatu Eux et nous op. cit. et A. Grosser Affaires extérieures - La politique de la France, 1944-1984, Paris, Flammarion, 1984 p.288-295, 311-313

By 1984, obvious changes in the international situation led the President to revize his foreign policy. After the failure of repeated Soviet attempts at preventing the deployment of American missiles in Europe (the implantation of the first Pershings and cruise missiles began in November 1983), he thought it advisable to resume a dialogue with Moscow, whither he went in June 1984.
Nothing much came out of this visit, which could be described as a type of preliminary skirmish. Nevertheless, secretary general Gorbachev was invited on an official visit to France.

Thaw Tinged with Distrust (1985-1988)

Only after Gorbachev's visit to Paris in October 1985 and the first Soviet international attempts at opening up linked with the new policy of perestroïka and their new approach to international affairs[5], that relations between Paris and Moscow improved markedly.
Gorbachev's personality played a large part in this gradual thaw. F. Mitterrand paid him an unprecedented compliment when he described him, in July 1986, as the first "modern man" the Soviet Union had ever had at the helm, as a leader "who understands that he must behave differently from his predecessors", and whose primary goal was to improve the standard of living of the Soviet people[6]. An assessment which was in accord with that made by the opposition, after its return to power in France in 1986[7].
Relations between the two countries, still at odds on strategic matters, remained all the same rather strained. The Soviet Union was still seen as a threat, and its policy was interpreted as aimed, not at desarming, but dividing Western countries, at putting under pressure Western and in particular French strategic programs, and achieving the traditional goal of Soviet diplomacy : the de-nuclearization of Europe. Gorbachev's decision to come to France for his first visit in the West after his arrival to power was "an honor for France" (F. Mitterrand), but was considered as being first of all connected with the French reluctance to back U.S. research on SDI, a nightmare for the Soviets. This reluctance was confirmed by President Mitterrand, but there remained wide differences between the French and Soviet points of view. At the time the French President refused to take part in negotiations on SDI. However, a few months later the Chirac government took a much more positive view of the American program[8].

---

5   M. Gorbatchev Perestroïka - Vues neuves sur notre pays et le monde, Paris, Flammarion, 1987, 371 p et E. Chevardnadze L'avenir s'écrit liberté, Paris, O. Jacob, 1991, 357 p.
6   Herald Tribune july 5-6, 1986
7   See interview with Foreign secretary, J.B. Raimond, in the Chirac Cabinet, Le Monde sept. 10, 1986
8   On may 22, 1986, the new Prime minister says that "this movement is irreversible ant it is justified" and "France cannot afford not to be associated with this great research program" Herald Tribune may 23, 1986, Figaro may 28, 1986 and Le

Soviet insistence on including the French strategic forces in nuclear arms limitation negotiations fed French distrust and remained, until the 1989 East European revolutions, the stumbling block in relations between the two countries. In October 1985, M. Gorbachev proposed "direct (French-Soviet) talks" leading to nuclear forces reductions[9]. Afterwards, he asked France repeatedly to join Soviet-American talks, which Mitterrand refused flatly to do as long as the bi-polar terms of strategic balance were not fully reappraised. In 1985, F. Mitterrand refrained from commenting on Gorbachev's proposal and in Moscow, in July 1986, he declared once more France's support for the nuclear deterrent, "the basis of our independence and of our security", and stated again "the necessary conditions for France to consider taking part in any future negotiations" : (1) to agree to such cuts in Soviet and American strategic weapons as to make it possible for "the nature of their relationship to the other nuclear powers to be fundamentally altered"; (2) an allround realignment in levels of conventional and chemical weapons; (3) no further reinforcement in anti-nuclear defense systems, such as SDI or ABM, which would adversely affect the credibility of the French strategic riposte[10].

Given these limits, French reactions to Gorbachev's disarmament proposals and to current Soviet-American negotiations had to remain cautious. When Gorbachev suggested on January 15, 1986 a total nuclear disarmament program for the year 2 000, Roland Dumas, Foreign Affairs Minister, admitted that such proposals were pointing "in the right direction", but he reminded his French audience of the overwhelming Soviet superiority in conventional and chemical weapons in Europe, emphasizing that European security "must be analyzed while taking into account all the elements involved"[11]. When the two superpowers seemed ready at the Reykjavik summit, in October 1986, to reach a final agreement on the dismantling of intermediate-range ballistic missiles, the then Prime Minister, Jacques Chirac, was worried about the obvious fact that "decisions vital to the security of Europe could be taken without Europe really having any say in the matter"[12]. However, because "it is better to disarm than to overarm" (F. Mitterrand, May 1987[13]), the subsequent signature of this treaty, in December 1987, was greeted by France as a strategic disarmament success[14]. For the first time in its history the Soviet Union

Monde july 23, 1986
[9]   Press conference on october 4, 1985, Documents d'actualité internationale n22, nov. 15, 1985
[10]   Le Monde july 9, 1986. F. Mitterrand already expressed this position in 1983 at the United Nations and will again express it afterwards, see Le Monde october 13, 1988
[11]   January 28, 1986 speech at the opening of the ninth round of Disarmament Conference in Europe
[12]   December 2, 1986 speech at the WEU, Herald Tribune dec. 3, 1986, Le Monde dec. 4, 1986. See also J. B. Raimond Le Choix de Gorbatchev, Paris, O. Jacob, 1992 p.92-93
[13]   Le Monde may 13, 1987. See also F. Mitterrand's "Letter to the French people", Le Monde april 8, 1988
[14]   B. Racine "La France et les FNI" Politique Etrangère 1988 n1 p.79-91. See also

agreed to the effective and complete destruction of a whole category of strategic weapons targetted on Europe, to a quantitatively unbalanced dismantling of weapons and to on-site inspections for verification. This proved to the French an unprecedented, new element in Soviet strategic thinking and such a good will as to make them greatly appreciated by France. Nonetheless, Paris feared the consequences of this IMBM treaty[15]. Because of Soviet superiority in conventional and chemical weapons, Europe's security was paradoxically more vulnerable after the IMBM treaty had been signed in Washington than ever before. And France was afraid of Moscow taking advantage of the impetus given by this agreement to obtain a reduction of American strategic presence in Europe and to weaken the link between Europe and the United States. It was feared that pressures in favour of strategic disarmament would become stronger and in Europe they would ultimately lead towards much feared denuclearization.

    These fears were not entirely groundless. French public opinion was still very suspicious of the Soviet Union. In April 1987 62 % of people interviewed in a SOFRES poll asserted that they had a bad opinion of Soviet behaviour in international politics; only 18 % had a good opinion. During a survey done in June-July 1987 among French opinion makers, 14% said they trusted the Soviet Union (46 % in Germany and 62 % in Italy)[16]. During the same period, to a question asked by SOFRES: "who believes the most sincerely in world peace ?", 10 % answered the Soviet Union and 38 %, the United States[17]. However, French public opinion could change very quickly. Within three months, French people had changed their minds in respect of the INF agreement. 45 % of the people interviewed in April 1987 thought that the double zero option was a trap, because it would leave the Soviets with a large military superiority in Europe. In July 1987, only 28 % continued to maintain this opinion. The number of French people who approved this option rose from 35 % in April to 53 % in July. The French government had thus good reasons to fear the "Gorbachev effect", the influence that the Soviet leader exercised on public opinion.

    In fact the Soviet Union tried to take advantage of the impetus generated by the treaty. In particular it denounced the modernization of tactical nuclear weapons (of less than 500 km range)[18], decided in 1983 at Montebello by NATO member countries (which was

F. Mitterrand's press conference in Buenos Aires on october 9, 1987 and J. Chirac's speech on december 12, 1987 at the IASND, in La politique de défense de la France, texts and documents presented by D. David. Paris, FSND, 1989, p.296-303

[15]   L'Express's file, sept. 25-oct. 1, 1987 "Unprotected Europe" reflects how deep are French fears.

[16]   Surveys done in France by TMO Consultants, in Germany by Sample Institute and in Italy by Pragma

[17]   See also SOFRES L' Etat de l'Opinion, Paris, 1987, ch. 11 "L'image de l'Union Soviétique" and I. Egorov "Francuzy i perestroïka" MEiMO 1988 n5 p.87-95

[18]   France calls weapons of this category not tactical, but pre-strategic. It works at this time on the successor of the Pluton missile, the Hadès, whose range is shortly less

said to transgress the treaty's spirit) and suggested destroying them (triple zero option). This divided Western countries[19]. J. Chirac refused emphatically, in the present circumstances, this "triple zero option", which "would inevitably lead to the departure of the Americans from Europe". He denounced the "salami strategy" adopted by the Soviet Union[20], underlining that "we do not see any slowing down of the Soviet military effort"[21] and stressing that France's nuclear forces "represent the minimum needed for her security", while Soviet and American forces were of "disproportionately large"[22].

In spite of the "new approach" to international affairs adopted by the Soviet Union, France emphasized that Soviet policy had not fundamentally changed. In addition Europe remained divided (the existence of a wall in the heart of Europe was "unbearable", said the French Prime Minister during his visit to Berlin on March 1, 1988). Concerning human rights, in spite of improvements, "a lot has still to be done". Moreover the Soviets still occupied Afghanistan[23].

Serious commercial difficulties made the situation even more difficult. Trade between the two countries dropped in 1986 by 26 % in comparison with 1985 and, between 1985 and 1990, by 33 %. France's share in the Soviet foreign trade, which was 4 % in 1980, was only 2,7 % in 1985 and 1,8 % in 1989. It was not only with France that Soviet trade relations got worse. But the situation was worse for France than for any other industrialized country. France was the third partner of the Soviet Union in 1985. This position was reduced to seventh in 1989. In 1980, her share was 11,9 % of Soviet trade with Western countries; in 1989 it was only 6,9%. Moreover, the trade balance, positive for France during the 1970s, became negative from 1979 henceforth (7,6 billions FF deficit in 1986 and 4,8 in 1987)[24].

than 500 km.
[19]   Germans, directly concerned by these missiles, wish a reduction of their number; Americans, French and British think it is too early to do so. See J.B. Raimond Le choix... op. cit. p.94-97, P. Lellouche "L'après-Washington" Politique Etrangère 1988 n 1 p. 153-167 and V.Y. Ghebali "Le traité de Washington et l'avenir du désarmement" Problèmes politiques et sociaux sept. 30, 1988, p.33-48.
[20]   Le Monde may 5, 1987 and october 6, 1987. Former Prime minister, R. Barre, also denounces at the same time the Soviet "indirect strategy" whose purpose is "victory without war by putting the enemy in front of the choice between surrender or apocalypse", Le Monde march 28, 1987 and dec. 31, 1987. The opposition is also very careful, see Michel Rocard Le Monde march 18, 1987.
[21]   J. Chirac will say once more the same thing a few months later, on november 15, 1988, in Munich.
[22]   Press conference, march 1, 1988
[23]   France strengthens at this time its help to Afghan resistance and receives in Paris in june 1986 M. Rabbani, spokesman of the Islamic alliance of the mujahidins.
[24]   A. de Tinguy Le Courrier des pays de l'Est op. cit.

Thus at a time when a dialogue with Washington was a priority for the Soviet Union[25], French-Soviet relations remained difficult[26] and only rare meetings at the highest level took place. F. Mitterrand, after his trip to Moscow in July 1986, waited until November 1988 to repeat the experience. And the French Prime Minister's visit to Moscow in May 1987 revealed more than differences of opinion. Thus, J. Chirac was impressed by M. Gorbachev's "clear vision of things to come" and his will "to make things change"[27]. However, he stated again that the French nuclear force and its modernization were "under no circumstances negotiable". His Soviet counterpart, N. Ryzhkov, spoke of "frightening elements" in the French strategic policy and accused Paris of giving to a **rapprochement** with the Soviet Union "a very low priority"[28].

II - France's Shift to Support of Perestroïka

From 1988, relations became less tense. However only after the autumn of 1989 and 'velvet' revolutions in Eastern Europe did relations really improve.

A relationship which "resembles détente"

Despite changes in the Soviet Union and the withdrawal of Soviet forces from Afghanistan, the year 1988 and the first months of 1989 were still difficult. President Mitterrand's trip to Moscow on November 25-26, 1988 was hardly more significant than those before that date. He was in a sense just re-establishing contacts [29].

The atmosphere in Mosocw was undoubtedly more relaxed : "nowadays we can take a great step forward", said F. Mitterrand on June 7, 1988[30], and his Foreign Minister added a few weeks later : "even if we are not in a period of détente, we are experiencing something very close to it"[31]. This détente, which manifested itself, among other things, by French political interest in Eastern Europe being given a new lease of life, with Moscow looking benevolently on [32], was possible because East and West were close to an agreement in their negotiations on the reduction of conventional forces, which Paris

---

[25]   See Horst Ehmke "Le rôle de la France et de la RFA dans les relations Est-Ouest" Politique Etrangère 1988 n4, p.855-860

[26]   See for example Vl. Bolchakov Pravda sept. 28, 1987

[27]   Le Monde may 16, 17-18 and 19, Liberation may 16-17, 1987

[28]   May 14, 1987 speech

[29]   See Gorbachev's description of his talks with F. Mitterrand in Moscow in november 1988, Avant-Mémoires, Paris, O. Jacob, 1993 p.55-66

[30]   Le Monde june 9, 1988

[31]   R. Dumas' interview, Le Monde sept. 9, 1988

[32]   F. Mitterrand goes to Tchecoslovakia in december 1988, in Bulgaria in january 1989 and then to Poland in following june...

considered a precondition for good relations[33]. Moreover France took into account the progress of Gorbachev's democratization policy (constitutionnal reform of December 1988, Andréï Sakharov being permitted to travel outside the Soviet territory)[34]... This led Paris to agree, after much hesitation, to the principle of a conference on Human Rights, under the auspices of the CSCE, to be held in Moscow in 1991. This thaw was moreover clearly linked to France's concern not to allow the United States to do the running in the field of detente. "Europe must be more and more active in deciding on the new international order under discussion by the two superpowers", declared R. Dumas in the autumn of 1988[35].

However, basically, nothing had changed. Disagreements about strategic matters persisted: "Perestroïka had (still) not acquired a military meaning"[36]. F. Mitterrand therefore kept on refusing to have the French nuclear force taken into consideration in international negotiations. He stated again, on May 18, 1989, that "it is not yet time, far from it, for a third zero option to be considered"[37]. Moreover he remained doubtful of Gorbachev's European visions : "the idea of a common European House is 'attractive', but there still exists in Europe 'a wall' and 'limitations on individual freedom'"[38]. "For the first time in 50 years", he added to Gorbachev's face, when greeting him in Paris in July 1989, "the possibility of making Europe emerge from an era of division and confrontation...is within an arm's reach, but between the two halves of Europe, there are still many difficulties to be sorted out"[39]. If France remained skeptical, this was also due to her being convinced that the Soviets still intended to evince the Americans from Europe in order to have a dominant influence there [40].

Whatever the Soviet aims, the "Gorbachev effect" tended to turn into a "Gorbachev shock" as far as French public opinion was concerned. His popularity jumped by twenty points between June 1987 and May 1989 : in 1987 Gorbachev was referred to as their

---

[33]   See R. Dumas' interview in France-URSS Magazine, july 1989

[34]   After a trip to the United States, A. Sakharov is allowed to come to France in december 1988.

[35]   Interview, Le Monde sept. 9, 1988

[36]   Prime minister Rocard's statement on november 15, 1988, Le Monde Nov. 16, 1988. His secretary of defence, J.P. Chevènement, said the same thing during an official visit in Moscow in april 1989.

[37]   Press conference, may 18, 1989, Le Monde may 20, 1989. In spite of this refusal, on july 6, 1989, in Strasbourg, M. Gorbachev offers a unilateral reduction of Soviet nuclear tactical missiles in Europe "if it becomes clear that NATO countries are willing to open negotiations", Le Monde july 7, 1989.

[38]   F. Mitterrand's interview to Soviet television, quoted by Le Monde nov. 26, 1989 and press conference of may 18, 1989, Le Monde may 20, 1989.

[39]   Le Monde july 6, 1989

[40]   Concerning European policy of the Soviet Union, see R. Fritsch-Bournazel "De Rapallo à Zavidovo : réflexions sur le devenir des relations germano-russes" Les Cahiers du CREST n11, sept. 1993.

favourite statesman by 31 % of French people; in 1989 by 51 % and he occupied a second place after the Pope, John-Paul II. On the scale of confidence in heads of state or government, he was third in June 1989, with 60 % of the opinions poll for him, just after Chancellor Kohl (61 %) and President Mitterrand (65 %) and well in adavance of President Bush (51 %). Gorbachev's popularity was reflected in the high opinion the French held his country. By June 1989 42 % of people professed a favorable opinion of Soviet international action (as compared to 9 % in November 1985 and 18 % in April 1987). Moreover, 51 % thought that "the Soviet Union sincerely wants peace" (29 % in December 1983 and 33 % in April 1986)[41] As a direct consequence of this feeling, French people were increasingly sympathetic to Soviet ideas. In June 1989, 51 % of them said they were ready to accept denuclearization of Europe; and only 40 % thought that, in this case, Western Europe would be without a deterrent to face the Soviet Union which enjoyed a large superiority in conventional weapons[42]. This confidence in M. Gorbachev and his country was, however, tinged with skepticism. While 82 % Germans said, at the beginning of the summer 1989, they believed that M. Gorbachev's reform policy would succeed, 52 % French thought his power was fragile[43]. When J. Chirac said in June 1989 that "in Moscow, powerful forces are only waiting for an opportunity to impose a return to the most rigid totalitarian regime"[44], he reflected a widespread anxiety in France, shared by President Mitterrand. "One must not go faster than is necessary", was the latter's comment on May 18, 1989. "The democratic evolution has to be confirmed. History often moves in leaps and bound after which, it stagnates. Forces of opposition get organized..."[45].

<u>"To help by all possible means..."</u>

Revolutions occurring in Eastern Europe during the autumn of 1989, swept away all these French reservations. "To help by all possible means and in the best possible conditions the great changes undertaken in the Soviet Union" became the guiding principle of France's Eastern policy. "It is in everyone's interest", declared F. Mitterrand declared "that the changes under way in Central and Eastern Europe may succeed"[46]. "Accordingly we have to help M. Gorbachev, 'a man of vision', who has an important, historic part to play, because he is in fact the cornerstone of the whole enterprise"[47]. This

---

[41]   Olivier Noc "Le choc Gorbatchev" in SOFRES <u>L'Etat de l'opinion</u>, Paris 1990 p.51-68.
[42]   O. Noc "Le choc Gorbatchev" op. cit.
[43]   Michel Tatu <u>Le Monde</u> july 2-3, 1989
[44]   <u>Le Monde</u> june 10, 1989
[45]   Press conference, <u>Le Monde</u> may 20, 1989
[46]   <u>Le Monde</u> oct. 30 and june 20, 1990. See also F. Mitterrand's televised speech on july 14, 1990, <u>Le Monde</u> july 17, 1990
[47]   F. Mitterrand, in Strasbourg, on october 25, 1989 and on French television on

position was repeatedly acknowledged and upheld by the French opposition[48]. Nonetheless, disagreements on strategic initiative as well as disappointment with mutual economic and commercial exchanges remained an obstacle of further rapprochement. More ancient causes of tension, such as the affair of the reimbursement of tsarist pre-WWI loans, made their appearance again as if by magic. But seen in a completely different international context, these new problems could no longer prevent a gradual normalization of relations between the two countries.

Contacts of all kinds were now taking place. The two heads of state, Mitterrand and Gorbachev, met in December 1989 in Kiev, then in May 1990 in Moscow, and in October 1990 in Paris. Pierre Joxe went to the Soviet Union on an official visit in December 1989 : he was the first French Minister of the Interior of any Western country to do so. J. P. Chevènement, another (defence) minister, went to the Soviet Union in April 1989 : the last visit of a French Defense Minister was in 1977.

F. Mitterrand's support of M. Gorbachev did not stop at words. At a time when the Soviet Union was losing its hold in Eastern Europe, he made every effort to have factors affecting Soviet security taken into account by the West. As he was convinced that it was important to prevent the Soviet Union from becoming isolated, he was the first Western leader to back the call Gorbachev made in Rome on November 29, 1989 for holding a summit meeting in 1990[49] of the thirty five member countries of the CSCE , while on December 31, 1989, he launched the idea of an European confederation, which the Soviet Union might join[50].

F. Mitterrand was willing to take Soviet security interests into account, because he was worried about the consequences of European security imbalance[51] and shared some of the Soviet fears, in particular as far as united Germany was concerned. He stated in November 1989 that "he had no ideological or political objection to the idea of reunification"[52], but emphasized in December that "the new German balance cannot be built to the detriment of the European balance of power as a whole"[53]. One had to respect "the right of the German people to decide their future freely", R. Dumas asserted two

dec. 10, 1989, Le Monde oct.27 and dec.12, 1989

[48]   "Perestroïka is also in our interest", says for example J. Chirac, Le Monde oct. 21, 1989. "So we have to go with this process".

[49]   F. Mitterrand backs this proposal when he meet M. Gorbachev in Kiev, Pravda dec. 8, 1989. The week before, at the Malta summit meeting, president Bush refrained from endorsing Mr Gorbachev's call, Herald Tribune dec. 7, 1989. Concerning Soviet position on the CSCE, see A. Arbatov, S. Karagonov and Vl. Lobov The Soviet Union and European security, pSIS papers, n4, 1990, 29 p.

[50]   Televised statement, dec.31, 1989, Le Monde jan. 2, 1990

[51]   "The whole of Europe is moving. We are going to go through a very tense period", says F. Mitterrand in Paris-Match, quoted by Le Monde nov.24, 1989.

[52]   Interview with The Wall Street Journal, nov. 22, 1989, quoted by Le Monde nov. 23, 1989.

[53]   Televised statement on dec. 31, 1989, Le Monde jan. 2, 1990

days later, but it was not possible "to cut corners", because this would result in Europe "taking unwarranted risks" with its own security[54]. At the same time, F. Mitterrand echoed Soviet anxiety due to their "having (in Germany) genuine strategic, geopolitical and historic interests"[55] and quoting M. Gorbachev ("the very day when reunification of Germany was announced, a press release will announce that a Soviet marshal sits in my chair as President"), he stressed that "Soviet military power is still very powerful" and has to be taken into account[56]. Was the President concerned about overreactions to German re-unification among the Soviet population and the state bureaucracies? Did he real want to lean on Moscow to slow down the process of re-unification [57] ? The meeting taking place on December 6 in Kiev, at the instigation of Paris, showed similar uneasiness in the minds of both French and Soviet leaders. Without the knowledge of a secret deal between Gorbachev and Kohl and siding with Mikhail Gorbachev, President Mitterrand distanced himself from Bonn and warned: "no European country can act without taking the others into account"[58].

Later on, however, the French President accepted re-unification without demurr. Henceforth he just tried to keep the upheaval in Eastern Europe under some sort of control. During the "2 plus 4" negotiations between the two German states and the four victorious powers, which since the war had assumed special responsibilities in Germany, as well as with his Western partners, he asked the Soviet Union to agree to German sovereignty being restored and to the future unified Germany becoming a member of the North Atlantic Alliance. At the same time, he tried to reassure Moscow, to give substance to the idea that its acceptance of German re-unification could lead to a substantial change in Western attitudes towards the Soviet Union. He even tried to help Gorbachev in the pacification of the Soviet population, when Soviet humiliation in Germany became obvious. He redoubled his backing of Gorbachev's efforts to obtain economic assistance from the West[59]. F. Mitterrand particularly supported the wish expressed in July 1989 by M. Gorbachev of "a full involvement of the Soviet Union in the world economy"[60]. If he

[54]   Speech on dec. 12, 1989 at the parliament, Le Quotidien de Paris, dec. 13, 1989
[55]   Interview already quoted with The Wall Street Journal, nov. 22, 1989, quoted by Le Monde, nov. 23, 1989.
[56]   Le Monde nov. 24, 1989
[57]   Margaret Thatcher confirms in 10,Downing Street - Mémoires, Paris, 1994 p.658, 662-665, that F. Mitterrand was filled with concern. She writes that the president got closer to Great-Britain in order to try to find a mean "to stop or slow down the reunification".
[58]   Joint press conference in Kiev, Pravda dec. 8, 1989. On dec. 7, Pravda says it is very pleased about the turn of Soviet-French dialogue. F. Mitterrand's policy towards the reunification of Germany will be severely criticized, see J. Amalric Le Monde august 27, 1991
[59]   The idea that it was necessary to reassure Moscow was already expressed by R. Dumas in july 1989, see his interview in France-URSS Magazine july 1989.
[60]   M. Gorbachev's letter, dated july 14, 1989, to F. Mitterrand as president of the G7

pleaded for the Soviet Union to take part in the EBRD, the Bank for Reconstruction and Development of Eastern Europe, if he argued, like Chancellor Kohl, at the European Council in Dublin and in July 1990 at the G7 meeting in Houston, in favour of granting the Soviet Union Western assistance, his pleas were intended precisely to help the Soviet Union bear the burden of reforms, but also to swallow the 'bitter pill' of German reunification[61]. During this time of adjustment in East-West relations, the United States became the Soviet Union's first and chief partner[62]. However, France was also providing a significant political assistance to Moscow.

The treaty of friendship and cooperation, signed by F. Mitterrand and M. Gorbachev at Rambouillet on October 29, 1990 -the first one signed between the two countries since the December 10, 1944 treaty- confirmed, on both sides, the turning-point reached at the beginning of the summer of 1990. On July 6, members of the NATO admitted publicly that the Soviet Union was no longer considered an enemy. In the French-Soviet treaty, the two signatories state that "they consider each other as friendly states"[63]. Reconciliation between East and West was confirmed in November 1990 in Paris. The historical agreement on conventional forces, signed on the 19th by members of the NATO and of the Warsaw Pact, was considered by the Western countries as the cornerstone of the new European order[64]. This was the price the Soviet Union had to pay for achieving what it had been asking for since the 1970s : the institutionalization of the CSCE, which was given it a formal say in European affairs[65]. All these events were greeted enthusiastically by F. Mitterrand : "Yalta ended today in Paris... no enemy remains in Europe"[66].

---

meeting in Paris.

[61]   Public opinion does not agree with the president on this matter. At the end of 1990, only 6 % are in favour of an economic assistance to the Soviet Union, Le Monde, dec.18, 1990.

[62]   See for example C.D. Blacker Hostage to revolution - Gorbachev and Soviet security policy, New York 1993, 239 p. and R. Fritsch-Bournazel De Rapallo à Zavidovo... op. cit. p.33-41

[63]   This treaty, which provides in case of "threat against peace" only "consultations", goes much less far than the september 1990 treaty between the Soviet Union and Germany. See Le Monde oct.28-29, 1990 (Claire Tréan) and Herald Tribune oct. 29 and 30, 1990

[64]   J. Klein "Désarmement régional en Europe et sécurité collective" Politique Etrangère 1991 n1, p.41-57

[65]   The "Charter for the new Europe", signed on november 21 by the 34 signatories of the Helsinki Final Act, says that "the era of confrontation and of division in Europe is over". The text of the charter is published in Pravda nov.22,1990. See also Gorbachev's speech in Paris, Pravda, nov. 20, 1990.

[66]   Press conference on nov. 21, 1990, Le Monde nov. 23, 1990

Cautiousness or Error of Judgment ?

Signs of changes in Soviet attitudes during the winter 1990-91 (return to power of conservative forces, bypassing of the agreement on conventional disarmament, use of force in the Baltic states etc.) undermined this new friendship based, at least on the French side, on a wish to help the process of democratization in the Soviet Union and its integration on new terms in the international community. Despite these warning signs Mitterrand remained convinced that Mikhail Gorbachev still intended to push through his perestroika policy and that he was still in a position to do so. He thought it necessary to continue to support him [67].

In 1991, during the days of the USSR's break-up the French President refrained from taking any initiative which would hasten the collapse. He reacted with extreme caution to the first declarations of independence made by the Soviet republics, especially the Baltic states, whose annexation by the USSR France had never recognized. After Lithuania's declaration of independence in March 1990, he stated that his "role is not to pour oil on the fire"[68]. A few days later, with Chancelor Kohl, he asked Vilnius for patience and willingness to joint negotiations[69]. Up to December 1991, French policy rested on considering the central authorities as the only official internationally recognized representatives. In April 1991, when Boris Yeltsin was in Strasbourg and Paris on a private visit, the French authorities cold shouldered the future supreme leader who became shortly afterwards the first Russian President to be elected by universal suffrage[70]. Two weeks later, on May 6, in Moscow, F. Mitterrand fully supported M. Gorbachev, at the very moment when Soviet military authorities intervened brutally in Armenia[71]. Only after the August 1991 putsch, which F. Mitterrand seemed ready to accept at least for a while[72] , his policy towards the USSR changed completely. On August 27, at the same time as the other EC members, he decided to establish diplomatic relations with the three Baltic republics. However he kept on giving priority to relation with the Soviet Union and its President who was entertained at his country house on October 30, the day after the opening of the Madrid Conference on the Middle East. He

---

[67]   This conviction is clearly expressed by R. Dumas, Le Monde, march 12, 1991.
[68]   Le Monde march 27, 1990. French government will maintain this position for several months. See R. Dumas Le Monde march 12, 1991 and E. Guigou Le Monde june 23-24, 1991.
[69]   French-German letter of april 29, 1990
[70]   The leader of the socialist group at the European parliament, J. P. Cot, says, on april 15, in Strasbourg inside parliament, hurtful words to B. Eltsine. At the Elysée, F. Mitterrand asks his general secretary to receive B. Eltsine and joins them only during the last minutes of the conversation.
[71]   Izvestia may 6, 7 and 8; Figaro may 7 and Le Monde may 8, 1991
[72]   At the end of the day, on august 19, 1991, F. Mitterrand says, in a televised statement, that "the new leaders...will be judged according to their acts".

declared again that France "will establish links of cooperation with those republics who wish to do so", but that she "will deal only with legal authorities"[73].

President Mitterrand's cautiousness stemmed from his wish not to hasten a disintegration process which might have frightful consequences for Europe and the world. In his dread of a "political vacuum" consequent on the Soviet collapse he feared especially a 'scattering of responsibilities in the nuclear field'. This is also the reason for his proposal of September 11, 1991 to hold a conference of the four European nuclear powers[74] and, later, for his recommendation of retaining central control of the Soviet nuclear deterrent [75].

But was not this cautious attitude due also to errors of judgment ? Did F. Mitterrand fully appreciate the meaning of the events occurring in the last months of the Soviet Union ? The French opposition, but also many political analysts, blamed him for remaining blind to the irresistible rise of the republics, for being too slow in accepting the independence of the Baltic states[76], for overestimating M. Gorbachev 's ability to keep control of the situation. At the time of the August 1991 putsch, he was justifiably accused of "losing his cool and being overtaken by events"[77].

In any case, after the Community of the Independent States was set up, on December 8, 1991, the demise of the Soviet Union and M. Gorbachev's resignation inevitable, F. Mitterrand turned completely around. After he assured himself that the newly independent succession states would respect the Soviet Union's international commitments and would sign the non nuclear proliferation treaty (requirements specified on December 16 by the twelve EC members), France promptly established diplomatic relations with the new states. The fall of the Soviet regime and of the Soviet Union signified also the end of the East-West conflict : a new era was opening.

III - A privileged partnership with Russia

__Russia, "the chief successor state of the Soviet Union", the only one among the fifteen new states to be recognized as a nuclear power, has since been a privileged partner of France and of the other industrialized countries. The Russian policy of partnership with the Western world makes now mutual cooperation a matter of routine. After paying official visits to London, Washington and Ottawa, President Yeltsin, in February 1992,

---

[73]   Le Monde nov. 1, 1991. M. Gorbachev's book-December 1991, Zug (Switzerland), CopArt, 1993, 238 p- shows clearly that up to the end of the Soviet Union, relations between himself and F. Mitterrand were quite good.
[74]   Le Monde sept. 13, 1991
[75]   Televised statement on oct. 30, 1991, Le Monde nov. 1, 1991
[76]   Many key figures sign in february 1991 a declaration in favour of the Baltic states, Le Monde feb. 21, 1991
[77]   Le Monde sept.3, 1991. See also Le Monde august 27, 1991 and march 12, 1993 (F. de Rose); Herald Tribune sept. 3, 1991.

came at long last to Paris, where he asked for economic assistance and was given a favorable answer. France allocated to Russia most of the credits awarded to the demised Soviet Union and promised that she would support its candidacy to the IMF, the World Bank and the Council of Europe. The signature of the "treaty between France and Russia" and of many other agreements renewed the traditional ties stemming from a long French-Russian history and put the relationship between the two countries on a new footing[78]. During the following months, after they visited Moscow, F. Mitterrand in March 1993[79] and t new Prime Minister, E. Balladur, in November (just after the October confrontation drama between the President and Parliament which resulted in military assault of the White House in Moscow), both underlined France's willingness to back the process of reform and democratization[80]. Disagreements on disarmament, which have for so long poisoned relations betweeen the two countries, became muted. France did not take part in Russian-American strategic negotiations. However it did not stay away from the international process of negotiations. Since 1991, important measures of nuclear disarmament were implemented. Credits for equipment were reduced, some programs were restricted and spread over a longer period, some pre-strategic weapons were withdrawn earlier than expected (AN-52 bombs and Pluto missiles), the Hades program was stopped (June 1992)[81], nuclear tests were suspended.

Even if the relations with Russia were given priority, France took an interest in the other succession states. The fate of nuclear arms in the former Soviet Union remained of paramount importance. Together with the other Western countries, great efforts were made to oblige the newly formed republics with strategic weapons stationed on their territory (Ukraine, Kazakhstan and Bielorussia) to sign the non-proliferation treaty and become nuclear free countries. President Shoushkevich of Bielorussia was invited to Paris in April 1992 to discuss the non-proliferation problems; President Kravchuk of Ukraine in June and President Nazarbaev of Kazakhstan in September of the same year; with those last two, treaties of cooperation were signed. Afterwards, F. Mitterrand tightened French links with Kazakhstan, whose strategic policy was considered as sound, and went to Alma-Ata on an official visit in September 1993. In addition France paid special attention to the Baltic states. F. Mitterrand, in May 1992, visited these three countries and strongly supported their position in the conflict opposing them to Russia

---

[78]   The "new friendship" is based on "trust, solidarity, cooperation", on "attachment to the values of liberty and democracy" and on the willingness to establish armaments, in particular the nuclear ones, "at a level of minimum sufficiency" Izvestia feb. 6 and 7, Le Monde feb. 9-10, 1992.

[79]   Nezavisimaia Gazeta march 17, 1993

[80]   Izvestia oct. 20, 1993, Nezavisimaia Gazeta nov. 3 and Rossiiskaia Gazeta nov. 2 : French attitude versus Russia is at that time considered by Russians "as a whole, friendly and constructive". See also the statement of A. Juppé, Foreign secretary, Le Monde oct. 9, 1993.

[81]   Le Monde march 19, 1993

regarding the withdrawal of the former Soviet military forces [82]. Two years later, when Moscow sent to these states a warning, considered as unacceptable, the Minister for European Affairs, A. Lamassoure, went there in order to show that they were backed by France at least diplomatically[83]. Contacts were also established with Armenia (a treaty was signed between the two countries in March 1993 during President Ter Petrossian's visit to Paris), Adzerbeijan (President Aliev came to Paris in December 1993), Uzbekistan (President Karimov was in Paris on a state visit in October 1993), Turkmenistan (President Niazov came to Paris on a private visit in May 1993).

The collapse of the Soviet Union and the emergence of a new Russia in the international community raised excessive hopes and expectations of permanent peace. Within about two years, this early euphoria gave way to "a measure of disappointment" and gave rise to some concern[84]. By 1993 the relationship of Russia with France, as with the other Western states, entered a more difficult period. After the "romantic"[85]period engendered by the fall of communism, Russia, in turmoil, hardened its attitude towards the West, tried to find a new balance in foreign policy, even attempting to re-create a sphere of dominant influence in the area of former USSR. In particular Russian foreign policy makers insisted on an international community recognition of their rights to conduct peacekeeping operations in the area. However, the days of partnership with the West were not over. But the latter were no longer regarded by Russia as her priority. In addition the identity crisis, which she was going through, rendered cooperation in Europe more complicated. East is not, for France and for the other Western countries, an homogeneous area as the Russians insist on thinking. However, they are all careful to avoid any decision that could isolate Russia diplomatically or let her believe the West wants to isolate her again as under communism and thereby weaken her.

In this respect France made her position clear in March 1994, when the enlargement of the European Community was discussed: according to her the six countries of Central and Eastern Europe and the three Baltic states " are destined to become an integral part of the EC" and thereby become associated members of the WEU[86]. However, two months earlier, largely in answer to Russia's security objections, Paris and its Western allies refused to enlarge NATO to include Central European countries and instead put forward a formula of "partnership for peace", open to all the former communist countries,

---

[82]   F. Mitterrand suggests to discuss about this conflict in an international forum which could be the CSCE Izvestia may 13, 14 and 15, Le Monde may 15, 16, 17-18, 1992.

[83]   Le Monde jan. 23-24, 1994

[84]   A. Juppé, statement during IFRI-La Croix's seminar on Russia, march 22, 1994. See also S. Neil MacFarlane "Russia, the West and European security" Survival aut. 1993, vot. 35 n3 p.3-25.

[85]   Expression of the President of Russia'press secretary, V. Kostikov, Herald Tribune april 9-10 1994

[86]   A. Juppé, statement already quoted of march 22, 1994

including Russia. Thus, trying to show special consideration to the latter and at the same time asking her to observe a few rules of the international game, without creating resentment in Central and Eastern Europe and without encouraging Russia to think that it has a particular role to play in the area, she appeared pacified. Nonetheless, all this security and diplomatic commotion, within a few months, has created a highly complex situation. As a result what seems at stake is a peaceful reconciliation of once divided Europe, which could lead to bipolarization again.

Perestroika and European Strategy

Dominique David

Most people think that historical events occur in a rational way. This is why they believed that the Soviet system, after its collapse, would be replaced immediately by a new strategic European concept. We know now that it is not as simple as that, The countries of the former USSR are far from entering the final phase of reorganisation, on the contrary they are still experiencing the first stages of desintegration.

A better focus might be gained from looking at the process of decomposition, as this is the only name that can be given to the phenomenon without risk of misinterpretation. Europe has evolved from a situation where things were clear-cut and simple to one of flux, in which people come and go, according to no preordained pattern. Instead of there being a limited number of deciders who obey few and well-known rules, there is now multiple choice. New states appear , Germany is reunited, the USSR breaks up together with the countries of Central Europe. Other nations which had never lost their legal existence, recover strategic significance, that is the possibility to choose their allies, a prerogative which had been denied to them after becoming part of the Eastern bloc.

Simultaneously, the weakening of central power in Eastern Europe, though accompanied by loud claims of sovereignty, makes for an increased number of local political entities eager to play a role in international strategy, with their own ambitions and resources. Though these communities can hardly aspire to nationhood, they can still interfere and be of nuisance value in the overall strategy.

There can be new regional alliances, beyond the sphere of nations, to add their voices to the many-sided levels of decision-making already in place, so that the number of participants to any international gathering , conferences, forums and confederations becomes a factor of greater complexity in the concept of European strategy. This does not include outlying areas which may also have interests in Europe, and intervene for reasons other than in the past, as for example the United States or Turkey.

Thus the first finding of the enquiry is that the parties involved in European strategy have multiplied, instead of belonging to two close-knit blocs as in recent years, they now are scattered. The collective means of control in Europe have either disappeared or are ageing. Not only has the Warsaw Pact vanished, but it has not left behind any bridging machinery which could regulate relations between the various members or even some of them. The Atlantic Alliance is alive and well, but the price paid for retaining its political legitimacy was a marked decrease of military value. Instead of holding a semi-monopoly of all Western military-political questions, it represents now just one among several institutions concerned with matters of security on the Continent. The ECSC which looked for a while as if it would be the main forum for all the new European entities, as the November 1990 Paris Charter stated, has become in reality less important, in proportion with the emergence of new competing institutions (for example, the North Atlantic Council for Cooperation set up by Washington).

The most striking feature of present day Europe is its fragmentation. The demand for sovereignty - taken as legally independent nations - necessarily implies, everywhere except in Western Europe, a period of weak collective organisations, such as is the case in what used to be Yugoslavia. The ultimate emergence of a new European order will only take place after an endless series of implosions, each creating more potential causes of conflicts all over Europe.

This dual character (multiplicity of separate authorities and potential causes of conflicts) makes the situation all the more dangerous as there are huge arms arsenals in Europe. In spite of some achievements in reducing armaments, thanks mostly to the new approach of the USSR in international negotiations under Gorbachev, the arms arsenals existing at present in Europe are different, but not much, from what they were ten years ago. Intermediate nuclear ballistic missiles have disappeared of course. Agreements were signed to limit conventional weapons, or long range nuclear missiles, and there should be drastic reductions of short range nuclear missiles. Yet the application of these agreements will take time, probably a long time. In the meantime the weapons are available, it will take years to withdraw and destroy them, and the next stages of negotiations are just as uncertain as the future of political leaders in Central and Eastern Europe.

The financial and technical difficulties of armament destruction; uncertainty as to further negotiations; the impossibility of quick reconversion for national economies based for the most part on military production, and therefore on a large output in producing and exporting military equipment; finally the weakening of power at the center, all these factors make for the continuance of large stockpiles of arms in Europe, while at the same time the political systems, which in the past controled them, have gone for good. There is no saying that some time the arms will not be appropriated by a myriad of local leaders in a vast movement of "Libanization" which will engulf a large area of Europe.

The effects of the collapse of the dual Soviet empire tend to make all the regions affected increasingly difficult to rule. The unavoidable partition of the old territories was accompanied by political phenomena of major significance. One is a trend towards the disappearance of American influence in Europe in the long term. The United States will not succomb to the temptation of isolationism, it would make no sense for such a political, military and economic power to put it into effect. Yet the disappearance of the Soviet adversary in the short or middle term, the fragmentation of the European strategic theater, allowing for conflicts beyond the comprehension and the grasp of the Americans, the emergence in Western Europe of a political power able to capitalize on the economic edge acquired by the Community, lastly the size of social and economic problems in the United States, are strong factors pointing not to a withdrawal of the United States from Europe,but at least to a rethinking of their influence on the Continent.

The flamboyance of American diplomacy, its much heralded initiatives sometimes lacking in coherence cannot deceive the Europeans for long, and together with a decrease in American forces, necessarily a new set of rules in relations between Europe and America will have to be devized. Undoubtedly the United States will continue to play a significant part , but it will probably be more remote, whether the Continent slides into anarchy, or whether it reorganizes along new political lines. The United States are and will remain a very great power. However, whether we like it or not, European problems will increasingly become a matter of local concern. In other areas of the world, Washington, in spite of the Gulf War, has neither the means nor the intention presumably, to become the leader of a world which has ceased to be bi-polar. The men in power in Washington may be capable in the future to prevent new alliances in Europe , but they will not be able to organize the Continent as they wish.

Another compelling factor is the disappearance of the Soviet Union. Events happened so fast that not only has the enemy vanished, but also the partner involved in world affairs, so that it will no longer in the short and middle term pose a major threat. No imaginable scenario can show a new massive military capability emerging in the near future to threaten directly NATO members. Instead of a threat, there are now multiple dangers, arising from the instability of political powers, local quarrels between the new independent states, and also the sheer weight of military capability in the old establishments. Even if the Red Army is no longer capable of launching a large scale offensive of the East-West kind, it still can intervene decisively in local conflicts.

Apart from the difficulties in relations between the old members of the USSR, the political dangers besetting the Russian territories are such that the central rule of Moscow might cease to exist as a contributing factor to reorganizing Europe. There was a time when it was possible to dream of the USSR under Gorbachev, losing its threatening posture to cooperate, in a lesser fashion than it could have in the past, to a restoration of order in Europe. It is now out of the question, and the Russian authorities are now exclusively concerned with problems of economic and political survival, thereby always giving preference to bi-lateral agreements which promise financial gains, while the Russian diplomatic and military establishments are in disarray. This is why there is no chance of the advocates of the "common home" cooperating in an effort to reorganize

Europe. Enormous problems arise from this state of general anarchy in which Eastern Europe has fallen, as well as from the de facto disappearance of the political authority of Russia. The aim of reorganization seems to have been erased, no one knows for how long, from the mental processes of post-Soviet society. Russian authorities are henceforth a liability in the context of unstable East-European situation and cannot play a part in most international negotiations.

There is a third danger to consider: Intra-state or supra-state institutions are at present out of date. They were not set up to deal with these altered circumstances; NATO, WEU, ECCS, and the Community were in fact devized to function in conditions exactly opposite, that is to say the need to manage the central confrontation in Europe. They are not equiped to react to a fluctuating or chaotic situation as the case may be, which at present, and even less in the future, cannot fit into simple mental categories, nor institutions. The ECSC failed to fulfill the hopes that the Paris Charter had raised, as it was made ineffective by major partners such as the United States which went so far as setting up a rival organization, the North Atlantic Council for Cooperation. NATO remains in place as an institution, but its list of competences is now rather hazy, and its military commitments come under scrutiny, as evidenced by the difficulty in implementing the military reform passed last year. As for the idea of a confederation of European countries, it has so far failed to take shape, due to the hostility of the United States and the reluctance of Central Europeans powers which are now driven by an obsessive wish to enter fully the European Community in the near future. The Community indeed has been making good progress. Yet the heated debate on the Maastricht Treaty ratification seems out of proportion with the extreme caution of its provisions in foreign affairs and security; it is only mentioned that there will be an arrangement to this effect in the future...In reality, the situation in Yugoslavia offers a symbol of present day Europe on two counts: it shows its irreversible slide into a puzzle of fragmented nationalisms and ethnic communities, together with the passive attitude of European collective bodies and their failure to act in defense of stability.

Once again, not only is the disintegration of Europe, or part of it, unavoidable, but it is already happening. The only question is whether it will spread in an uncontrolable way, or whether it can be slowed down and chaneled into new regional arrangements. The former alternative is not the least likely.

It is enough to imagine the Western European Community going back to the fantasies of a free trade area, under pressure from the United States and in the wake of the Maastricht Treaty's failure, or as a result of a sudden influx of new members. If one adds the failure of the countries of Central Europe to form a confederation, as they prefer to continue their search for bi-lateral agreements which so far have been at the core of their foreign policy, the likelihood of disaster increases. Inequalities would worsen and the map of Europe would resemble a kind of leopard skin, in which remained vast areas of underdevelopment at the core. Then economic disorder would follow political anarchy, quarrels of irredentism and frontiers would increase ten-fold, and due to lack of real international structures, the only policy available to deal with crises would be to stop them spreading to neighboring areas. All this would happen on a continent where arm production continues unabated and where formal agreements are often ignored, while new ones, though necessary, cannot be negotiated. Thus, after the fall of the Berlin Wall, the new European unity would only prove to be a sham.

Yet it is possible to imagine another scenario, in which European disintegration would be stopped by collective organizations. There would need to be a great number of them, of a complex character and they would be interrelated. There could be two different systems, probably complementing each other.

One would give pride of place to regional centers under whose authority a limited number of partners would rally, with similar interests and preoccupations, and there would be a pooling of resources, in the economic and political field. The best example of course is the European Community which will assume a dual role: guarantee security and stable relations between individual states, on part of the continent at least, and serve as an engine to pull other regions in Europe on the way to economic modernization. Other regional administrations could spring up in Europe, and develop contacts with the EEC. In its actual configuration the map of Europe shows too many cultural, political and economic disparities to come under the same rules. It is useless to try and establish an European union stretching from the Atlantic to Vladivostock or even the Urals, obeying the same international laws. The end of the East-West divide, in which the two parts came under different empires, makes it imperative to create new regional systems.

In spite of its diversity, the European continent offers also specific features and even if no supra national figure can emerge, there must be regular consultations between the various European states, whose interests are at the same time close, interrelated and contradictory. The system of alliance may vary, it could be a reformed ECSC with stronger institutions, or an European confederation or even, as the United States would have it, a large alliance embracing huge territories from Vancouver to Vladovostock. The situation is deteriorating so fast that there is a spontaneous need for stabilizing forces such as economic cooperation, or cultural exchanges, control of disarmament, and a forum to prevent or at least manage politically the crises looming ahead.

As regards disarmament control, the nuclear aspect of it will concern the United States and Russia primarily. Yet establishing new regulations for the forces of dissuasion in Europe, or for disarmament in conventional forces, and even for cooperation in finding new structures for their military machines, is and will remain within the scope of the Europeans. The ECSC is the natural setting for consultations which are no longer possible between the two Alliances, for obvious reasons. Once again the management of the stockpiles of weapons scattered all over Europe will remain a vital element of the continent's future. One of the positive consequences of the events of the past five years is undoubtedly the fact that each of the main partners finds it possible to lower the level of its armed forces without endangering its security. In other words security is no longer seen as related to the amount of armament (either way). This doctrinal change has produced tangible results, in the form of a number of international agreements. The next stages are more hazardous because of recent developments in Europe. New avenues of negotiations on armaments will have to be found (announced by unilateral and "lightning" agreements between the United States and Russia); ways of enforcing the agreements will also have to be found, to control withdrawals and destruction of weapons, to convert military plants etc.; new checks will be needed in Europe as the superpowers can no longer act as watchdogs.

Disarmament in Europe is the only sensible option (what would result from a distribution of existing stockpiles among all the new national entities ?) and undoubtedly it is also the road to the emergence of a commonwealth of all continental nations, paved with difficulties, yet the only alternative to a catastrophe. The political basis on which to build is undoubtedly, come what may, independent states, as a return to sovereignty is the outstanding element of the changes taking place in Europe in the last ten years. Each nation has insisted on having political structures of its own, with legal independence and a clear strategic policy. This general trend to create new national units, hardly viable because they constitute a regression to pre-industrial times, (with its accompaniment of border disputes, along lines of ethnic "purification", etc.) is the reason why it is imperative to find fresh collective arrangements, in an attempt not to reverse the movement, which would be impossible, but to circumscribe it and render it less dangerous. Nobody can be sure of the end result either way.

This trend towards scattered national entities, which will continue for a long time, whatever the form taken by Europe in the future, will make a reappraisal of national defense establishments necessary. The enemy is no longer the same, in some cases the old one becomes threatening again, in others it has vanished. In any case, in the future, disputes will be settled by means that military authorities had not contemplated before, as there is no longer a superpower to face. Together with the configuration of battles, war aims have to be altered and with them military dispositions. This applies to all the countries involved, but especially to the major partners in the European game.

As regards France, the changes are far-reaching, they involve the physical theater of an armed confrontation to come. For centuries France has been threatened at home and defended herself with huge armies stationed near the North-East borders. This protection of the national territory is obsolete, since the vital regions are guarded by nuclear power and the crises in which France might have to intervene in years will take place far from home, and anyhow not on the border. A major point of French defense, that of manoeuvring on land at home and for national ends, has been erased form France's agenda. Next there is a change in war aims: if France is to intervene in a given crisis in Europe, if she has to use her military arm, it will not necessarily mean "going to war", in the ordinary sense (there could be miltary interventions to remedy "civilian" disasters, or to act as barrier, or for humanitarian missions etc.). If armaments have to be used, it will be in a different manner from the one envisaged during forty years of cold war, limited forces sent to far-away places will be a new feature of military action. Lastly a change in the specificity of armed forces is involved, guarding an open frontier is not the same as intervening over a length of five hundred kilometers. Moreover, many war scenarios would imply sending collective forces to the scene of action, ECSC, WEU, EEC, Alliance, UNO mandates, etc. This preference for collective manoeuvers means that compatible military systems have to be set up, flexible enough to adapt to individual situations.

These alterations to military forces will have to fit also possible interventions in the South, in the case of political powers which are present there and have economic interests in the area. Thus changes in Europe will be felt far outside, as some regions are left without military protection after the disappearance of the American and Soviet umbrellas and fall prey to their old demons. Furthermore competition between arms salesmen makes for higher and higher stockpiles of weapons, while the diversification of investments from rich countries to Central and Eastern Europe means that entire regions of the Third World, already living in extreme poverty (for example, the Maghreb, and worse still, the Sahel...) are completely destabilized. In short, the unsettled situation in the "South", especially in areas that are not far from France (Southern Mediterranean, Near East, the southern regions of what used to be the USSR, etc.) is likely to get worse, posing indirect risks, if not a threat to developed countries: problems of security for refugees and of internal stability in neighboring areas.

The bulk of these hypotheses does not require military solutions, but in so far as the use of armed forces could prove necessary, there is a need for sufficient forces of the right kind for intervention. In other words, if some Northern countries decide to intervene, in the event of conflicts in the Third World requiring it, which could only be in limited cases, such as a French action in Africa, or for a major power such as the United States, there must be a change in institutional machineries, particularly the military.

The tuning of military systems will prove delicate, since it would be disastrous to make our neighbors in the South think that a more or less united North wishes to acquire the means to rule over its backyards. The difficult situation in which Europe finds itself, which we are well aware of, does not appear so to countries in the South, which see it merely as the turbulences of a rich world, intent on building up an economic and military machine to threaten the "Other", the Third World. This picture was recently made most credible by the Gulf War.

Thus, alterations to national defense machineries, necessary for all concerned, must be all embracing and include nuclear forces. The nuclear arm is not "threatened" in Europe, either quantitatively (it will take decades to bring about structural changes in nuclear weapons already deployed, even if disarmament talks have made good progress in recent years) or qualitatively - what good reason could there be to give up the ultimate recourse at a time when the continent is more and more the prey of chaos ?. Yet, the strategic status of the nuclear weapons available in Europe will have to be revized.

Even though things unfortunately change too slowly, theater nuclear weapons will disappear in Europe (middle range or long range). Ultimately the American nuclear cover will disappear from Europe, it will no longer be deployed physically, in terms of material, on the continent. The divorce between demands for security and quantities of armaments eventually should lead to a fresh, "minimalist" approach to nuclear strategy (small nuclear forces can give political clout). The European Community, if it becomes a political power, will probably have to examine the collective status of the French and British dissuasion forces. The proliferation of countries with a nuclear capability, in Europe and outside, as a result of the break up of the East-West polarization, and later of the USSR, might alter our conception of "world nuclear strategy". Lastly the likely disappearance of the threat of nuclear war in Europe (until recently any local dispute could develop into a nuclear confrontation, but soon a nuclear solution to any kind of European crisis will become unthinkable) will make for increased expenditure in conventional forces, at the expense of nuclear programs.

A reappraisal of defense needs, including nuclear forces, is thus on the agenda. The operation should be a collective undertaking, and findings should be brought together for final decisions. As a precondition, a common authority should be created to manage the area of greatest danger, that of armaments, even though old territorial units would continue to break up into smaller ones.

Forty five years of stability have created an image of Europe though far from gentle, at least simple. Nowadays complex situations arise everywhere and they will multiply in years to come until complete fragmentation is possible. A precarious balance between rabid separatists and the forces of cooperation will be difficult to maintain in Europe. History cannot provide guidelines in this matter: the old collective arrangements have gone from the map of Europe, or been replaced by sclerotic bureaucracies no longer adapted to present day conditions.

The changes that have taken place in recent years should give a new sense of identity to the various parts of Europe, enabling them to avoid becoming a theater for endless clashes of overarmed sovereign entities as in the past. The situation of chaos which prevails at the moment is reflected in the contrary opinions it evokes: many countries to the south of the Mediterranean are convinced that the "North" is uniting to turn against them later, while many European countries seek salvation in claims for legal independence ad infinitum. Neither solution seems sensible and the question now is whether the idea of European unity will win the day rather than the other nighmarish visions, to provide a fitful but beneficial ray of hope.

***

Selected Bibliography

David D., Conflits, puissances et strategies en Europe (Bruxelles 1992); Est-Ouest 1945-1990 (Paris 1992)

Perestroika and Economic Reforms

Jacques Sapir

In the light of experience our opinion of Gorbachev and of the movement he launched Perestroyka, has sunk quite low. The years when the last President of the USSR was in power, almost seven in all, left a legacy of half baked reforms, moves and countermoves that raised many unfulfilled hopes. After his departure in 1991, confusion was at its height. Inflation coincided with acute shortages, industrial production was 10% down, while trade between regions and Republics was completely disrupted.

However, in 1939, Roosevelt's New Deal might have appeared equally lackluster, had he lost the 1940 elections. Even now the results of the Gaidar reform which started in January 1992 are not at all promising. Inflation reached 1% a day in May, commercial networks are seizing up, and industrial production, down by 14% in the first quarter, may well fall to 25% of its former level. Let us hope the situation will improve; if such a trend were to continue the ensuing social and political upheavals would make a conversion to the market economy out of the question.

Thus it is premature to try and evaluate a far reaching process of change such as Perestroyka, but it is tempting to do so and we may derive an insight on what is to come. Drawing a balance sheet of the last seven years can also serve to decide on the best policies to replace the Soviet system. This is still topical in many ways, but to do so one has to go back to the Brezhnev era which will put into relief the reasons behind Perestroyka. This is the only way to understand the ambiguous approach to reform of the Gorbachev years and the mistakes which led to the situation going out of control in recent times until it plunged into disaster in the last few months.

First of all, it should be made clear that Perestroyka cannot be held responsible for the economic crisis that is gripping the Soviet Union. It may have brought it to a pitch after exposing it, but the situation was hopeless when Gorbachev took over. This is the only reason why a self confessed reformer was allowed to become supreme ruler.

In the early 80s it was not obvious that the Soviet economy was in deep trouble, though all the signs were there. Allowing for the in built bias of Soviet statistics, it seems that growth came to a stop in the late 70s. This was mainly the result of an end in productivity gains, though the momentum continued for a while. When production was no longer boosted by such factors as cheap labor, it inevitably fell to a point of no growth at the start of the 80s.

This situation did not result from a slow process of deterioration to be blamed on further distances from natural resources (further and further eastwards). The Soviet economy had enjoyed a burst of growth in the second half of the 59s and after a deep recession in 1961-1964, another one up to 1971. The crisis in the 80s could not blamed either on central planning and its congenital inefficiency, since in that case it would have become apparent much earlier. The crisis was not due to outside events, as the embargo which affected exports of machinery to the USSR from 1981, as well as fluctuating oil prices (whose exports are the main currency earner for any Russian government) are not enough to explain a phenomenon with its roots in the mid 70s. As for military expenditures, though heavy, they had not been increased since the end of the 70s.

The recession goes back a long way, to the seesaw variations which had plagued the Soviet economy since the late 30s. These economic cycles were a reflection of circumstances inherent to a particular type of economic system, not due to the vagaries of a political leader, nor to errors in central planning. A study of the pattern of the Soviet economy since 1930 totally disproves political theories, it makes nonsense of analyses invoking totalitarian factors. There is also a striking absence in this crisis of any of the forces which used to reawaken the economy in the past. It appears as the end product of a logical system as small variations can be observed which affect institutions, general behavior and organization grids in the 60s. These changes gradually neutralized all the normal processes which might have led to a return to full working capacity. The cycle used to imply bursts of growth at regular intervals, but since this came to an end late in the 70s, there is evidence that the crisis reached structural proportions. Unable to perpetuate itself, the system had to either change or disappear, not to say change and disappear.

Indeed the crisis had far-reaching consequences, an end to economic growth rendered the leaders vulnerable by depriving them of the power to redistribute wealth, as was their wont in a society built round patrimonial logic. It also meant the failure of the attempt to bring the country on an equal economic footing with the West, as the distance with developed countries would inevitably increase. The leadership would be on unsure ground on the question of legitimacy henceforth, since it seemed incapable of enforcing some of the rules which had ensured internal stability since the demise of the Stalin regime, or of pursuing its aims in international strategy. To start with, instead of facing up to the situation, the Brezhnev leadership chose to take evasive action. It cut investments and infrastructures, while allowing deficits to increase. This only made the situation more ominous and after 1976 social and economic infrastructures deteriorated in such a way as to threaten internal stability while putting paid to any hope of returning to industrial growth. Meanwhile the hierarchy at the time of the Brezhnev freeze lost all credit with the new generation of cadres and administrators that was waiting in the wings. Perestroyka was both an attempt to solve the three crises that were coming to a head, in the economy, society at large and lack of legitimacy, together with a settling of accounts between two generations.

In 1985, when M.S. Gorbachev came to power, reform was in the air. Just another one, some cynics might have thought, since after 1957, reform had become the norm in the Soviet system. Krushchev had tried to encourage initiatives in the regions by doing away with production ministries in favor of local sovnarkozes. When the attempt failed, the emphasis swung again to industry. The 1965 reform, strongly influenced by E.Liberman's research, offered a mixture of increased autonomy for individual firms and more controls. The repercussion of the Prague Spring meant a reinforcement of the control side which was backed by the creation in 1973 of Industrial Unions. Under Brezhnev's influence, reform took the shape of a mere reorganization of the administration. This trend remained in evidence in the 1979 measures which gave more power to ministries and increased centralization. Then in 1983, Andropov, who was terminally ill, tried once again to combine experiments in autonomy, on the pattern of what the GDR was establishing at the time, with increased central controls.

This balancing act seemed doubtful and the first statements made by Gorbachev were far from clear. There were obvious signs of a wish to change the economy and to remedy the most striking deficiencies. Yet, only in the late 1985, did some plain speaking find its way into official speeches. The terms Perestroyka, Uskorenie and Glasnost became more pointed and more frequent. At the 27th Congress of the CPSU in January 1986 the notion of radical reform was finally announced in full. There were still some ambiguities, since Gorbachev stressed the need for Peresztroyka, that is to say a complete overhaul of society, while the Prime Minister, N.Ryzkhov, emphasized the necessity of increasing growth and development. The first measures that were taken did nothing to dispel uncertainties. Conflicting interpretations can be made of the March 1986 decree on running Agriculture, as well as laws on autonomy in industrial plants, cooperatives or joint-ventures, passed from January 1987 to January 1988.

These measures could be perceived as the first steps on the road to radical changes, or they could equally be taken as limited improvements of the system. Basically the Perestroyka looked ambivalent for several reasons, one of which was that Gorbachev was forced to compromize with more conservative elements in the Party. He fully remembered Krushchev's failure twenty five years earlier, and constantly sought to isolate the most conservative wing of the apparat to create the right political conditions for his reform to succeed. This is why he fought for democratization and cutting down on the Party's influence in favor of the State. Gorbachev and his entourage, foremost among which was A. Yakovlev, wanted to build a social and political basis for economic reform. From this point of view it is nonsense to blame them for excessive caution. After all it was taken as Gospel's truth that Soviet type systems were impervious to change. In 1986-88 most observers forecast that the reform would fail and conservatives would be back in power before long. It is true also that political manoeuvering was not the only reason for dithering. Gorbachev was an acknowledged champion of reform within the Soviet Socialist system, but he probably was more aware of signs of malfunctioning in the economy and society than he was of the sources of this phenomenon. He only reflected the conflicting views of economic experts, at a time when the frequent use of such a phrase as "market socialism" showed deep seated discrepancies in analysis. Was it only a matter of providing opportunites that were already present in the Soviet economy, or was the USSR entering a period of transition to full market economy, still including a good deal of social protection, as happens in Northern Europe?

These contradictions were not without consequences for economic policies. The support given to Uskorenie up to late 1987 meant a wave of investments which was the main factor in increased budget deficit. The aura of uncertainty surrounding the real meaning of Perestroyka led to ignoring some problems which proved to be of paramount importance later. Thus the worsening of the monetary situation was in 1988 still not perceived as one of the main threats to a continuation of reform. The consequences of the law on commercial banks, already in the air in 1988, on money supply were not taken into account until much later. Finally the process of devolving responsibilities from the Communist Party to State administration revitalized federal bodies which had been kept dormant under Party centralization. In reality there were in the system in-built tendencies to collapse because forces for dilution of power were stronger than effective decentralization in decision making.

The year 1989 was crucial for the history of Perestroyka. On the one hand it achieved a lot for democratization. The new assembly that had been elected the same year was, in part, a proper democratic assembly. A point of no return had been reached in the devolution of power from the Party to State administration. Yet on the other hand the economic situation had undoubtedly taken a turn for the worse. The old crisis was still gripping the country and simultaneously the measures taken in 1987 and 1988, though they had made the old system weaker, were quite inadequate for setting up new controls. The cumulative impact of shortages and excessive increase in the money supply led to break downs in movements of goods and to speculation. Support for Persestroyka was frittering away while it became more and more obvious that the ultimate goal was still unclear. Moreover the economic crisis coincided with various ominous political crises in the regions, as far flung as the Baltic countries and the Caucasus.

Gorbachev and his entourage desperately looked for remedies throughout the 1989-90 winter to regain control. The best policy seemed to be putting the economic reform into higher gear as well as making it more radical. The "Program for 500 days" introduced in the late summer 1990, was conceived at this time. In view of the crisis, a choice had to be made, and some of the original ambiguities disappeared then. The acknowledged aim was now to turn the Soviet economy into a market economy. But was there a Soviet economy left? The crisis had strong centrifugal effects. As supplies were becoming more and more erratic, subsidiary networks were appearing in the regions, doing nothing to solve difficulties. Whatever Gorbachev could do to decentralize economic power came too late to be effective. In many ways, the Union had come to be seen in irrational terms, by 1990. Local political authorities, whether belonging to the Communist Party, or independent and representing the new democratic forces, saw the Center as intrisically bad. When their legitimacy was reinforced by elections in the Republics in 1990, these authorities started systematically to question federal power.

Of course the latter was also to blame, repeated reform plans (the November 1989 Abalkin Plan, December 1989 Ryzhkov Program, May 1990 Ryzhkov Plan, August 1990 Shatalin Project) could only give an impression of confusion. At an early stage, the intended reform still greatly reflected old practices. The plan devized by Shatalin and his collaborators, under the name of "500 days Plan", was a curious mix of idealism and realism, trying to put market forces into play while retaining central control. Basically the economic debate was an instrument used by conflicting political factions. The rise of B.N. Yeltsin marked increased competition on the contents of the notion of reform. As soon as Gorbachev's economic advisers launched an idea, on privatization of Agriculture or foreign investments, immediately their opponents answered with a more radical version. The debate was no longer centered on viable alternatives, it now rested on attacks on central power which had lost its legitimacy. This made for increasingly unrealistic schemes, more and more removed from the daily worsening economic situation .

In the circumstances, it is easy to understand why, in late 1990, Gorbachev chose to put the emphasis on stabilization rather than pushing forward with economic reform. What is known as his "right hand turn" was probably an expression of fear arising from the wild suggestions of the more radical reformers. In the field of the economy, the managers of the Industrial-Military Complex, who also looked after a large section of production as a whole, had no trouble in showing him how unrealistic all the ideas put forward were. Just as Gorbachev and his team lacked legitimacy, the reformers lacked all credibility. This was the break-up of the alliance that had produced Perestroyka, a point of no return was reached between October and December 1990.

It is one thing to say that Perestroyka was dead and quite another to envisage a return to the Brezhnev type of power. It only means that a specific approach to reshaping the old system was abandoned. A zone of disturbance followed with political and economic conflicts coming to a head and the Union breaking apart, as in the Baltic countries. Some of the Republics stopped paying taxes, making budget deficit quite unmanageable. The "Law War" in which each tier of government denied the other any legitimacy gave rise to an avalanche of reforms, all equally vain since they were never enacted.

Yet Gorbachev insisted on fighting. He first attempted to solve the economic crisis by price control under the aegis of the new Prime Minister, V. Pavlov, in April 1990. The result was inconclusive, but partial stabilization was achieved in May and June, which could be a real achievement compared to the effects of the end of price regulations, under I. Gaidar early in 1992. Gorbachev also desperately tried to prevent the Union collapsing , first by holding a referendum on March 17, 1991, later by concluding an agreement with the leaders of the nine main Republics, the 9 plus 1 agreement, in May 1991.

These last efforts failed miserably, but probably for political reasons rather than economic ones. No longer acceptable to reformers, Gorbachev now had to stop relying on the moderate conservatives who had been his allies for a while. The latter labored under the delusion that they could solve the crisis on their own, after seeing the successful March referendum and the partial achievement of price reform. The result was the aborted putsch in August, which marked not only their departure from the political arena, but also an end to any hope of reviving an alliance to champion Perestroyka in the near future. The gradual eviction of Gorbachev, the rebellion of the Russian authorities which came to a head with the undignified break up of the USSR on December 9, were only logical consequences of previous events.

It is always dangerous to give estimations of historical events still in the making. Perestroyka has not yet its niche in History, but it lies like a corpse that can never be resurrected, and its shadow inspires such feelings of fear that it has to be exorcized. Would Russia, indeed, have launched the risky operation of deregulating prices, if her leaders had not been intent on exorcized at any cost the notion of gradual change, that is to say Perestroyka? The fact that B.Yeltsin, late in May 1992, reacted violently to declarations made by Gorbachev, though the latter has no official standing now, while Khasbulatov, the President of the Russian Assembly, makes even louder noises, shows that there are ghosts still haunting him.

The first half of 1992 has been a disaster. Price deregulation was supposed to mop up excess currency as living expenses would go up suddenly and bring about stabilization. Advisers to the Gaidar government reckoned that the situation would be the same as in 1990 in Poland, and with the population suffering increased hardship, shortages would become a thing of the past. Nothing of the kind happened. Price deregulation was not followed by equilibrium, because economic exchanges were too fragmented. Prices rose very high with inflation accelerating (1% daily early in May 1992), but shortages are still there. The new price system is totally dependent on monopoly agreements by industrial firms or local managers. Prices may vary from 1 to 10 according to the town where one is. Industrial relations are disorganized, with corresponding drop in output, which in turn leads to more shortages. As plants are unable to produce goods, for lack of supplies, or to sell their product, for lack of customers, they increase their deficits, and chronic insolvency threatens to bring about a general financial crisis. In the circumstances, the chances to operate normal macroeconomic means of manoueuver are minimal. The State cannot balance its budget since its tax returns are shrinking under the impact of reduced production; the central bank cannot impose tight monetary control for fear of a financial crisis engulfing the whole country. The economy, Russian now, is increasingly split up into geographical separate units while local authorities become more powerful. Firms and local authorities print their own money, either as bonds or "shares" that are given out to employees instead of the bank notes in short supply under the impact of inflation.

The shock therapy that Gaidar administered created just the situation people feared would be established by Perestroyka and the gradual measures taken by Gorbachev. Therefore it is not surprising to see the managers of the Milatary Industrial Complex raise their heads from the middle of May 1992. Their influence is felt through the Industrial Union of A. Volsky and several of its members joined the government in June. They are seen as saviors after the failure of radical economic changes. It is easy to understand Yeltsin's outbursts when Gorbachev openly criticized his policies. He may well be forced into the same channels as his rival and then how will he claim legitimacy for himself and his entourage?

Meanwhile another corpse threatens to be resurrected. Yeltsin liquidated the Union which had been approved in principle by a majority of the people in March 1991. In order to evict Gorbachev, the man who embodied all democratic hopes, after his assent to power following on the failed putsch, lost no time in slighting the authority of universal suffrage. Undoubtedly all claims to economic independence put forward by individual States are without foundation. The USSR was well integrated economically and remains so. The failure of the CIS would bring about a collapse of economic relations and consequently of the economies of each new State. A precondition for an end to the present crisis is a new treaty of Union, at least in the economic field. This was Gorbachev's aim not so very long ago.

Perestroyka may look different in six months' time, but to assess its value it is essential to distinguish between what it sought to achieve and what it actually performed. It is obvious that the reformed socialist society that Gorbachev dreamt of in 1987 and 1988 will never exist. As for the passage to a market economy, it is not sure that the slow pace of Gorbachev's reform could not have ensured it better than the hurried one of Gaidar's.

***

Selected Bibliography

Sapir J., Pays de l'Est: vers la crise generalisee? (Paris 1980); Rytmes d'accumulation et modes de regulation de l'economie sovietique (Paris X (Nanterre) 1986); (ed.) L'URSS au tournant (Paris 1990); Les fluctuations economiques en URSS: 1941-85 (Paris 1989)

Chavance B. (ed.), Regulation, cycles et crises dans les economies socialistes (Paris 1987)

Drewnowski J. (ed.), Crisis in the East European Economy: the spread of the Polish disease (London 1982)

Ericson R.E., The Soviet Statistical Debate: Khanin vs the TsSU (Palo Alto 1988)

Lewin M., The Gorbachev Phenomenon (Berkeley 1988)

Hewett Ed. A., Reforming the Soviet Economy (Washington DC 1988)

Soviet Economy in a Time of Change (Washington DC 1979)

Soviet Economy in the 1980s (Washington DC 1982)

Kushnirsky F.I., Soviet Economic Planning 1965-80 (Boulder 1982)

Desai P., Perestroika in Perspective (Princeton 1989)

Yasin E.G., Khozaistvennye sistemy i radikalnaya reforma (Moscow 1989)

Perekhod k rynku, kontseptsiya i programma (Moscow 1990)

Beyond Perestroyka: The Soviet Economy in Crisis (Washington DC 1991)

Guetta B., Eloge de la tortue. L'URSS de Gorbatchev, 1985-1991 (Paris 1991)

Perestroika and Constitutionalism

D. G. Lavroff

Who in 1985 could have imagined that the Soviet Union, an immense landmass of nearly 300 millions inhabitants, with huge natural resources, and a military machine equal to that of the United States in the field of strategic weapons, would simply fade away in 1992. Soviet disintegration occurred in spite of its superiority in conventional forces and the fact that the USSR represented an ideal for a large section of the planet's population in both 'socialist' (totalitarian) and 'capitalist' (liberal democratic) countries. Many people believed in various degree in the ultimate triumph of 'socialism', naturally with the assistance of the Soviet 'motherland' whose edicts, for this reason, they were prepared to obey most faithfully. Moreover the sudden collapse of the USSR was not the result of a world war, but of internal decay comparable to that of a building undermined by termites. Only a few people, such as Solzhenitsyn and Zinoviev, who had to pay dearly for their farsightedness, realized that the 'mystical beast of communism' was terminally ill, because it drew nourishment from an empty dogma and was powerless against reality-truth battering continuously its evil structures. Political scientists (H. Carrere d'Encausse, for example) and economists, such as F. Hayek, did expose in the clearest possible way the deepseated flaws of the 'evil empire'. It was gradually torn apart by tensions among its member nations, the chronic shortages of a subsistence economy in which all available resources were diverted to armaments and a costly expansion policy in international affairs. Such an intellectual stand required courage and strong convictions in the climate of Marxist sympathy and pro-Soviet attitudes prevalent in Western intellectual circles at the time, which allowed naive preconceptions on the ultimate advent of communism to be widespread. Yet it became evident in the 'post revolutionary' era that these old assumptions were wrong, especially in the wake of mass protest demonstrations in the 1980's against the installation of the Pershing missiles in Western Europe to counterbalance the SS 20s in the USSR and in the Peoples' Democracies of Central and Eastern Europe.

The disappearance of the Soviet Union as a nation state, the official rejection of Marxism-Leninism in favor of a market economy, and the emergence of independent states from the ruins of the Soviet Union, completely altered the political structures of this vast area with far-reaching consequences for the whole world. It may be appropriate at this stage to examine recent institutional changes embodied in the new constitutions. Though these changes at first sight look insignificant compared to the upheavals taking place in politics, they are, nevertheless, important. If one considers the Marxist concept of Law as an element of the power apparatus imposed by the State on production forces and completely dependent upon it, it could be inferred that the rules of Law are consequences but not prime causes of the development. If examined in this sense, they do not throw any light on a given situation. Nonetheless, such a concept of law was advocated by the Soviet authorities and was invariably presented in a simplistic manner by them. As for the Constitution, as a body of rules defining the system, organs and instruments of political power, it reflects, according to them, a point of development reached in the class struggle at a certain time. Soviet authors have always developed a mechanistic concept of the Constitution; it is obviously a tool in the hands of the ruling class. As Brezhnev and Stalin expressed it in different terms in 1936 and 1977, the Constitution is meant to be a landmark in the class struggle and has no intrisic value, except as an official statement of the stage reached. It lacks any authority which would enable it to curb the revolutionary appetite of the proletariat, as supposedly expressed by the governing elite. It is an instrument, not a supreme authority, as is the case in a liberal society. The Constitution in the Soviet Marxist doctrine is an acknowlegement of a state of affairs as well as a symbol. Into the drafts of the Constitution, Soviet rulers have often inserted clauses which were never meant to be applied, nor to represent even an ideal, but were intended to inspire admiration in the Soviet people and among foreigners. Such is the case, for example, of the Declaration of Human Rights, the Declaration of the Rights of the Working People which has been used since 1918, or the tenth chapter of the 1936 Constitution and the 1977 Human Rights Declaration. These texts had no legal value and could not be used by ordinary citizens in getting redress from the State for abuse of power on the part of their rulers. This interpretation of the Law was confirmed by the fact that in the heyday of Marxism in the Soviet Union, that is to say from the end of the NEP to that of the Brezhnev era, whenever the demand for the application of dispositions laid down in declarations of Human Rights or any rules of a constitutional character was raised, it was considered as counterrevolutionary or treasonable, and thereby punishable with heavy sentences. The serious difficulties encountered by A.Sakharov and other Human Rights activists, such as Siniavsky, Daniel, Pliushch, are proof of the symbolic value of the main constitutional rules concerning the rights and liberties of individuals. This point was raised by the author as early as 1958, when Western legal experts, especially the French, still believed blindly that in the Soviet Union individual freedoms and Human Rights were "real" and only "formal" or without 'substance' in Western democracies. Unfortunately, this misapprehension, surprising if it was genuine, but scandalous if it was not,came to light only in recent years with changes occurring in the Soviet regime and satellite countries. As late as 1990, a French lawyer could describe as a remarkable achievement the establishment of the rule of law that President Gorbachev declared as his aim, while in reality this notion was absolutely incompatible with Marxism-Leninism and in practice was constantly violated. Since it has been 'scientifically' established that Soviet Law, especially Constitutional Law, has no relevance to social reality and is not intended to serve as a yardstick to both rulers and ruled, calls for a Rechtsstaat were symbolic. Still it is worth examining such reforms, as, on the whole, they reflect the picture that the Soviet authorities and their allies would like to present to the world of the kind of society they were building and putting in place 'by force'. It also gives an idea of the powerful forces for change that took hold of the Soviet people and the populations of the Peoples' Democracies in recent years. Thus, on the one hand, Constitutional amendments will be examined, as reflections of "perestroika" in the Soviet Union. On the other hand the new version of Constitutional Law which accompanied the end of Marxism in the Soviet Union and the disappearance of the USSR will be discussed.

When Mikhail Gorbachev, in March 1985, came to power and became General Secretary of the CPSU, he announced that he intended to modernize the political and economic systems, a reform made necessary by the "stagnation afflicting the country in the Brezhnev era." The words 'transparency' (glasnost) and 'restructuring' (perestroika) were to be the rallying cry of the **new policy**.

The Constitution of October 7, 1977, heralding the disappearance of social classes in the Soviet Union, with the State representing the people as a whole, had preserved roughly the constitutional arrangements of 1936. However, it seemed to limit the field of State interference and gave a greater scope for political action to the Federal Republics. Despite appearances nothing fundamental had been altered, since the CP was still in full control of society and all the instruments of government were in its hands. It ran the system according to the principles intrisically based on the explicit concepts of Marxism-Leninism.

Thus the 1977 Constitution was first amended by a constitutional ruling on December 1, 1988, which expressed Gorbachev's intention to transform the Soviet Union into a **law governed state (Rechtsstaat)**. The formula sounded impressive and could be used as a propaganda slogan, but in no way did it coincide with the traditional legal meaning of it. The constitutional innovation brought about by Gorbachev's political initiative was automatically curtailed by the 'higher judiciary-ideological' authority as incompatible with the tenets of Marxism-Leninism. The only reforms enacted under this much advertised clause had little impact: the use of the idea of popular sovereignty to establish a system of decision by assembly; the creation of a Congress of People's Deputies of the USSR which partially restored the 1924 Congress of People's Deputies of the USSR abolished in 1936. This measure was intended to ensure larger popular representation. Neither was the creation of a President of the Supreme Spoviet of greater importance.

The December 1990 Constitutional reform was of even less practical significance. It brought electoral laws nearer to those of the democratic countries because it allowed multiple candidates, but on condition that they be put forward by organizations of the Party or social and professional bodies. It also set up a Committee of Constitutional Surveillance of the kind that exists elsewhere in Europe under the name of the Constitutional Courts. However, in the Soviet Union constitutional rulings remained incomparable in character with those of liberal democracies.

On March 14, 1990, however, adopted amendments altered the balance of the constitution much further by instituting a President of the USSR who had the same powers as the President of the Supreme Soviet, together with new ones turning him into the Chief Executive in a Presidential regime, but with the additional power of being also General Secretary of the CPSU and therefore all powerful. The Congress of the People's Deputies was made into the supreme organ of State power (art. 108-1) to deal with essential decisions of policy, arbitrating in conflicts between various bodies at the top of Soviet power, and able to impeach the President of the Union in the event of violation of the Constitution or Law (art. 127-7). In reality this organ of power consisting of 2.250 deputies who assembled for a few days every year was quite incapable of fulfilling its constitutional role. The Supreme Soviet turned by the Constitutional Reform of December 1st, 1988, into something resembling Western Parliaments, both in numbers (500) and length of sittings (two sittings of three or four months each), was "the legislative organ controlling the power of the State in the USSR, permanently, even when not in session." (art. 11-1) As such it became the supreme lawmaker and more importantly a body which approved government decisions or could force its resignation. In this power arrangement the President of the USSR occupied a key position. It was probably the most appropriate role for him, necessary for the Soviet Union: a strong central figure was needed to take urgent modernization measures. It also answered Gorbachev's desire to be independent of the Party, not to run the risk of being dismissed, like Khrushchev, after a debate of the Central Committee. He demanded and got a guarantee of stability of tenure and in a sense a constitutional mandate. This proved to be a pious hope when ultimately Gorbachev was forced to resign without any constitutional reason. The intention to bring the Constitution into step with the American one was obvious, since it was announced that the President of the USSR would be elected by direct universal suffrage, thereby increasing his legitimacy, and that he would be assisted by a Vice-President and a Presidential Council consisting of ministers appointed by the President and accountable to him only.

These constitutional reforms were not enough to prevent centrifugal forces coming to the fore, in the shape of national claims put forward by Republics at the periphery of the Empire (Armenia and Baltic Provinces) together with Russian republican pressures exerted by President Boris Yeltsin. This was the start of the legitimacy controversy and the move to abandon Marxism at the same time as burying the Soviet Union.

The August 18, 1991, coup d'Etat was a crucial moment in the evolution of the Soviet Union. It seemed to mark the last effort made by the Communists to save the regime established in 1917 and its failure generated an acceleration in the fatal decline of Soviet power. It also resulted in individual Republics declaring independence. At the same time radical changes were occurring, though tentatively, in the constitutional arrangements between Russia and other Republics of the old Empire.

In the autumn of 1990 the Soviet Union seemed to enter a period of opposition on the part of the Communist regime to all attempts at modernization. Gorbachev had always proclaimed his faith in Marxism-Leninism and the reforms he suggested, some of which to do with privileges enjoyed by the **apparachiki** and their way of life, aimed primarily at running Soviet society in a more efficient manner, so as to pacify the detractors of the system. Communist representatives of the 'progressive movement' expressed their misgivings on hearing of the most important plants of the industrial-military complex being taken over by hard-line Communists bent on resisting **all** changes. Thus on December 20, 1990, E. Shevardnadze, the Foreign Minister who favored carrying out reforms, resigned from his post and warned of the risk of a coup d'Etat initiated by the 'conservatives'. A few months later, A. Yakovlev, the top advisor of Gorbachev and the man who formulated the theory of perestroika, announced that a coup d'Etat was planned for July 21, 1991. All these revelations were taken seriously since they coincided with accusations made by hardliners, such as the head of KGB, that the Soviet Union was allowed to disintegrate by default, due to the Western secret services and their Soviet accomplices. Gorbachev alone kept quiet and did nothing other than impress on Western powers that he played a vital part in the changes and there was no alternative to his policy, thus justifying the need to grant him financial assistance. The key questions had to wait until the 29th Party Congress which was to be held in the summer of 1991. Only then, in the course of this party hapenning, new directions would be adopted for a Social Democratic program. A new Union statute would be defined in the Pact of Union which had been accepted in principle by three Republics on August 20, 1990. It was clear that the Soviet Union was engaged on a course of change which could only be abbhorent to the 'conservatives'.

The coup d'Etat was rather like a Palace revolution (a proletarian palace of course). The main instigators were few in numbers, they were all of equal rank and members of the USSR government (G.Yanaev, Vice-President of the USSR, V.S.Pavlov, Prime Minister; B.K.Pugo, Minister of the Interior; D.T.Yazov, Defense Minister) either KGB chief or heads of large social and economic institutions, therefore enjoying political influence. As if this were happening in some Third World country, the plotters took advantage of President Gorbachev's stay in the Crimea on holiday to declare him incapable of exercizing office due to illness. G.I.Yanaev replaced him temporarily, as his function of Vice-President allowed, under the article 127-4 of the Constitution. He proceeded to apply article 127-3-15, and assumed special powers, appointing a State Committee made up of eight men on August 18, 1991, to take whatever measures were required in the circumstances, provided they were approved subsequently by the Supreme Soviet. On August 19, 1991, a second decree re-established censorship and martial law in Moscow, while detachments of soldiers backed by armored vehicles were positioned in strategic places in Moscow , Leningrad and the capitals of the Baltic Provinces. The putsch did not meet with much resistance from the population, and did not occasion much violence on the part of its instigators, who made serious tactical errors (they failed to take control of communications, to order mass arrests of all likely opponents etc.). After the initial shock, Russian President Boris Yeltsin's courageous declarations caused thousands of demonstrators to crowd streets in Moscow. A. Sobchak, the progressive Mayor of Leningrad, succeeded in returning to his city,giving moral support to the numerous demonstrators defying the putschists' tanks there. In the Baltic Provinces strong resistance was immediate, since the putsch was seen as mortal to the nationalist movement. By August 21, at 7.19 p.m. the putsch was over and Gorbachev was back in Moscow, a free man. However, the victory was Yeltsin's as he had shown outstanding determination and courage as well as strategic flair in combat, and promised real reform. Gorbachev emerged from the ordeal substantially weakened. His obstinate support of Marxism-Leninism alienated from him those more radical reformers who rightly thought that, only after discarding the dead doctrines, would the USSR evolve towards greater freedom and happiness. He had shown lack of judgment in appointing to the highest positions in government and the economy men completely without dignity or even ability, committed to a totalitarian system , who would not hesitate to use violence to secure their personal interests. It was obvious that his excessive reluctance in forging ahead with democratic reforms had brought on the crisis.

The ignominious failure of the putsch gave much hope to the populations of the USSR. For the first time in its history, popular opposition as well as the refusal of the security and armed forces to commit themselves to repression, had ensured the collapse of a putsch carried out according to all the rules of Marxism-Leninism, but applied clumsily and lacking a firm ideological basis. Suddenly thousands, if not millions of citizens were no longer dependent on the mercy of the party **apparachiki**, backed by professional soldiers and KGBists. This was the reverse of the Petrograd coup d'Etat of 1917.

The most significant result of the coup was the collapse of the Communist Party. It had already lost its dominant position in the State, but it survived to provide a kind of framework for central power, the economy and society as a whole. As soon as the crisis was over, Yeltsin decreed a ban on the Party in Russia and its property was confiscated. This decision was of course without any legal foundation, as it was taken on the initiative of the President instead of being embodied in a Law. The same happened in various Republics which seized the opportunity to declare themselves independent (Byelorussia, Moldavia and the Baltic countries). Moreover a decree suspending the CPSU, not a ban which could only be ordered in a Constitutional Law or a decree of the Constitutional Court of the USSR, was approved in a vote on August 30, 1991, by the Supreme Soviet of the USSR, consisting of a large communist majority. This endorsed a situation which brought to an end the process of dissolution of the Party started in 1990 by President Boris Yeltsin in Russia, culminating in President Gorbachev's resignation from his job as General Secretary of the CP on August 24, 1991. At his expressed wish the Central Committtee of the CPSU dissolved itself peacefully. It should be said that it had survived the putsch in name only. Thus, the actual demise of the CP was a deathknell of the totalitarian regime purporting to hold the key to the world's future. The partisans of the old regime protested strongly against the 'illegality' of a ban on the Party's activities and expropriation of all its property by the authorities of the new Republics. It is ironic to see the very men who had infringed the Law when in power, in the name of the revolution, or because they controlled power means, invoke immunity when subjected to similar injustice. It is questionable whether one is entitled to use the same power means that helped totalitarian regimes to stay in power in order to topple them. But it seems that at this early stage, in the revolutionary period that followed the August 1991 putsch, the answer had to be yes. On the other hand, if, as it is hoped, Russia and the other Republics intend to follow the path of democracy, the matter of a statute governing political parties, including the Communist Party, will have to be considered. The Russian Constitutional Court is at the moment engaged in a legal action in which the CPSU and its leaders stand accused; it will be a difficult task to bring it to a satisfactory conclusion, as the people in power in the Republics which used to belong to the Soviet Union, were all in the past leading members of the very party whose misdeeds they are supposed to condemn.

From the early days of Marxist-Leninist rule in the Soviet Union, political leaders and law experts expressing their theories held that the communist ideology was the only way to solve the problem of nationalities, which had kept many European countries in turmoil almost continuously since the beginning of the 20th century. According to them, the proletarian revolution was unique in shaping the nature of power and therefore relations between individuals and nationalities. Just as national struggles for independence against bourgeois governments oppressing the people were justified, so proletarians would be willing to cooperate with a regime which gave power to the proletariat, whatever its nationality, since it no longer suffered any injustice. As proletarian power could not deal unfairly with the proletariat, there would be no call for national entities. Thus independent from one another, they would, on the contrary, prefer to be part of a large proletarian and socialist state. In the years following the revolution, Stalin became a specialist of the question of nationalities, which came to the fore after the political upheavals in what was left of the huge Russian Empire. The Empire consisted of hundreds of different nationalities which had been subjugated by the Russians. The new Soviet rulers had no intention of allowing the various national units to break away. As a Georgian, Stalin firmly believed that all nations were from then on equal, and should coexist peacefully according to the principles of Marxism-Leninism. The 1924 Federal Constitution was his own creation. It instituted an Union of Soviet Socialist Republics, which was a Federation of a new kind, according to him, comprising Republics as well as regions and territories, enjoying wide powers of internal autonomy and sharing federal power. The 1936 Constitution ran on the same lines with a few slight modifications. It ensured that populations of different ethnic origin could coexist in the same State in spite of linguistic, cultural and historical barriers, of varying levels of economic development or the fact that a section of the population acted as masters and the rest as subordinates. The only link between them was that they used to belong to the Russian Empire, and could communicate through a common language, Russian, at least as far as the national elites were concerned. In addition they had to adopt the ideology of Marxism-Leninism, at any rate officially and the nationality problem was solved. Such a theory of Soviet federation settling nationality problems proved also invaluable for the preservation the 'new-old empire'. It could also be called colonial, since its peoples had been incorporated by conquest. At the same time the Soviet Union was spared the stigma of using force to keep them in order, even though in actual fact force was necessary to curb troublesome national masses. Soviet writers and sympathisers in the West lost no opportunity to stress the basic difference between bourgeois federalism, as an instrument for the proletariat to be kept in chains by the middle class and colonized peoples by their masters, and Soviet federalism, a means for the liberation of peoples and for the various populations to cohabit and work together as equals in their march towards freedom and progress. Between 1924 and April 26, 1990, when a Constitutional Law was promulgated, which once again altered the balance of responsibilities between the Federal Government and member states of the Federation, many structural changes were enacted, but the framework remained the same. Thus, ideologically, the 1977 Constitution constituted a significant advance in the Soviet society's march towards communism. It contained several indications of a weakening of the central state and of changing relations between the peoples making up the Soviet Union; a greater emphasis on autonomy for the federal republics became evident.

However, Soviet federalism could only grant a semblance of autonomy to member nations. In this constitutional as well as in other areas, the official recognition of the right for federal republics to manage certain sectors of public life had no effect on decision making on the spot. Above all the right to secede from the Union did not exist, though it was duly stated in the Constitution. It was simply unthinkable that a people should leave the Soviet Union, blessed as it was with the advantages procured for it by Marxism-Leninism and a proletarian government. Such ideological contradictions, if persisted on, would be treated as counterrevolutionary and punished. In fact the recognized rights and legal guarantees granted to federal member-republics were of little value for independent national decisions. For the top leadership of the CPSU made up of representatives of the Parties of federal republics, was inevitably Russian dominated. In the system of democratic centralism which required absolute subservience of national minorities to the Russian majority and enforced such hierarchical co-relations at all levels, it was inevitable. Thus the Russian communist leaders maintained throughout a monopoly of decision making in politics, the state administration and the economy. Despite the fact that republican CPs were often headed by a national First Secretary, real power was exercised by of the Second Secretary who was almost invariably Russian. The collapse of the federation in 1992 proved conclusively how artificial it was. Finally, there could be no real autonomy in the economy because the system was meant to run according to a centralized plan, covering the whole Federation whose requirements had to be met at all costs. The only remaining hope was the preservation of the cultural heritage of the individual peoples. It is probably in this area that some achievements were made, especially in the field of newspapers and publications in national languages, but this did not prevent enormous pressure put on the use of Russian in public life, since it had to be taught from primary school age and was a requisite for any administrative career. It is remarkable that the need to spread the knowledge of Russian among populations belonging to other cultures has led to the language losing in quality and becoming a kind of Pidgin Russian, much to the chagrin of many an intellectual. This so-called multinational paradise witnessed the most cruel campaigns of repression against some reluctant nationalities, such as the Germans of the Volga, Tatars, Georgians and Jews who, despite assimilation, were also treated as a separate nationality. Helene Carrere d'Encausse was quick in detecting the centrifugal effect of nationalism in the Soviet Union and a dangerous imbalance between the birthrate of the Slavic populations and the others.

After 1985 it seemed likely that Marxist principles and perestroika would improve relations between the various nationalities of the Union. However, nothing of the sort happened. On the contrary, the federation reached a breaking point. By 1989 it became increasingly difficult to satisfy the demand for greater autonomy made by many national minorities, the Balts and Caucasians claiming complete independence. The whole system was undermined by the rejection of federalism as a means of integration. The Law of April 26, 1990, tried to establish a new kind of federation, more decentralized, so as to fit the declarations of independence made by many large republics, among which the Russian. This process occurred in the parliaments elected in a less undemocratic manner than usual, as a result of the December 1st, 1988 Law amending the Constitution and the existing electoral law. Yet the new parliaments remained under even greater control by members of the Communist Party than before. On November 16, 1990, Gorbachev submitted to the Supreme Soviet a draft of his Treaty of Union which included 25 new articles replacing articles 70 to 75 of the Constitution. Having been approved by the Supreme Soviet, the Treaty had to be ratified by a popular referendum. The new arrangements was intended to turn the Soviet Union into an Union of Sovereign Republics (USR) in which each Republic would have full national responsiblities on its territory while the Federal State would be in charge of coordinating foreign affairs, and regulating the economy and finances inside the Union. It would also be responsible for policies in defense and foreign affairs as well as their application. To carry out these aims each Republic was entitled to raise taxes on its territory and the Union had its own budget and resources levied directly on citizens. Transports, energy and the space industry were a federal responsibility. The right for the Republics to secede was not acknowledged formally. Hardly had it been unveiled that the project met with strong opposition. Presidents Yeltsin and Landsbergis (Lithania) criticized it on the ground of too much centralism; Ukrainian leaders refused to sign the treaty before their country had adopted its own Constitution; while several Caucasian Republics rejected outright the new arrangements. Gorbachev reacted sharply and in a conservative way as he stressed the importance of a multinational State and the primary role of the Communist Party. The Central Committee of the CPSU followed him. For several months, Gorbachev tried hard to find ways to reassert his authority which was under attack in the outlying areas of the Union. He tried to increase his personal power to remedy institutional weaknesses. The 4th Congress of Peoples' Deputies met late in December,1990, in the absence of the Balts and Moldavians who had left when they realized that Russian speaking deputies from their states were in attendance. It approved the principle of a referendum on the question of the Union, which had been suggested by Gorbachev, thus the continuance of the USSR; the principle of a referendum on private property to oppose a reform aiming at privatization of land passed in Russia; and finally a Constitutional reform concerning executive power. The resignation of E.Shevardnaze on December 26, 1990, underlined the dangers threatening the reforms. The law of December 26, 1990, added to the Constitution of the USSR a chapter 15-2 (articles 127-8,9 and 10) under the title of "Federal Council". This body consisting of the President and Vice-President of the USSR with the Presidents of the 15 federal republics and those of the 20 autonomous republics, was intended to act as the powerhouse of the treaty as well as its guarantor, as it represented both central and peripheral leadership and could combine demands for independence with the need for Union. The Council was to adopt motions by a two third majority, which could bring about a paralysis in the event of certain republics withdrawing from the proceedings. The law of December 26, 1990, also instituted three new bodies: the Security Council whose members were appointed by the President, after he had taken advice from the Federal Council and sought approval from the Supreme Soviet; the Cabinet of Ministers which was described in the Constitution (art. 128) as the executive and administrative body of the USSR; as well as a High Court of Arbitration. The Procurator's office was modified to give more power to the Republics. Nevertheless these reforms did nothing to prevent relations between the Union and the Republics worsening, as the latter became more restless about independence and eager for full sovereignty. The failure of the putsch revealed deep divisions and the fragility of the structures meant to remedy them. Thus in a decree of September 5, 1991, the Congress of the Peoples' Deputies ordered a speedy conclusion of the draft Treaty of Union and its adoption "by everyone concerned ". The republics could choose freely their way of association with the Union. The latter had to be based on the principles of territorial independence and integrity, observance of Human Rights and the rights of Peoples, social justice and democracy. Finally, agreements on inter-republican cooperation in the field of economy, finance, environment, collective security and defense had to be signed. The same law covered the transition period, with the Supreme Soviet acting as a high council to represent the power of State. It was made up of two chambers, the Soviet of Nationalities-Republics and the Soviet of the Union; there was a Council of State drawn from all Republics and an inter-republican Economic Council. After sitting for four days the Congress of the Peoples' Deputies of the USSR was abolished.

The resignation of President Gorbachev coincided with the 'abolition' of the USSR. No one could have imagined this upheaval taking place without violence, such was the general belief in the power of Soviet leaders and, in spite of so much evidence to the contrary, in the soundness of Marxism. The Soviet Union had broken up as a result of the reawakening of nationalisms and general desire for liberalization. Since the bolsheviks had taken advantage of Marxism to tighten the bonds between the various nations of the ex-Russian Empire, in the name of internationalism, they had to repress national aspirations whenever they contradicted Soviet and therefore Russian power.Thus it came as no surprise that national demands led to rejection of Soviet power in 1992. This was obvious in the case of the Baltic Republics, which were the first to break loose from the Union. They asserted their right to self-determination against the Soviet and Russian power which had forcibly kept them in the Soviet Union. The same phenomenon occurred in the Caucasian Republics where feelings of national identity were intense and later in Central Asian Republics. In the European ones nationalism was rather a pretext than cause of rejection. Thus in the Ukraine and Byelorussia which are basically part of the Russian territory, even though there are some regional differences, the national claims put forward by a section of the population were used by Communist leaders in each Republic to gain political initiative against Russian leaders. It is likely that national feelings in the Ukraine and Byelorussia will grow in intensity over the years, but at the moment (1992), they are only of tactical interest in the struggle for power between various factions.

Can the creation of independent Republics in the ruins of the old Soviet Union or the old Russian Empire solve all problems and ensure stabilitity in the area? This seems hardly likely. First of all, it is clear that none of the new Republics is ethnically or nationally homogenous. The Russian Empire and later the Soviet Union have continuously mixed various populations in the huge territory and encouraged Russian nationals to move in large numbers to the most distant parts of the country. There are many Russians in the Caucasus, going back to the 19th century, as well as in the Baltic Republics which were always strongly influenced by their neighbor. Siberia was also considered as a land fit for pioneers, while in the Central Asian Republics the primary reason for colonisation was to keep so called underdeveloped populations under control, later "to colonize virgin land" according to the slogan of N. Krushchev and L. Brezhnev. A few figures will demonstrate this point: Armenia has 1,6% Russians and 1,7% Azeris; Azerbaijan, 5,6% Russians and Armenians; Byelorussia, 13,1% Russians and significant Polish, Ukrainian and Jewish minorities; Georgia contains 29,9% other nationalities, 8,1% of which are Russians; Kazakhstan, 60,3% other nationalities, of which 37,8% Russians; Kirghistan, 47,6% other nationalities, of which 21,5% Russians; Moldavia,

35,5% other nationalities, of which 35,5% Ukrainians and 13,8% Russians; Uzbekistan 28,6% other nationalities, of which 8,3% Russians; Russia 18,5% other nationalities, of which 3,8% Tatars and 3% Ukrainians; Tadjikistan, 37,7% other nationalities of which 23,5% Uzbeks and 7,6% Russians; Turkmenistan, 28% other nationalities, of which 9,5% Russians; the Ukraine, 27,3% other nationalities of which 22% Russians; Estonia, 38,5% other nationalities, of which 30% Russians; Lithuania, 20,4% other nationalities, of which 9,4% Russians. These figures help to understand why the creation of independent and sovereign Republics cannot take place without taking into account and guaranteeing the legitimate interests of national minorities. A partition which would grant the largest section of the population full powers would only give rise to instability. It should be added that the nationality question in the ex-Soviet Union cannot be seen simply in terms of opposition between the Russians, on the one hand, as representing the master race, and other populations, more or less colonized. Indeed, now in the 1990s, just as in the days of the Empire, the words Russian and Russia do not only have an ethnic and geographical meaning, but also a wider one which brings them closer to Russian or Soviet Empire and citizens of such. The Russian language has two words closely related applying to Russian: russki, meaning a member of the Russian ethnic group, and russkoe, applied to members of the Russian body consisting of various nationalities and ethnic groupings with the same cultural and historical background. Since 1924, the notion sovestkoe narod was used (Soviet people) instead of Russkoe narod giving it an ideological connotation. This explains why the disappearance of the Soviet Union caused such deep feelings of hopelessness, even in the minds of those who wanted inedependence for their Republic. They were suddenly deprived of an important part of their identity. There is a greater sense of frustration about the breakup in Ukraine and Georgia than among the other nationalities. A Georgian or an Ukrainian who was proud of his nationality was equally happy to be a Soviet citizen or a Russian one before that.

The federal institutions dating back to the 1977 Constitution and revized in 1988, 1989 and 1990, were suspended **sine die** early in September 1991. On September 5, 1991, the Congress of Peoples' Deputies voted and thus sanctioned several important measures. First of all, a decree of the Congress drew the consequences of the joint declaration of the President of the USSR and leaders of the Federal Republics and of the decisions of the Presidium of the Supreme Soviet of the USSR. It approved the ten measures taken by the Presidents of the USSR and the Republics, including the most important ones: the CPSU was suspended; the Supreme Soviet abolished; a new Pact of Union was to be speedily drafted and signed; temporary bodies were set up to govern the country. The President stayed in his job, but a new Supreme Soviet and Council of State were elected, inaugurating a transition period. The declarations of independence made by various Republics were ratified, on condition that negotiations with the USSR were started and the treaties banning nuclear arms proliferation were ratified as well as the final Helsinki agreement and treaties guaranteeing Human Rights and individual freedom be drafted. This decree was of purely political value and of no significance for the future. However, the Constitutional Law on State institutions for the USSR in the transition period was the most meaningful document, due to its legal character as well as the contents. It was difficult to have it approved because of the opposition of a large number of deputies to the far-reaching changes that were taking place. This law suspended most of the arrangements of the 1977 Constitution for an unlimited period, together with its amendments of 1988, 1989 and 1990 and became in fact a new Constitution. The supreme representative body was the Supreme Soviet made up of the Soviet of the Republics counting 20 deputies for each Republic and another deputy for each autonomous republics whose members were elected in proportion to their population. It inherited the powers of the old Supreme Soviet, with a few minor differences. The Council of State, under the chairmanship of the President of the USSR, consisted of the Presidents of the Federal Republics and exercized some executive power through a small number of Federal Ministries still in existence. The new Supreme Soviet was to meet on October 2, 1991, at the latest. In the end it met only on October 20, 1991 and no more than seven Republics sent representatives (Russia, Byelorussia, and the Central Asian Republics). This Constitution in reality was never applied, since the President of the USSR resigned and above all because each Republic had become fully independent and did not wish to belong to such a Federation. The third document was the Declaration of Human Rights and Liberties, which was adopted by 1.724 votes to 4, with 13 abstentions and 41 deputies not participating. This declaration included some of the propositions of the 1977 Constitution, but any mention of Marxism or Socialism was cut out and new rights were added (wider scope for freedom of conscience, right to life, right to equal justice for all, freedom of movement, right to speak one's mother tongue, protection for minorities, right to strike under the same conditions as in liberal societies, right of entering the Civil Service for all, wider scope for the right to own property, right to protect the environment). Mention was made that the protection of Human Rights takes precedence over the right of peoples to self-determination, which means that the USSR claims to be entitled not to recognize the independence of a Republic which would establish a regime not guaranteeing these freedoms. These dispositions remained a dead letter since there was no State to apply them. Once again it is remarkable that in the Soviet Union the most significant changes occur in real life before being turned into Law and that the rules of Law are almost never applied. Let us hope that this will be the last occurrence of the Soviet concept of a pseudo Law that has nothing in common with the rules of law known in liberal societies. There was nothing left of formal institutions in the USSR, everything was in ruins.

Late in October 1991, there were only two Republics still belonging to the Union (Russia and Kazakhstan), ten Republics had entered into the transitionial arrangements, twelve had approved the Economic Union Treaty on October 18, 1991, and seven wanted a seat on the Supreme Soviet. Where was the rigorous "order" of the former Soviet Union? In this institutional confusion, Russia spared no efforts in trying to set up an organization, however limited, to re-establish a measure of harmony between the affiliated Republics, to ensure internal peace and reassure the West. These efforts resulted in several treaties.

The so called Minsk Conference, a gathering of Presidents of the Slavic Republics at Brest, issued the following statement: "We, Republics of Byelorussia, of the Russian and Ukrainian Federation, as States founding members of the USSR and signatories of the 1922 Pact of Union, thereafter called the highest contractual parties, recognize that the USSR as a subject in international law and geopolitical reality has ceased to exist." A final agreement reached at this conference consisted of political and technical dispositions. Each State acknowledged the independence of the others. It undertook to cooperate by means of specific treaties in the field of politics, economics, culture, education, health, science, commerce, environment and any other area to be agreed on. Each State recognized the inviolability of the other signatories' borders and freedom of movement for all nationals. They also stated their intention to cooperate in safeguarding peace and disarmament and to 'liquidate' strategic weapons in order to denuclearize their countries. They decided on joint foreign policies, economic development, establishing an economic community, a common policy as regards immigration, transport and communications. They also agreed on the fight against organized crime, and protection of the environment. They undertook to honour the treaties signed by the former USSR. They declared that the Community will be open to other states which would be willing to accept the same principles and obligations. They decided on common action to prevent accidents of the Chernobyl kind. The Community was to have Minsk as its administrative centre.

To the main document was added a declaration of Heads of State, explaining the need for creating a new organization because of the disappearance of the Soviet Union and laying down the aims of the Community. There followed a more technical declaration of heads of Government.

Thus, all the other republics had been faced with a fait accompli following the Minsk agreement. Despite legitimate objections to start with, they had no other option than to join the CIS. This was done at Alma Ata where an agreement of December 21, 1991, was signed by all the republics of the former Union, except for the Baltic States and Georgia. Several propositionss were approved.

The Alma Ata declaration acknowledged the disappearance of the USSR and on the whole endorsed the explanations given at Minsk as well as stating the signatories' intention to subscribe to the standing commitments of the USSR.

The protocol of the Heads of States' Conference announced the reorganizing of armed forces under the command of Air Marshal Shaposhnikov.

The Council of Heads of State of the Community decided to give the seat of the UN Security Council to Russia. The three members of UNO (Byelorussia, Russia and Ukraine) undertook to do their best to help the other states with admission to UNO and other international organizations.

Then the Community had its institutions well defined. Four main bodies were created, with the Council of Heads of State the most important. Evidently it consisted of the heads of all the Republics which signed the Treaty. Two annual ordinary sessions were to be held and extraordinary ones could be convened, whenever necessary. This body is supposed to make the most important decisions. The Council of Heads of Government meets at the same time as Heads of State. It is subordinate to the latter Council and seems to be charged with the application of the broad directives issued by the Heads of State. Six ministerial committees were set up in Defense, Economy, Finance, Transports and Communications, Social Security and Home Affairs. They had to coordinate national policies in these fields. Each Committee met at least four times a year. Lastly, a Committee of Overall Supervision was created, the only permanent body in the new structures, consisting of one representative per member state. It had its seat at Minsk and had to ensure continuity, check that decisions made by the political bodies were carried out, study any difficulty that might arise and find solutions to them. Lastly, it was supposed to keep the Heads of States and Governments informed about problems as well as pass on to them proposals.

The CIS obviously has nothing in common with the old Soviet Union. It is not a Federation nor a Confederation by any means, since these usually have a Diet on which representatives of national parliaments sit, enpowered to pass laws which can be applied to the whole Confederation. It is also clear that the CIS is not a subject in International Law, as each State retains full responsibility in defense and foreign relations. It seems to be a inter-State consultative body in pre-determined areas. Until we have evidence to the contrary, the rule for adoption of motions appears to be unanimous agreement. No threshold of majority was laid down and no mention was made of individual republics being under any obligation to carry out the decisions taken by CIS bodies.

The momentous political and institutional changes that occurred in the former Soviet Union, have not always been followed by a new draft of the Republics' Constitutions after independence. In the old system constitutional arrangements for the federal or federated republic were a reproduction of that of the Union, with minor modifications. This is not surprising, the Constitution reflecting the level of development in the building of Communism that had been reached by a Republic. All the sections of Soviet society were in theory at the same stage. Up till now no new Constitution has been drafted and the independent republics remain under the old constitutional arrangements, subject only to a few amendments. However, this applies only for the duration of drafting which is undertaken in most of the republics. A majority of those tend to adopt a regime of the presidential kind.

It is interesting to look at the constitutional situation of the Federated Republic of Russia in view of its importance within the CIS and because the solutions chosen there will probably serve as a model for the others.

The Constitution, as it is at the moment, dates back to April 12, 1978, with amendments adopted in 1989, 1990 and 1991. The document promulgated under

Brezhnev, is Marxist-Leninist in nature, to fit a "State for all the Peoples". It claims to apply to one of the last stages before reaching the historical goal of full Communism. The modifications brought about in 1990 and 1991 partially reorganized the distribution of power in favor of the president. The main levers of power were then the Congress of People's Deputies of the Russian Federation; the Supreme Soviet of the Russian Federation under a presidium; the President of the Supreme Soviet; the President of the Russian Federation; the Council of Ministers; the Constitutional Court and other legal organizations in that order.

The Congress of People's Deputies of the Russian Federation which was elected in its present form in 1990, with a five year mandate, by a uninominal poll with a second ballot, is made up of 1.068 deputies representing the population and 900 deputies representing the various national and administrative units: 4 to each autonomous republic, 2 to each autonomous region, 1 per autonomous district and 84 for the six territories, 49 regions and the cities of Moscow and Saint Petersburg). In keeping with Soviet constitutional tradition, this body retains the people's sovereignty and enjoys the powers of a Constituant and Legislative Assembly. It defines the main economic, political and social objectives for the civil society, elects the other Federal political bodies such as the Supreme Soviet, the President of the Supreme Soviet as well as Vice-Presidents and the Constitutional Court.

The Supreme Soviet of the Russian Federation is a bi-cameral Parliament consisting of the Republic's Soviet, representing the population and the Nationalities' Soviet counting 129 deputies, representing national units (3 deputies per autonomous republic, 1 per autonomous region or district and 66 for other territories). This Parliament enjoys legislative power. The main difference with the Supreme Soviet of old is the number of deputies, smaller and more in line with traditional parliamentary assemblies. Until recently it was a kind of talking forum for several thousand representatives which made it impossible to get any work done. The number of weeks of each sitting has been modified (on average eight months a year, instead of two weeks previously).

The presidium of the Supreme Soviet is the executive office of Parliament. It comprises a President, a first Vice-President, Presidents for each chambre, and chairmen of commissions and of permanent committees of the Supreme Soviet. Like the administrative office of parliamentary assemblies, it takes care of organizing the assemblies' agenda and representing them in public life. The President of the Supreme Soviet nowadays no longer exercizes the functions of a head of State as he did in the 1936 Constitution.

The Presidency of the Russian Federation was instituted by a referendum held on March, 17, 1991. It comes under direct universal suffrage, in a uninominal poll with a second ballot. The President is assisted by a Vice-President elected likewise. President Yeltsin insisted on creating such a post, whose incumbent was also legitimized by direct universal suffrage. Thus, he could counteract the authority of the then President of the Union and oppose the conservative attitudes prevalent in the Supreme Soviet dominated by the old Communist apparat. On June 2, 1991, Boris Yeltsin was elected President of the Federation polling 57,3% of the votes; Colonel A.Rutskoy was elected as Vice-President. While the Constitution does not contain any clause to that effect, President Yeltsin added to his functions that of Prime Minister and Defense Minister in April 1992. This is not without similarity to the situation of the Soviet leaders in the past who took over the most important jobs at State and Party level, to avoid competition and enjoy absolute power. Seeing that President Yeltsin was granted full powers in economic and administrative matters by a vote of the 5th Congress (renewed at the 6th Congress), he seems to exercize unlimited power.

The Council of Ministers comes under the authority of the President of the Republic. The ministers are politically responsible to the Supreme Soviet. They apply laws and direct the administration.

The Constitutional Court and other legal institutions in the country also figure in the Constitution. The creation of a constitutional juridiction is one of the elements for the establishment of a rule of law and a pre-condition for the democratization of state institutions. The Constitutional Court is elected by Congress. It comprises a President, a Vice-President and ten judges. It is empowered to pronounce on the legality of motions passed by constitutionally approved institutions. It has issued several decrees since its inauguration but seems hesitant about its competence.

The drafting of a new Constitution for the Russian Federation, which was set up by a constituent treaty endorsed by 14 of the 16 autonomous Republics (the Tatar Republic and the Chechen-Ingush Republic refused to sign) is proceeding. The treaty signed on 31 March 1992 confers on the Federation full constitutional powers, entitling it to decide on border changes - a matter of consequence - responsibility in foreign Affairs and defense, and minting currency. Individual republics and national units are in charge of the administration and economy and participate in the conduct of foreign affairs. The constitutional debate is difficult, because of disagreement between political movements on several major points. The character of the Federation itself is a matter for discussion. The old Soviet Socialist Republic of Russia (RSFSR) received the name of Russian Federation in the Minsk agreement; later the Congress called it Russia and finally Russo-Russian Federation. The debate goes deeper than linguistics, as the name Russia is pre-Revolutionary and has an imperialist, or even colonialist connotation and is rejected by the other republics, unless the adjective Russian is taken as covering the whole of the political entity (Rosskoe) rather than applying to nationality or ethnic group. In the end it will probably be the term Russian Federation which will be adopted. Some deputies insist on Soviet and Socialist to be revived, but this would be unpopular. The question of the nature of the regime is also hazy; some advocate a parliamentary system to retain the division of powers, while others led by President Yeltsin aim at a Presidential regime such as exists in the United States. This regime gives the President enough authority and stability to govern, while leaving Parliament legislative and budgetary powers. In these days of internal disunity and deep social differences, the presidential regime seems more appropriate than a parliamentary one. The character of the new Constitution is crucial in the debate; the fact that the Supreme Soviet is in charge of drafting bills is dangerous. With the old ideology still in force, the constitution could be turned into a framework for society as a whole, instead of limiting itself to the definitions of the divisions of political power. This danger was stressed by Alexeev, former Chairman of the Committee of Constitutional Control in the old system and by A.Sobchak, Mayor of St Petersburg and a lawyer, in a series of articles published by Izvestia on April 1 and 2, 1992. They favor a Constituent Assembly to prepare a Constitution which would ensure the separation of political powers, thus instituting a law-governed state (Rechtsstaat), as well as establishing proper federal institutions solving the question of nationalities, so far swept under the carpet.

In the meantime, a constitutional commission of the Supreme Soviet has issued the first draft of 143 articles including a long list of rights and liberties as well as general principles for the organization of society. The draft also upholds the Federal principles and proposes the creation of other organizations, such as the State Duma, to consist of 300 deputies representing the population and the Federal Council of three deputies per Republic and Land. The President of the Russian Federation is to be elected for four years, renewable for another term, to be flanked by a Council of State and a Security Council, a Council of Ministers under the President of the Federation's authority helping him to carry out his objectives as executive power, with a Constitutional Court and magistrates appointed by the assemblies for life. Early in August, President Yeltsin declared that he wished to give a wide scope to the referendum process, since it would allow the people to make their views known on the most important issues and also, no doubt, because it is an invaluable means for the Head of State to press his will on assemblies eager to increase their own power. The republics on the whole are in favor of a presidential regime similar to that of the United States, since it is the most powerful country in the world and has always served as a model. They also like the U.S. system because it maintains an equitable balance of power between the three branches of power and is compatible with efficiency. Nonetheless, it should be born in mind that the political system of the United States is not the result of a Constitution but rather that American society created and evolved it from a constitutional framework acquired two centuries earlier. In an effort to imitate U.S. constitutional institutions blindly, Russia may risk by-passing what is at the core of the American political system.

Thus, all the new constitutional drafts lack a clear expression of the democratic ideal to which the leaders of the new Republics are committed, at least in words. This is also the reason for keeping the old constitutions in place, while experimenting. There may be some modifications here, such as strengthening the authority of the Head of State, or there, electing the President of the Republic by universal suffrage (Azerbaijan, Georgia, Moldavia, Russia, Tadjikistan..), of the possibility of organizing a referendum, giving full powers for reforming the economy and putting new institutions in place (Yeltsin was voted full powers in these matters on November 1, 1991 and he added to his function of

President of the Federation that of Prime Minister on November 6, 1991), but no fundamental statement of democratic aims is forthcoming. It is also curious to see that the new assemblies are still controlled by communist majorities (deputies who were either converted to democracy or still believe in the old doctrine). Most curiously the Presidents of the new republics are more often than not the former republican 1st secretaries of the CPSU. This situation may be even more difficult if the publicly proclaimed changes to democracy are to be enforced by men trained by the Communist regime and used to the old system. How can they adopt the democratic ways and the principles of liberal democracy? It should also be stressed that it is no easy task, perhaps an impossible one, to find new men in a country where every leader even of middle rank standing, be it in politics, the economy, culture or with social responsibilities, was necessarily a party member and has always lived under its control.

   Thus, the main hurdles for the Republics of the CIS to surmount are not of institutional character, though this is also part of the problem. The tragedy gripping these countries is primarily to do with the fact that society is split into a myriad of individuals who no longer recognize any values to guide them in the search for private morality or social behavior. The blind pursuit of money acquired without effort seems to be the only aim left in life. Moreover the old levers of the economic system have collapsed and have not been replaced yet by those of a market economy. These simply cannot materialize by a dictate from on high, but will take a long time to emerge as a result of hard work, dedication and patience. Finally the break up of the Soviet Union which had succeeded the old Russian Empire, gratifies demands for independence, some of which are justified, but it also serves as a spring board for the gratification of selfish ambitions and factional interests. It can also become the cause of conflicts between various territorial and national units. One dreads to think of a political situation similar to the Yugoslav one, but the possibility is there. If the worst is to be avoided, cooperation between the Republics must be increased, political institutions capable of dealing with problems in the widest possible context have to be devized, while real autonomy must be granted to the republics, members of the Community. It is clear that the path to democracy is straight and narrow, but the hope of building it still attracts the majority of Soviet citizens. Democracy, however, will not be the instant remedy of all past evils it was once thought to be. On the other hand, it is essential that the Russian people do not give way to political despair, but discard the possibility of an easy way out of the present troubled situation, particularly if the easy way is offered by a political leader or an ideology.

***

Selected Bibliogrpahy

Carrere d'Encausse Helene, L'Empire eclate (Paris 1978); Le malheur russe (1988); La gloire des Nations (1990)

Hajek F., La route de la servitude (Paris 1990)

Pasukanis, La theorie general du droit et le marxisme (Moscow 1924)

Vyshinsky A. Ya., Voprosy gosudarstva i prava (Moscow 1948)

Tumanov V., L'Etat sovietique et le droit (Moscow 1971)

Lavroff D.G., Les libertes publiques en Union sovietique (Paris 1963)

Lesage M., La crise du federalisme sovietique (Paris 1990)

Lesage M., F. Barry, L'URSS la dislocation du pouvoir (Paris 1991)

Perestroika and Central Asia

Catherine Slater

Historically Central Asia designates a much larger area than it currently encompasses. Today the term covers the Soviet Union's former republics: Kazakhstan, Uzbekistan, Turkmenistan, Tadjikistan, and Kyrgyzstan. The area has been subject to invasions throughout its history from Scythians, the Macedonians, Turks, Uighurs, Oyrats, Khitans, Mongols and others. It is a melting pot of nationalities having been a land of opportunity for Russians and a dumping ground for fractious minorities. The defining characteristic of the region is a common religion: Islam, which spread to the region within a few decades of Muhammad's *hijirah* in AD 622. Another notable feature is its rapidly growing population. Central Asia was one of the last great tracts of land to be incorporated into the Russian empire in the 19th century. The Russian czars encountered little opposition from the mainly nomadic peoples and even less from their rulers, who in a sense retained their limited independence. Under the Soviets Central Asia was made up of Kazakhstan, Uzbekistan, Turkmenistan, Tadjikistan, and Kirghizia-Kyrgyzstan. It was ruled from Moscow directly by the communist party. At first through the intermediary of local communists, but since Stalin found them unreliable and purged (killed) them, Russian viceroys were in charge. Brezhnev was for some time linked with Kazakhstan and many secondary figures made their party careers in these Asian 'provinces'. After 1985 Gorbachev continued to treat these provinces the same way as before. His replacement of Kunaev in Kazakhstan by a Russian caused nationalistic rioting. All of these provinces were largely unaffected by the perestroika reforms going on in Russia and the other Soviet republics. They were rather more affected by the centre's drive against corruption which uncovered local communist mafias.

Kazakhstan

Kazakhstan has a population of over 16 million. It is situated at the centre of the Eurasian landmass.It covers 2,717, 300 sq km and lies mainly to the east of the Ural

River. It stretches from the Caspian Sea to the Tien Shan Mountains. It is the second largest state to emerge from the break-up of the former Soviet Union. It has a wealth of natural resources, including oil, lead, copper, coal, iron ores, zinc, bauxite, and many other minerals. It also produces sheep, grain, vegetables and other agricultural produce. It is a land of many nationalities, having been colonized by Slavic peoples for several centuries. The native Kazakhs represent about 40 percent of the population. The Russians make up about 38 percent and Ukrainians 5.5 percent. Muslim settlers arrived in the late 19th century. Uighurs and Dungans from China settled the southern parts of Kazakhstan. During World War II many nationalities were deported to Kazakhstan, including the Volga Germans, Crimean Tatars, and Meskhetians. There are also Uzbeks and Kyrgyz living in the south.

The Kazakhs are descended from the Turkic and Mongol peoples who settled in the area at the end of the first century BC. In the sixth century these nomadic peoples formed part of the Turkish empire - a loose grouping of nomads. During the eighth century they came under pressure from Mongolians from the east. In the tenth century the Mongolian Khitans were the dominant tribe in the area. They were followed by the Karakitai, who were themselves ousted by a group of formidable Mongols led by Genghis Khan. These Mongols, known as the Golden Horde, swept aside all opposition as they drove westward and in 1240 the Russian city of Kiev fell to them. Meanwhile an offshoot of the main Mongol army, known as the White Horde and led by Orda, Genghis Khan's grandson, dominated the area of Kazakhstan.

These Mongol armies, however, were beset by internal problems as rivals challenged the leaders, and other nomadic peoples developed their own fighting skills. By the end of the fourteenth century the Mongol empire was falling apart. Two new powers emerged the Nogais (another offshoot of the Mongols) and the Uzbeks. The term Kazakh began to be used around 1520, when the people of Kazakhstan were known as the Uzbek Kazakhs. At the time two leaders from the White Horde moved to neighboring Mongolistan and began to build up a Kazakh dominion, or "khanate." By the early sixteenth century Kazakhs were united under Kassim Khan, who ruled 1511-18, and had 200,000 horsemen. Under Kassim Khan, the Kazakhs controlled the steppes. His three sons succeeded him, but by the seventeenth century the khan's power weakened. The Kazakhs split into three hordes. The Greater, Middle, and Lesser Hordes spread between the Tien Shan Mountains and the Ural River.

During the seventeenth century the Kazakh hordes faced attacks from the powerful Oyrats in the east. They temporarily united under Tauke Khan (1680-1718) and in the 1720s succeeded in defeating the Oyrats. This success was short-lived, however, the alliance soon fell apart as new power struggles flared up. Meanwhile the Russians were beginning to advance through the Kazakh steppe. The Romanov dynasty was pursuing an expansionist policy. In 1718 the Russians established a fort at Semipalatinsk, and a year later at Ust-Kamenogorsk. The Kazakhs thought the Russians might protect them against eastern invaders, and accepted the czar's offer of protection.

At first the Russians left the Kazakhs to rule themselves but in the 1820s, the czar abolished the power of the khans. This resulted in a Kazakh uprising but by the mid-nineteenth century Russia was firmly in control. The Kazakh lands were divided into four provinces, and Russian and Ukrainian peasants were encouraged to settle there and farm the steppes. The Russian rulers allowed the Tatars to move in and convert the Kazakhs to Islam. Although the Kazakh khans had followed Islam, their people had continued to follow older religions. The czars may have thought Islam would make the Kazakhs easier to rule.

Kazakh nobles received Russian education and became influenced by nationalist ideas. Kazakh culture became more developed and resentment grew against Slavic settlers and Russian rule. In 1916 Nicholas II tried to mobilize the Kazakhs to take on non-combat duties and defend the Russian empire in World War I but the Kazakhs objected violently. More than 50,000 took part in the uprising but many were massacred by the Russian army. In 1917 the czarist government in Kazakhstan collapsed, and the nationalists, known as Alash Orda backed the communists, who had seized power in Moscow and St Petersburg. There followed several years of bitter fighting but by 1920 the Kazakhs were part of an autonomous republic within the newly created Soviet Union.

Some 1.5 million people were thought to have died during the fighting in Kazakhstan. Just over a decade later, a further million are thought to have died as a result of the forced collectivization of agriculture in the area. In 1897 there has been 3,800,000 Kazakhs by 1934 the number had fallen to 2,900,000. During World War II the Soviet leader, Joseph Stalin, deported troublesome nationalities to Kazakhstan and other parts of Central Asia, including the Soviet Germans, the Crimean Tatars, the Meskhetians, Balkars, Chechen, Ingush, Karachais, Ossetians, Kurds, and Koreans.

Under Leonid Brezhnev's leadership of the Soviet Communist Party, Dinmukhamed Kunaev was the First Secretary of Kazakhstan. He dominated political life in Kazakhstan for well over 30 years and represented the republic on the Politburo. He used this powerful position to secure Soviet resources for his republic. Northern Kazakhstan became an industrial centre and its cities were developed. Alma Ata saw a great expansion with monumental government buildings rising up, some even decorated with gold leaf. It was a time of seemingly great prosperity and many people enjoyed a higher standard of living but in real terms the republic was slipping behind the Caucasian republics in terms of economic development.

Kunaev ran the republic as a family enterprise. He and his family had enormous privileges and wealth. His brother, Asqar Kunaev, was President of the Academy of Sciences. Other family members held jobs in the provinces for which they were overpaid. The Minister of Higher and Secondary Education was fired for taking bribes. The group around Kunaev controlled 247 hotels, 414 guest flats, 84 cottages, 22 hunting lodges, 350 hospital beds, and other facilities, such as private aircraft.

After Brezhnev's death in 1982, his replacement as General Secretary, Yuri Andropov, the former head of the KGB, launched an anti-corruption drive. Teams of anti-corruption agents toured the republics purging the Communist Party of corrupt elements. In 1984 they were busy in neighboring Uzbekistan. Kunaev knew they would soon turn to Kazakhstan so he publicly helped to uncover a corrupt Russian minister in Kazakhstan. In 1985 the Soviet Communist Party politbyro elected Mikhail Gorbachev as its new General Secretary. He immediately started talking about reforming the Soviet system and tried to speed up the anti-corruption drive. In December 1986, it was announced that Kunaev was being replaced as First Secretary by a Russian, Gennadii Kolbin. There was an immediate response - young Kazakh people in Alma Ata protested over the appointment of a Russian. Official accounts stated there were 3,000 demonstrators and in the ensuing riots two people were thought to have died and 200 were injured. This was the first political mass demonstration in Soviet history since 1927. Essentially it was an anti-Russian demonstration by Kazakh students anxious that their people retain their leading position in the republic. By 1986 the birth rate had made the numbers of Kazakh and Russians roughly equal - especially since Slavic peoples were leaving Kazakhstan for improved economic opportunities in the Baltic states.

However, soon after Gorbachev's *glasnost* policy was launched Kunaev's corruption was exposed. Kunaev's dismissal was followed by that of many of his retinue, including his brother. Thousands were fired for corruption and public officials were forced to take tests to prove they could do their jobs. Many of the exclusive shops run for the Kazakh elite were shut. The newspapers began to report political and social problems more openly. Magazines also reported on the drug problem and youth crime. Some also reported on environmental protests in the Semipalatinsk area, where there had been nuclear-weapons testing.

Kolbin remained in charge and tried to placate the Kazakhs by creating committees on interethnic problems. In January 1987 he presented a plan to set up a body to make sure that all institutions maintained a fair ethnic representation. The Second Secretary was a Kazakh, Sagidulla Kubashev. A special commission discovered that there was much antipathy over language: Kazakhs felt their's was a second-class language as the administration would only deal with Russian requests and Russian rarely bothered to learn Kazakh. Eventually in September 1989 Kazakh was made the official language of the republic. In June 1989 Kolbin was replaced by Nursultan Nazarbayev, a reforming Kazakh who had previously criticized Kunaev.

In September 1989 reforms of the administrative system were introduced making the Kazakh Supreme Soviet a full-time legislature and cutting the number of deputies. These reforms implied that more than one candidate could be nominated for a seat. Meanwhile the reforms of the Soviet economy were leading to severe problems in Kazakhstan. There were food shortages and a severe housing shortage as the building programs could not keep pace with population increases.

The advent of *glasnost* had uncovered a sorry tale of environmental degradation. There were pollution problems as both industry and agriculture damaged the environment and created health problems. The massive irrigation projects in the south of Kazakhstan had deprived the Aral Sea of the waters of the Syr Darya and Amu Darya.It had shrunk by 13,000 sq km (5,000 sq miles). From 1960 to 1975 the level of the Caspian Sea had dropped by 2.5 meters (8 feet). Already in 1989 a Semipalatinsk Oblast Peace Committee had announced that there had been radiation leaks in the area as a result of nuclear weapons testing. In September 1990 an explosion at the Ulba nuclear-fuel processing plant at Ust-Kamenogorsk led to beryllium gas being released into the atmosphere. A week later 60,000 people demanded the closure of the plant and Nazarbayev pressed for compensation. Without *glasnost* no one would have known about these protests.

Already Nazarbayev was trying to detach his republic from its historic dependence on Moscow and Russian/Soviet demands. In April 1990 Kazakhstan stopped exporting goods to other republics and in June the five Central Asian republics (Kazakhstan, Uzbekistan, Kyrgyzstan, Tadjikistan, and Turkmenistan) signed an economic alliance. Nazarbayev's government has set in train various moves to control trade, economic activity and land. There is a privatization program in hand which would put land and industry in private hands - after nearly 70 years of state ownership.

In August 1991 the news broke that the Soviet army and anti-Gorbachev leaders had tried to seize power. In its aftermath the Soviet Union disintegrated and Nazarbayev led the drafting sessions to form a new, looser organization. Nazarbayev arrived in Moscow in early December to join the Russian, Ukrainian, and Belarussian leaders in forming a Commonwealth of Independent States (C.I.S.). He retained Kazakhstan's nuclear weapons, thus ensuring its leading role in Central Asia.

Following the coup the Kazakh Communist Party changed its name but it retained power. In late 1991 Nazarbayev's position as Kazakh leader was confirmed when he was elected president of the republic - the first democratically elected president in the history of the Kazakh people. On December 16, Kazakhstan declared its independence.

In a sense *perestroika* was a preparation for nationhood of Kazakhstan, as reliance on Moscow for direction and subsidies was gradually withdrawn. However the country cannot afford to alienate its non-Kazakh minorities, as they provide many skilled industrial workers. Kazakhstan has some economic and political assets but it needs economic partners to develop and privatize its industry. Despite the lack of political freedom - Nazarbayev has not allowed the Alash opposition group to register as a political party - Kazakhstan is relatively stable and despite the economic problems, it should prosper. By 1993 several Western oil companies invested in prospecting in the country, while the Baykonur space station is under Kazakh control.

Uzbekistan

With a population of just over 20,000,000, Uzbekistan has the third largest population of the states to emerge from the breakup of the Soviet Union. It extends from the foothills of the Tien Shan and Pamir mountains to land just west of the Aral Sea and includes the Kyzylkum desert. It is in the area near the Aral Sea that cotton is grown -

Uzbekistan was the largest cotton-growing area in the Soviet Union. Other important products include grapes, melons, and other fruit, milk, rice, vegetables, and wool. The country also produces coal, copper, gold, natural gas, and petroleum. It manufactures agricultural machinery, chemicals, food products, and textiles. Tashkent is the fourth largest city in the C.I.S. with a population of over 2,000,000. The city is modern as it was rebuilt after an earthquake in the 1960s. There are many different ethnic groups in Uzbekistan but the largest group, comprising 70 percent of the population are the Uzbeks. Russians make up less than 10 percent of the population. Other groups living in the country include Tatars, Kazakhs, Tadjiks, and Karakalpaks. Most people in Uzbekistan are Muslims and Islam is an important, unifying force in the country.

The Uzbeks are a people of Turkic origins, descended from the nomadic peoples who swept over Central Asia - the Mongols of the Golden Horde, Persians, and others. Since the days of the Persian Empire in the sixth century B.C., the lands of Uzbekistan were important as they lay on the Silk Road - one of the world's oldest roads linking China with Central Asia, the Middle East, and the Mediterranean Sea. It was a major trade route and some of world's oldest cities sprang up along its route, including Samarkand. Trade was mainly in silk from China, cotton from India, jade from Central Asia, and glass from the Mediterranean. The Silk Road was also a conduit for ideas and religion and in the eighth century the Muslim armies that conquered Transoxiana, as the region was known at the time, demanded that their subjects convert to Islam.

In 1040 the Seldjuk Turks swept through Transoxiana and conquered much of Central Asia. They controlled land from Turkey to Central Asia, which now became known as Turkestan. Then the lands were overrun by Genghis Khan and the Mongols, who easily overwhelmed Bukhara and Samarkand. After two centuries in power Mongol rule in the area declined and the last khan of any importance was Tamerlane, whose court was based at Samarkand. The region disintegrated into rival Muslim khanates, based at Khiva, Bukhara, and Kokand.

Russia was beginning to look at the area with interest, especially given British interests in India and Afghanistan. By 1864 the Russians decided they could no longer let the khanates be independent and sent an invasion force. Tashkent fell in 1865, Samarkand in 1868, and Khiva in 1876. However Russian rule proved to be fairly lax. The social and political changes were relatively minor; in fact the most significant event was the building of Trans-Caspian Railway, begun in 1880, which opened up the area to outside influences and ideas. The Central Asians came into contact with other Muslims within the empire, such as the Tatars of the Volga and Crimea, and the Azerbaijanis, both were known as *jadidists* as they were keen on reform. They wanted to modernize the educational system and opened their first school in Tashkent in 1901.

In late 1917 Soviet rule tentatively replaced the Czarist rule. It was not consolidated until April 1919 and there was much fighting in the area as a result of the civil war between the Reds and the Whites. Once the Soviets were firmly in control they set about changing Central Asia, by dividing the area along national lines. On October 27, 1924 the

Uzbek SSR was created composed of the districts of Amu Darya, Syr Darya, Samarkand and Fergana, part of the Bukharan state, and part of the Khivan state. It included Tadjik ASSR until 1929, which then became a union republic. In 1936 the Karakalpak ASSR was incorporated into the Uzbek republic.

The Soviet Union's leaders soon set about trying to bring the Muslim republic in line and an anti-religious campaign was launched at the end of the 1920s. Mosques were closed, Muslim schools and courts were gradually run down. The social and economic structures were transformed through the five year plans, which ran from 1928-38. Skilled labour and during World War II entire plants were brought in from Russia in order to achieve rapid economic development. Land was brought under state control as agriculture was collectivized. Nomads had to abandon centuries-old traditions and live and work within the state-run farms. Uzbek land was increasingly set aside to grow cotton for the rest of the Soviet Union. Nomad herders were reluctant to give up their livestock to the state and preferred to kill their animals. These disruptive policies led to famine in the early 1930s. During the 1930s Josef Stalin launched several purges in Moscow and in the outer regions, which resulted in party officials and others being sentenced to death or long incarceration.

The Uzbek economy began to take off during the war years, stimulated by the Soviet need to move industry eastward but by the 1950s this dynamism had petered out. By the 1960s increased cotton production produced some growth as ambitious irrigation projects drained the Syr and Amu Darya rivers. However compared to the rest of the Soviet Union Uzbekistan remained backward with low life expectancy, high infant mortality, and surprisingly the highest birth rate in the union. There were severe environmental problems. The Aral Sea had been shrinking over two decades so that its main port Aralsk was 60 miles from the shore. The dry beds of the Aral Sea had been eroded, dust storms had become a major hazard, allowing the salts - residues of fertilizers and pesticides - to damage fertile land.

As the new brooms swept through the Soviet system promising *perestroika* and *glasnost,* Uzbekistan had already faced the attentions of the anti-corruption drive launched by Andropov in 1984. Teams of investigators arrived and soon Uzbekistan became a byword for all that was bad about the Soviet system. It emerged that much of the annual cotton crop, announced by Uzbekistan at six million tonnes, existed only on paper. Satellite photography demonstrated the falsity of Uzbek leaders' claims. The Uzbek Communist Party attacked its leaders Charaf Rachidov and Prime Minister Khudaiberdiev. In 1988 some of the ringleaders were brought to trial and convicted and sentenced to long prison terms, but the Mafia-style gangs still thrive. The trials revealed that the whole system was corrupt - based as it was on the traditional deference to elders (*aqsaqaly* - or white beards). The education system allowed those with connections or with the means to pay bribes access to higher education. Jobs were allocated on similar lines. The weekly magazine *Ogoniok* also uncovered evidence of a criminal Mafia that controlled the economic system and, operating in a similar manner to the Sicilian Mafia, provided protection. So Uzbekistan became a prime casualty of *glasnost*, as its status went from being the Soviet Union's leading cotton producer to a backward nation riddled with the worst aspects of corrupt capitalism.

The other byproducts of *glasnost* was information about the environmental and economic problems facing Uzbekistan. This stretches from the Aral Sea catastrophe, to the degradation of the soil because of the monoculture of cotton, the pollution of soil and water supplies because of the overuse of fertilizers and pesticides, all of these leading to severe health problems. Children and women, who traditionally picked the cotton were in the front line of chemical exposure. The infant mortality rate is officially 118 per 1,000 live births, while the Soviet average is 25.4 per 1,000 live births.

Gorbachev's restructuring drive did lead to greater religious freedom in Uzbekistan. In 1989 popular pressure led to the fall of the officially appointed mufti and the installation of a more acceptable figure, Muhammad Sadyq Mahammed Yusuf Hoja-ogli. This was followed by the opening up of more mosques, the distribution of copies of the *Quran*, and the preparation of a new edition of the *Quran*. It became much easier to practise Islam and Muslim leaders have taken on new responsibilities, including criticizing the popular violence against the Meskhetians in Fergana in June 1989. After the death of over one hundred Meskhetians, some 16,000 were evacuated to the Russian republic.

The revelations about corruption within the Communist Party did not weaken its hold on power. There has been a tradition of political repression and police brutality. Despite this in November 1988 a group of Uzbek intellectuals founded the *Birlik* (Unity) popular movement. It attracted a large following campaigning on several issues, including legal recognition of the Uzbek language, but after a year it collapsed under both internal and external pressure. Since then a few small organizations have sprung up but the Communist Party retained its political supremacy.

The Uzbek Communist Party reformed as the People's Democratic Party and in December 1991 its leader, Islam Karimov, was elected president of the state. The political climate remains repressive with few parties having gained legal recognition. The *Erk* or Freedom Party has only got 20 representatives out of a possible 550 in the national assembly. In January 1992 there were clashes between the police and demonstrators over a massive increase in the price of bread, which led to the death of two students. The rise in xenophobia does not bode well for the future.

Economically there are brighter prospects. In May 1992 major oil deposits were discovered, on the day that Uzbekistan joined the United Nations. President Karimov has been actively seeking economic partners, such as Turkey and Saudi Arabia, and in August 1992 signed three agreements with Pakistan on investment and economic cooperation. However the lack of political freedom and democracy may create tension and conflict, particularly with the increasingly confident Muslim elements in the country, who are based in the Fergana Valley in the east of the country.

Kyrgyzstan

Kyrgyzstan is a mountainous country sharing borders with Kazakhstan to the north, Tadjikistan to the south, Uzbekistan to the west, and China to the east. It covers 198,500 sq km. In the 1990 census it had a population of 4,400,000, of which only about half were Kyrgyz, the most important peoples being the Russians (22 percent) and Uzbeks (12 percent). There are also Tadjiks, Volga Germans, Ukrainians, and Uighurs. Economically Kyrgyzstan relies on livestock farming and for centuries the nomadic Kyrgyz have tended sheep and goats in the Tien Shan mountains. More recently the country has developed its hydroelectric potential by harnessing the power of its mountain rivers. There are few other natural resources beyond the mountain scenery.

The Kyrgyz are descended from the nomadic peoples who settled in the area - a mixture of Mongols, Turks, and Kypchaks. By the 16th century they formed a distinct group of people under Mongol rule. Then they came under the rule of the Jungarian Oyrats, until they in turn were conquered by the Chinese Manchus. At this time the Kyrgyz were mainly under the rule of local lords but in the early 19th century they came under the rule of the Khan of Kokand. In 1876 the Russians defeated the Khan of Kokand and incorporated the territory into their empire. Russian rule was resisted and there were numerous risings in the border territories, culminating in the 1916 uprising which was unsuccessful. Thousands were killed on both sides and up to 150,000 Kyrgyz fled to China. After the revolution and civil war, Soviet power was established in Kirgizia in 1919-20. In 1924 Kyrgyzstan was made into a self-governing region - *autonomous oblast* - called Kara-Kyrgyz. In 1936 the region became a Soviet republic called the Kyrgyz Soviet Socialist Republic.

One of the first changes the Soviet rulers imposed on this very backward country was land reform. Confiscated lands were returned to the Kyrgyz but in the 1930s the collectivization policy forced the nomadic farmers to settle on state-run farms and totally changed rural life. During the 1930s the purges hit the Kyrgyz elites and much of the local party leadership. After World War II there was a big push to develop industry such as engineering, metal-working, building, mining, the production of electricity and food. Although this led to a shift in population from the country to the cities the urban population stabilized at around 40 percent of the total in 1979.

During the Brezhnev era, the stagnation followed the same pattern in Kyrgyzstan it had elsewhere in Central Asia. Corruption in all the echelons of the party so the first signs of *glasnost* were the start of a campaign of criticism from the First Secretary of the Kyrgyz Communist Party, Turkadun Usubaliev. In June 1985 Usubaliev announced that 174 officials had been sacked, before retiring a few months later. In 1986 Usubaliev was in turn accused of all the usual crimes: nepotism and advancing his cronies. Many of his associates were purged.

Accompanying these political upheavals, there was a loosening up of the restraints on Kyrgyz culture. Some important Kyrgyz writers, Moldo Kylych and Kasmyn Tynystanov, were rehabilitated. Kyrgyz history came up for reevaluation and there was discussion of the need to improve Kyrgyz language teaching. Again as in other Central Asian republics the shackles on Islamic practice were removed and visits to Takht-Sleiman near Osh became a popular religious pilgrimage. This led to an upsurge in nationalism and there were the customary clashes between ethnic groups, this time between Kyrgyz and Uzbeks.

These were all small steps on the road to achieving sovereignty, which accelerated when the Soviet Union broke up in 1991. A reform-minded non-Communist, Askar Akayev, had already been elected president. His aim has been to create prosperity by opening up the economy to "the four corners of the World" and thus create a powerful, well-off middle class, who can guarantee Kyrgyzstan's stability. But Kyrgyzstan's economic problems are formidable: it used to rely on subsidies of cheap food and manufactured goods from the Soviet Union now it has to operate on the world market. In February 1992 fuel was in such short supply that only one flight a day was possible from Bishkek airport to Moscow. The country needs to modernize and develop its economy and build up economic links with neighboring countries. It faces a difficult task.

Turkmenistan

The 488,100 sq km of Turkmenistan is mainly desert and lies to the east of the Caspian Sea. It shares borders with Afghanistan and Iran to the south and Uzbekistan and Kazakhstan to the north. The Karakum desert lies within its borders and is the largest one within the C.I.S. Beneath the desert lies vast reserves of natural gas and oil and Turkmenistan is able to supply neighboring Uzbekistan, Iran, and other members of the C.I.S. with natural gas. Turkmenistan has a population of 3,630,000, of whom about 70 percent are Turkmen. The rest are Russians, Uzbeks, Kazakhs, Azerbaijanis, Baluchis, Tatars, Ukrainians, Armenians, and others. Like other Central Asian states it contains a large Muslim community.

As with all the Central Asian countries, the earliest inhabitants of the area were nomads. In the sixth century A.D., Turkic peoples settled the area and the term Turkmen dates from this period. Mongols, Turks, and Uzbeks controlled the area before the Russians completed their conquest of Central Asia by bringing the Turkmen lands into their empire in 1885. In 1917 following the revolution, there was some resistance to communist forces from the local tribes. By 1921 this had been overcome and the autonomous Turkmen region was formed and it became the Turkmen Soviet Socialist Republic in 1924. When the collectivization policy was enforced in the 1930s, there was armed resistance from nomadic herders. In 1928 the Soviet authorities launched an anti-Islamic campaign and closed down most of the country's mosques, Islamic law courts, and Islamic schools. This anti-Islam policy went with a general suppression of Turkmen culture. Again the purges had a profound effect on the educated Turkmen people as well as native political leaders.

Turkmenistan remained one of the most backward regions of the Soviet Union. Literacy rates were improved but industrial production grew very slowly. There was some industry centered on the extraction of oil and gas but most of Kyrgyzstan's output was agricultural. As in Uzbekistan there were ambitious irrigation projects geared toward cotton production. Cotton became the leading produce of the country. The Soviet authorities did provide subsidies which got roads, schools, housing, hospitals, and transportation systems built but the Turkmen people had one of the lowest standards of living in the Soviet Union.

As in the other Central Asian states, the effects of *glasnost* were to disclose evidence of environmental problems, in this case the damming of the strait between the Kara-Bogaz Gulf and the Caspian Sea and the drying up of the Aral Sea as a result of the Karakum Canal irrigation project. Complaints about Soviet rule proliferated, especially about the low level of investment in industry and infrastructure. Even under the Soviet system there was unemployment and housing shortages. There has also been a resurgence in pride in Turkmen culture and history. There were concessions to Turkmen Muslims and a new, large mosque was opened in the capital city, Ashkhabad. Again there were plans to distribute copies of the *Quran* in the Turkmen language. The Muslim feast of Kurban Bairam was restored on July 13, 1989. However communist officials were not keen to embark on reform programs because of the country's lack of resources, as well as their innate conservatism.

The long-term impact of *glasnost* and *perestroika* were inconsiderable. After Turkmenistan became an independent country in the wake of the breakup of the Soviet Union, President Sapamurad Ataevich Niyazov retained power as leader of the former Communist Party, now called the Democratic Party. There is very little political freedom and no opposition parties have been legally recognized. In 1990 the Islamic Renaissance Party was unofficially established and it enjoys much support from the Turkmen peoples. There have also been no plans of political or economic reforms. Turkmenistan's mineral reserves have attracted outside interest, especially from oil companies wanting to prospect for oil. Because of its proximity to Iran, communications with Teheran have been improved and a new road is being built to link the two capitals. There have also been overtures from Turkey, keen to establish good relations with the Turkic-speaking nations of Central Asia but Turkmenistan has a long way to go before it will achieve self-sufficiency in food production and anything approaching economic prosperity.

Tadjikistan

Curiously the Tajiks speak Farsi, which belongs to the Iranian family. This differentiates them considerably from the other Central Asian native peoples, whose language is of Turkic origins. Tadjikistan shares borders with China, Kyrgyzstan, Afghanistan, and Uzbekistan. It has a population of 5,250,000, of whom 62 percent are Tadjiks. Russians make up about 9 percent, the rest are Tatars, Kyrgyz, Kazakhs, and

Turkmen. Tadjiks have traditionally led a nomadic life, and there are substantial numbers of Tadjiks living in Uzbekistan and Afghanistan. Like Kyrgyzstan, the country is very mountainous, consisting of the Pamir and Zeravshan Mountains, and covers 143,000 sq km. The western part of Tajikistan slopes down to the plains of Central Asia, where there is farming and cotton is grown. There are few natural resources apart from hydroelectricity, and some mining of lead and bauxite.

Iranian peoples settled in what is now Tadjikistan at least a thousand years before the Turkish peoples arrived. They ruled the area until Alexander the Great gained control of the Persian empire in 331 B.C. After Alexander's death, part of Tadjikistan was absorbed by the Seleucids. Another part became part of Bactria. In the first century A.D. these tribes were overthrown by the Kushans, nomadic peoples from China, who dominated the area for three centuries. In the sixth century Turkish peoples from Eastern Persia and Central Asia gained the ascendancy. The name Tadjiks was used by other peoples to describe the Arabs at this time. Until the sixteenth century the area was subject to successive invasions from Turkish peoples and Mongols. Then the Uzbeks gained the upper hand until in the early nineteenth century modern-day Tadjikistan was divided between the two khanates of Bukhara and Kokand. Both fell prey to Russian dominance in the latter part of the nineteenth century: some lands were handed over to the Russian empire, other were nominally under Russian protection. As in other parts of Central Asia, Russian peasants were encouraged to move in and develop farming

In the wake of the Russian revolution, soviets were set up in the major towns and after some fighting the Bolsheviks controlled northern and eastern Tadjikistan by the end of 1918. The remaining territories were not incorporated into Turkestan ASSR until 1921, when the Emir of Bukhara's army was finally defeated. In spite of this anti-Bolsheviks continued to fight until 1926. In 1925 Tadjikistan formally became an autonomous republic within the Uzbek SSR. In 1929 it acquired further territory and became of Tadjik SSR. This very backward region was in great need of modernization and development and the Soviets built roads, railroads, schools, and houses. They also collectivized agriculture and increased the cultivation of cotton. Again collectivization met with considerable resistance. There was also a campaign to extend literacy and against the traditional Islamic beliefs.

The advent of the Gorbachev's reform plans had only a limited impact on this remote and backward region. As in the other Central Asian republics, nationalist sentiment strengthened and the dominance of the Russian language came under attack. By 1989 there were mass demonstrations in favor of making Tadjik the state language, which eventually happened in July of that year. This nationalist upswing was accompanied by violence toward Russians and Ukrainians and friction with Uzbekistan over its sizeable Tadjik minority. Economically, the situation worsened with unemployment rising as more people came into the labour force.

Politically, the Communist Party retained power under the leadership of President Rehman Nabiyev, who had dominated political life in the republic for 20 years. But in

May 1992 opposition forces, the Islamic Renaissance Party and the Democratic Party, succeeded in forcing him to resign and the country has experienced civil war since then. Nabiyev (who died in 1993) had repressed opposition with force and once the restraints were off, it became impossible to restore order. Nabiyev was replaced by a Revolutionary Coalition Council but fighting intensified between the two opposition parties. In November Imoli Rakhmanov, a former Communist *apparatchik*, became acting president. The fighting is fueled by the support the Islamic Renaissance Party gets from Tadjik members of the Afghan *mujahedeen*, who fought communist forces in Afghanistan for over ten years. The outlook for the country is very bleak as it cannot come to grips with the economic problems as long as the civil war persists.

Conclusion

In Central Asia Gorbachev's perestroika coupled with glasnost and democratization has had the inevitable liberation impact on the largely Moslim and underdeveloped populations of this vast area. On the one hand it disclosed the corruption and general futility of Soviet communist rule. On the other hand the republics discovered that without some sort of association with the former Soviet Union modernization, development and prosperity were impossible. Nazarbayev's statesmanship has brought Kazakhstan not only political prestige, but also Western aid and modernization with it. Karimov's astuteness has also served Uzbekistan well, though such international agencies as IMF or EBRD are more reluctant to encourage investment in the country than in Kazakhstan. In the other three independent republics political instability requires Russian military presence and largely vitiates against the benefits flowing from national independence. Without perestroika there would not have been anything like it and stagnation would still be the most oustanding feature of this part of the world.

Bibliography

Akiner, S. *Islamic Peoples of the Soviet Union* (London, Kegan Paul International, 1983).

Allworth, E. (ed.) *The Nationality Question in Soviet Central Asia* (New York, Praeger 1973)

Bennigsen, A. and Wimbush, A. S. *Muslims of the Soviet Empire: a Guide* (London, C. Hurst & Co. 1986).

Carrere d'Encausse, H. *La Gloire des Nations ou la fin de l'Empire sovietique* (Paris, Fayard 1991)

Carrere d'Encausse, H. *L'Empire eclate* (Paris, Flammarion 1978)

Smith, G (ed.) *The Nationalities Question in the Soviet Union* (London, Longman 1990).

Perestroika and Russia's Democratization

Vladimir B. Pastukhov

Democratization has been the most dynamic element of perestroika and has dominated social life in Russia for the past few years. After the attempted coup in August 1991 this unique phenomenon has finally attracted the notice of political and social scientists . As a concept democratization is somewhat puzzling for several reasons : the sudden victory the reformists achieved in the struggle for power gave them the possibility to become the strongest political ruling force; yet inner contradictions revealed themselves very early after the drive was launched and prevented them from becoming a cohesive body politic.

The role of democratization in Russian society has long been underestimated, since it was not well known and has not been studied. Not until the CP political archives were made accessible to political science researchers, did democratization properly emerge from the limbo to be properly assessed. Then it suddenly appeared as the instrument for the solution of all Russia's problems. It was identified with civil society and compared with democratic movements in the West. Soon what had been at first a mere hypothetical concept became an axiom of further progress of perestroika. However, when an internal crisis among perestroika reformists broke open, many saw in it the end of democratization. Yet it is arguable that other options and interpretations are possible. Invariably the question whether the reformists' movement was really democratic has to be asked. Did it really form the backbone of civil society as it claimed? Answers to such pertinent questions will help with the defition of democratization as well as with the establishment of its limits. However, only concrete situations will be assessed, no generalization attempted.

Paradoxically, Russia's democratization is the product of the totalitarian system's gradual disintegration, not an objective for political parties or movements. In Russia totalitarian rule was self-sufficient; while the authoritarian state thrives on the weakness of and underdevelopment of society, it does not exterminate it. However, the Soviet totalitarian state absorbed society completely. It acted so for purely ideological reasons, leaving no room for individuals or their personality, using mass consciousness as an 'appendage' of the state and leaving in society nothing capable of developing into democracy.

The Soviet totalitarian system made social life identical with that of the state, which was the reason why any impulse for change towards democracy could only proceed from the top. At the same time all the totalitarian states weres impervious to any outside influence. Therefore, communist societies seemed incapable of evolution. Yet one aspect of societal development in the totalitarian set up had been overlooked, by researchers and critics alike. The totalitarian state decays from inside, because of accumulated tensions. Since society is absorbed, any social conflict acquires a state dimension. Thus, social tensions do not manifest themselves as new, possibly opposition, movements appearing before or after disorders. They thrive only in what was termed as 'the decay of state discipline'. Social unrest has always assumed the form of state machinery dysfunctioning, and not of a public social or political formation. Or as Churchill likened such struggles aptly to "the fight of bulldogs under the carpet".

As the state decay has advanced to a certain point a striking phenomenon appeared out of nowhere. This new factor was usually called "double thinking". People's lives were invariably split into official and non-official ones. In his official life every citizen remained a unthinking executor of the general will, an ideologically programmed machine. In his private - non-official -life he kept his own counsel about right and wrong, about truth and about realities of the surrounding world. In time something akin to schizophrenia developed in people's minds, as they went on thinking and speaking one way in public and another way at home, with their family or friends. "Private" lives diverged from official state life slowly but steadily.

Thus, double morality, double standards of behavior, gradually developed in all the departments of the social system. This type of social schizophremia left increasingly few "balanced persons" about, whether they were among supporters or enemies of the Soviet system (among the latter 'the balanced enemies' could be counted on one hand in the relatively small number of dissidents). However, the danger of this process lay in the fact that it was allpervading. In time internal contradictions and 'official discord' have reached critical levels. Non-official, "kitchen" mentality became the attribute of the ruling elite, reaching and affecting the very top of the CP and state hierarchy. By this time at long last, "kitchen" mentality became 'official', endorsed as a new way of thinking officially. Surprisingly this new thinking was presented to the whole world as perestroika in the broadest possible sense. In fact it was the expression of criticism of Soviet reality developed inside the totalitarian consciousness in the past decades.

Not only was Gorbachev a pure product of the "communist" system, but he is a striking example of double thinking. When he became the leader of the country, he and his entourage saw their opportunity to use the critical attitudes of people in all walks of life. A pre-condition for this was to free people from dogmatic inertia and fear, to do away with division between "official" and "non-official" thinking. Gorbachev used the state machinery at his disposal and the "incredible" happened: the totalitarian state put into motion the movement aimed at changing the system.

In the last stage of the crisis the totalitarian system suffered a split; it generated its "murderer", the force which drew its identity from the will to eliminate totalitarian rule. Democratization was the offspring of the totalitarian state, genetically and functionally bound to it. According to its laws, it does not express a movement of society trying to reform the system, rather it is auto-destruction on the part of the system, internal fight to the finish.

This explains why the dissidents _the few public opponents of totalitarian rule - stayed on the sidelines. This seems puzzling at first glance, since the six years of perestroika seemed to mean an improvement in the very areas which they had defended. In reality it is clear that the dissident's movement was supported by individuals, non-conformists rebelling against the "system". "We were not politicians", S.Kovalev wrote, "simply we were morally incompatible with the regime". (Komsomolskaya Pravda, 2.XII.1991). Democratization found supporters in the ranks of the majority, who saw in it a way of combining their own ego with the power game in which they were involved. It was a movement of conformists. The line between "dissidents" and "democrats" had nothing to do with principles, simply there was a moral and psychological barrier separating them.

There is no question here of attacking those who fought against the regime in the 70's, but rather those leaders who responded favorably to the call from on high for glasnost and democracy. Furthermore, the most eager were the very people who in the past had shown the most zealous conformism. There was no difficulty for them to turn from one way of thinking to another, the essential condition was that the change was initiated at the top.

The supporters of democratization were divided into two groups, separated not by profession but by age. Their function was quite distinct inside the movement. The first belonged to the 50-60 generation. Their world outlook was formed during a period of comparative weakening of totalitarian rule, in the years of the Khruschev's thaw. This is why there are many of them without dogmatic prejudices. However their active life started in the 60's and coincided with Brezhnev's reaction. Some "shestidesyatniki" repudiated reaction and formed the core of the party of law-defenders. Yet the majority adapted themselves to "external conditions", though they retained some of the romanticism of their youth, in spite of the fact that many of them made brilliant careers in government or scientific disciplines. They just kept quiet and waited for a better day. Thus they answered Mikhail Gorbachev's appeal enthusiastically and in large numbers.

The second group is made up of people in their 30's, born of those who were young at the time of Khrushchev's thaw. They, however, were brought up in different circumstances and in another climate. The 80's is a period of decay for totalitarian rule. Political, economic and moral degeneration of the regime was all too obvious. Corruption in all sectors, incompetence of the authorities turned the power into an object of ridicule. This was the subject of discussions at home, in the "kitchen", on the part of the older generation. The regime went on existing due to the monstrous force of 70 years of inertia. Having no chance to change anything, not even to protest, the younger generation turned out to be thoroughly disillusioned, having no faith in anything. Some of them tried to isolate themselves from reality, living in a world of their own. The children acted in the same conformist way as their parents, but there was an essential difference between them. The fathers had kept some of the idealism of the post-Stalin spring and a belief in the possibility to change the system for the better. While under the children's conformist attitudes were concealed pragmatism and cynicism.

During the years of perestroika the movement for democracy underwent a substantial evolution. Today with the totalitarian system in ruins, its life cycle is at an end, having gone from childhood to adolescence and maturity to end in decrepitude. Throughout it remained an expression of state policy, not a social movement. Every stage of its development was dictated by power requirements which colored its ideology.

The first stage of the development of democratization is the period of cooperation with the government. It ran from April 1985 to August 1987. The top leaders patronize it openly and the movement in turn declares publicly that it supports the new olicy of the government. The ideology is shaped by Gorbachev's policies and the stimulus goes almost entirely from top to bottom. Party plenums are still the most important milestones by which to determine the changes taking place in society. Vectors of development of power and democratization still coincide. Glasnost and openness are the main slogans of the time. The movement expresses itself merely in giving support to perestroika which was launched from above. The organization has not split yet and it is difficult to detect firm orientations.

The second stage is a period of competition between government and democratization. After gaining momentum, the movement develops according to its own laws and tries to fly by itself. This is the period covering August 1987 to March 1989. As it becomes more independent the movement aims its criticism not only at past mistakes but also present shortcomings. Then it transpired that the leadership is not ready to go the whole way, that Gorbachev aimed at limited political and economic reforms. He intended to breathe new life into the system by emancipating individual minds and allowing a measure of freedom of thought and expression. A conflict between power and democratization became apparent, but positions remained unclear. The leadership while criticizing what it considered extremist opinions, still encouraged the policy of glasnost and openness. Reformists, while insisting on accelerating the pace of change and accusing the authorities of inconsistenct, try their best to win Gorbachev over to their creed. Reform is gradually gaining the upper hand over the machinery of state. Every party plenum, every conference of the Central Committee is the occasion for new demands. To respond to them the leadership has to intensify reforms, but its decisions are half hearted and never come up to the expectations of the public, so that most of them are seen as concessions made under constraint.

Changing relations between the party of reform and government came to the fore in the autumn of 1987. The 70th anniversary of the October Revolution was approaching and the social climate was on the boil. A heated controversy arose over the part played by the Soviets and the revolution they carried out. A polarization occurred and nationalistic claims were put forward. High hopes of clarification rested with Gorbachev's report at the plenum of the of CPSU. What he eventually said came as a great disappointment both for the "left" and for the "right" of the public spectrum. The removal of Boris Yeltsin from his post exemplified the growing conflict between the party of the General Secretary and the democratic public. This juncture marked a change in the ideology of the movement for democratization. The word perestroika was retained but given a new meaning. Controversy raged over its being revolution or reform only, over the need for revolution "from above" or revolution "from below". Having parted company with government, the democrats concentrated on rousing public consciousness. They tried to woo the sympathy of the masses and in so doing often turned to populism. The most facile slogans were bandied about. Almost simultaneously two separate campaigns were launched. One supported Yeltsin, against every and any privilege; the other supported investigators Odlyan and Ivanov, and was aimed at corruption and the mafia. Ever since populism has been a consistent element of the ideology of perestroika. The democratic movement moved from support of Gorbachev to criticism of his policies.

Structural changes now occurred. During the process of estrangement from government policy two large groups appeared in the movement which differed in their attitude to state structures. They may be defined as "system" (liberals) and "non-system" (non-formal) democrats. A large section of people can be called "liberals" , including nunmerous scientific and creative members of the intelligentsia of the older generation, often enjoying a high social status, who responded positively to Gorbachev's "new course". As a rule they belonged to the same generation as the General Secretary, and resembled him in their mental set up. Yet in their criticism of the system they went further than Gorbachev and were more consistent. In part due to their romantic convictions of "socialism with a human face" inherited from the days of Khrushchev, and in part the comparatively high position which they enjoyed in society, led them to choose to keep within the framework of the existing system. Most of them were ideologists; using university chairs, contacts with the media and other available means, they exerted considerable pressure on public opinion and made sure of Gorbachev pursuing his policy of liberalization. Soon a group of the most popular publicists stood out against this strata. They were bound to be influential since every single statement they made created a stir in public life. Their only criteria were those of publicists so they judged the changes that had taken place and the amount of freedom newly granted by the extent to which criticism of the system could go.

"Non-formals" - is a group which did not play such a noticeable role in the early days of perestroika. From the beginning they refused to cooperate with power. They were mostly young people. They devoted all their energies to organizing themselves "outside the system". There were objective and subjective reasions for their approach. First of all, being young and having witnessed the decrepitude of Brezhnev's regime, they felt nothing but loathing for officialdom. Secondly, youth was not completely integrated into the system. On the one hand it enjoyed more freedom of choice since it was not afraid of losing a position in society like the older generation. On the other hand, being young they had no means or opportunities to defend their opinions within the framework of the system, or influence the situation in any way. This is why, after the end of 1986, small "non-formal" circles began to spring all over the country outside the framework of official structures. Thus, to start with, they were made up of isolated groups, each one counting no more than thirty people. Soon they became aware of the need for consolidation and at the end of the summer 1987 representatives of "non-formal" associations established themselves as an independent political force. For a year and a half fairly wide regional coalitions were created on this basis.

The membership of these non-formal circles is completely heterogeneous. First, there are some from the creative intelligentsia. Secondly, a small section of former dissidents who joined the movement. Thirdly, there is a fairly large group of people from various backgrounds for whom social action is an end in itself as a form of self-expression and/or an outlet for frustrated social ambition. Among them not a few could be failures, adventurers or misfits.

In their theories the "non-formals" follow roughly on the same lines as the older generation. In the field of policy they lead the way. As they are not bound by the need to cooperate with the system they put their views forward in a more aggressive fashion, ask more far-reaching questions. In order to push their policies they were the first to appeal directly to the masses.

During the period under consideration the structures of the democratic movement changed mainly under the impact of the growing importance of "non-formal" associations. A new stage of development was under way.

This was a stage of political opposition with government, lasting from the election of people's deputies of the USSR and Russia in March 1989 to March 1990. This is the rebellious youth of democracy. The "functions" of each side were at last clearly defined. The democrats went on the attack and demanded reforms. Now it is the only force radiating energy for change. The power keeps still and tries to stem the decay of the old machinery of state. They are not partners byt opponents manning different sides of the still symbolic barricades. A new electoral law contained a promise of legalization of the existing opposition.

Participation in the first "free" elections allowed the movement to consolidate its ideological and structural independence in relation to the state which had engendered it.

Anti-communism in its dual form of expression, direct and covert, has become the ideology of democratization. It manifests itself directly as the negation of communist postulates and the prerogatives of the communist party. A key moment was the fight for abolishing Article 6 of the Constitution of the USSR declaring the leading role of the

CPSU in state and society. In its covert form the movement shows its anticommunism in upholding principles antagonistic to communism such as parliamentary democracy, legal state, political rights and freedom, etc. As all negation of negation, the programme for democratization looked "positive", though it was in fact far from it. The movement became democratic only in so far as it was moving away from its opposite, i.e. from communism. An important landmark was reached went some of the organizers were elected as deputies. The situation was radically altered: the movement from existing de facto only, became recognized de jure and part of the political system. As it acquired legal recognition, its scope widened considerably: the institutions of government could be used to introduce reforms. Gorbachev would no longer be asked merely rhetorical questions through the press, but political ones, in Parliament. The leadership could not brush off questions, but would be obliged to answer them, may be to be pushed into action. Meanwhile the infrastructure of the movement took on its final form: deputies stood as the center of political action, access to mass media was provided through them. Groups of experts and analysts emerged and in the course of elections channels were created to gain influence on the population. Election coalitions were worked out in detail.

Structures also evolved to fit the new situation: since the democrats now represented the opposition to the system, the old division into "liberals" and "non-formal" lost its meaning. Preconditions for the new set up appeared in 1988-1989, when the theoricians of democratization in criticizing the system distanced themselves more and more, until they severed all links with official structures. "Non-formals" on their part increased their influence, tightening their grip on mass media, they acquired a reputation for fighting political battles to the finish. Under the impact of elections, the need for unification was obvious. In order to win elections the "supervisers of perestroika" need a team of helpers in the fight for deputy mandates. In turn "non-formals" sought out the support of well-know people in the regions, to rally voters round their names. As a result the old divisions in the movement became obsolete. The "non-formal" associations were replaced by a conglomerate of tentative groupings, unions, associations, fronts, etc. mobilized for gaining votes and being active in parliament, in short a proper opposition.

At this stage the democrats in their struggle for defeating communism, acquired a unified organization. They were all aware that disunity and confusion would weigh against them. Ideological differences amounted to very little, as all that mattered was to bring down communism. Their attitude to the authorities was identical, they were in opposition and appealed to the public to assist in the fight.

To start with the movement in that period may have been rather amorphous, but it gradually became more differentiated. On the one hand groups changed into parties adopting loud names but lacking in prestige, with their political image embodied in programs and charters. Soon the whole political spectrum was filled. On the other hand, the trend toward turning these groups into a bloc led to the formation of the movement called "Democratic Russia".

This is when it appeared as quite "civilized", on the lines of multiparty opposition of a western type. Yet this was a misleading appearance, as so-called parties were a mere facade. Real parties cannot be constituted where there is no free market forces, no large middle class, and hardly any democratic culture. The new parties were small pressure groups with a clientele of fellow campaigners gathered round one or more leaders who disposed of a modest newspaper and one or two representatives in the Supreme Soviet. Such structurization had no political meaning, neither then nor later. The error arose from the fact that real power had never belonged to these party corridors. It was also due to the fact that people voting "for" or "against" had not fully grasped the differences between various programs and intuitively chose to see one thing only: the movement's leaders were anticommunist. Real differentiation occurred only in the next stage.

The fourth stage started with coming to power. This was maturity when the full potential of the movement became apparent. This period lasted more than a year - from March 1990 up to August 1991. A complex process was at work for the democratic movement to gain power. The first step was the success of democrats at the elections to the Supreme Soviet of RSFSR and local Soviets of some large industrial centers.

This was the beginning of legalization of the movement as an instrument of power. As a result the political situation crystalized into opposition of two powers. The system reacted in the same way as with union power and treated the movement opposed to it as Russia's power. Political struggle in the conditions of "diarchy" left a mark on the ideology as well as structures of the democratic movement.

The "enemy" turned out to be "localized" in union structures of power and management. To get the upper hand the only policy was to raise the status of Russia and of other structures that were controlled by the democratic movement, and to claim independence. This colored the ideology of anticommunism with rigid nationalism and a rejection of empire. (There are other objective reasons which will be set aside here) The claim of Russia's sovereignty became central and helped the democrats to increase their influence steadily throughout the year.

The democratic movement coming to power brought about internal changes as the legislative and executive structures had to evolve along the lines of division of power. Some democrats joined executive organs and others concentrated around the Supreme Soviet and local Soviets. Their unity within the framework of "Democratic Russia" was preserved still ; the status of the movement as an alternative to power was intact, but only so far as the system was surviving. Yet the image of the party and Demrussia, above all toward the end of the period under consideration was getting fainter. Cracks appeared more and more in the facade of unityas contradictions between leaders of new administrations and new deputations became apparent. There was a general parting of the ways among various members of the movement.

In the natural order of events the democratic movement was bound to win the day and necessarily would experience a final stage of decay. But the putsch put a stop to the even flow of political life and victory came sooner than expected. When the dust settled it transpired that the democrats were in disarray.

One aim had been inscribed in the genetic code of the movement: the destruction of the totalitarian system. The communist party once removed from the political scene, the role had been fulfilled. It was clear then that the movement was doomed to self-destruction. First of all a crisis in the organization broke out. The so-called multiparty system, as portrayed by "Democratic Russia", had lost all political significance. Party leaders realized that the power they had created and escaped their reach and had become almost independent. Now representing power the movement lost its unity. It split into opposing factions, on the lines of state structures: State Soviet, Soviet of Ministers, deputy corps, President's apparatus, local executive power, etc.

The ideological crisis was less visible, though it carried the seed of decomposition. Curiously the democrats' victory made it plain that they had never had a positive doctrine. The only common denominator was anticommunism. Proper democratic, and even more national ideology were a parody of political program, it was anticommunism turned inside out. When communism ceased to exist the collapse came swiftly. There was no pivot for a new power to take toot. Lack of ideology means inevitable decay, every effort to stop it is futile and there is no energy left for influencing public processes. The fact that not a single reform was passed in the few months of democratic rule is an objective proof of this paralysis. The so-called democratic movement had no creativity in essence, as it grew from the state not from society. until it became the state and died. The new state is weak, it has no future. Who is to succeed it? All these years of struggle to bring communism down saw Russian society stir into consciousness after a prolonged coma. The new statehood can only come from the state itself. It could hardly be democratic, since neither cultural nor economic nor social conditions have come into existence for this in Russia. One can hazard a guess, but one thing is sure: the emerging power will correspond to the historical character and level of development of Russian culture as it reaches the end of the 20th century. Priority should be given to determining its nature.

What direction will political evolution take and what will happen to the "human material" once engaged in the movement and now in a position of power? The process can be gradual if the President of Russia relies directly on the masses and begins moving away from his former supporters in consolidating his position. Then after a few shocks, when real public forces manifest themselves more clearly, their representatives will be in the entourage of the President and will form the core of the new power which is to bring Russia out of its crisis. The process will be painful if the President chooses to ally himself with the old "democratic" team. Then Russia would have to undergo a revolution "from the bottom" The fate of the democratic political elite will be different, as part of it will join new public movements and another part will bind their career with that of the president and execute his will. The majority of the idols of perestroika will be thrown to the scrap heap of history.

The democratic movement received lavish praise at times, but not always well-founded. The time for it to be discredited is come, yet its historical role has to be gauged. At a particular moment of the development of Russia some pressing tasks were dealt with successfully and victory crowned these efforts. Expectations were often too high as to its capabilities. It could not become the backbone of civil society and had to exit from the political scene leaving to others the work of building a more enduring edifice.

Perestroika and Russia

Gerhard Simon

In the past five years events have taken place in Russia and Eastern Europe which will undoubtedly enter history textbooks. All communist regimes crumbledtaking with themselves into oblivion three states (Yugoslavia, the Soviet Union and Czechoslovakia), one of them considered to be a superpower right up to the end of its existence.

It seems natural that professional analysts and the public at large during the course of events should have been fascinated almost exclusively by the sweeping changes occurring in the East of Europe. As we tended to convince one another during the Brezhnev decades that almost everything in communist countries was stable and "normal", so now we were concentrating our efforts in describing and analyzing upheaval and collapse, and assumed that out of the "time of troubles" there would arise democracy and market economy.

Two years after the abortive coup in Moscow it seems in order to take stock and evaluate preliminary to what extent Russia has really changed, or in other words, how strong the forces of historical inertia are. As the western community earlier overemphasized stability and stagnation in the communist "bloc", so it tended to overestimate change after 1989. This holds true especially for Russia. At a glance reality seems to belie such a theory: the CPSU as the centre of the political system has been disbanded, the apparatus as the embodiment of real power no longer exists, the ideology of Marxism-Leninism has been denounced and ridiculed a hundredfold, and - most important of all - the Soviet Union as a whole has been broken into 15 independent states - all of which have been recognized by the international community.

Has a veritable revolution taken place in Russia? In 1917 the Russian revolution replaced the old regime by a new communist one, it decapitated the society of the Russian Empire and removed the old elite to make room for the new bolshevik nomenklatura, and it restored the Empire in the form of the Soviet Union. Lenin's bolsheviks did not hesitate to use brute force and terror to achieve their ends. They were motivated by the myth of knowing the laws of nature, history and society (Marxism) and of being the mouthpiece of history. Nothing similar to the 1917 revolution has happened in Russia in the late 1980s.

What we have witnessed was the downfall of the communist regime and in this respect the period of Russian history which started in 1917 is indeed over. The reason for the collapse was internal decay, which had accumulated for decades. Yet in contrast to 1917, there has not emerged a new social order and political system of power. There is no consensus as to the way the country should be run and how society should be organized. Neither is there a consensus on the best way to resolve these vital problems. Democratic values and procedures are far from being universally accepted. It is widely held in certain quarters of Russian society that only authoritarian rule or even a dictatorship can restore law and order. Two years after the end of communist rule, opinions have been voiced at home and abroad that the Russians are not able to govern themselves - in a modern democratic fashion. The term "democrat" has become almost an insult, meaning "traitor". Incidentally, the same sense was attached to it in Germany since the days of Bismarck until 1945.

We are faced with the paradox that, on the one hand, the communist regime was easily brought down without much resistance on the part of the communist establishment and its institutions. But this, on the other hand, does not mean that a new political and social order will be built up quickly and painlessly. It is arguable that the communist regime prevailed for so long not because people were convinced of its values or enjoyed its privileges, but for lack of generally acceptable alternative. It should be added that dissidents since the 1960s were unable to develop consistent political and social alternatives, let alone to come to an agreement between themselves. So the old order tumbled down before an alternative had been found. Lip service to democracy and the market economy - offered by almost everybody including most communists - serves only as a surrogate for a well defined political program. Since August 1991, Yeltsin and his crew have repeatedly and convincingly argued that their hesitations and mistakes were partly due to the fact that they were totally unprepared for taking over power from the communists at this time.

The absence of consensus about the future road for Russia may at least in part explain the amazing lack of popular enthusiasm when the totalitarian order broke down. The public mood could be described as horror vacui or postcommunist resignation and depression. This apocalyptic mood may be detected in all strata of society, including the intelligentsia and the political class. Postcommunist depression is in evidence in many former communist countries, but - it seems - nowhere as serious as in Russia.

Correspondingly, we witness a lack of emotional identification with the new Russa, the absence of positive myths and values that could fire society and the political class to action. There is no "Russian dream" to overcome cracks and tensions between social strata and political camps. The ideals of a pluralist democratic order, rule of law and a market economy fail to unite and mobilize the population and the intelligentsia. Most widespread is an overall anti-communist attitude which rejects the former ideology. Yeltsin standing on a tank and addressing the crowd during the August 1991 coup is a myth enjoying wide appeal. Yet the state holiday of June 12, the day when Russia declared herself a sovereign state, became a focus of controversy and the butt of outright rejection. This picture is in sharp contrast to the emotionally rich and varied myths offered by the reactionaries.

In spite of a general feeling that the communist order was dismal, we observe a strange inability and unwillingness for the public to dissociate itself from the communist past. True enough, a few national symbols - such as flag and anthem - have been changed, although Lenin is still on his podium in hundreds of cities and villages all over the country - quite unlike the Baltic states or Poland and Hungary. Accordingly, a number of key political institutions of the communist past are still in operation in Russia. These are first and formost the Soviets. There have been no general elections in the country after the disintegration of the apparatus of the CP. There is no freely and fairly elected parliament. Instead the Soviets have taken over the role of the defunct CP and claim - in keeping with the communist tradition - supreme power in the country. According to the current Russian constitution the Congress of People's Deputies "is entitled to discuss and decide any question" relevant to the Russian Federation (Article 104). Paradoxically, everybody is obliged to observe the constitution and the laws of a country no longer in existence, namely the USSR (article 4).

The Supreme Soviet in Moscow has been able to strike a pose as the only true defender of democracy and the constitution in Russia. Communists, chauvinists and the so-called centrists pretend that they stand for observing the law against the radical democrats who wish to turn the country upside down, to dissove the Soviets and introduce democracy by unlawful means. The small and weak democratic organizations and also Yeltsin and his entourage were quite unable to counteract these arguments.

The political class is either incapable or unwilling to understand that a new political order cannot be established within the framework of the old regime. The Soviet constitution cannot provide a framework for democracy. If Russia is to become a democracy the first requisite is to dissolve the Soviet regime. Could Nazi institutions and the Nazi elite - barely distancing themselves from Nazi ideology - have built a democratic society in Germany after 1945?

In Russia the old communist nomenklatura is fighting for its survival using the very instruments and arguments of a democratic order which they so despised earlier. The democrats are unable to cope with this situation. They are afraid of being labelled revolutionaries and bolsheviks, ready to disperse the Constituent Assembly, as occurred in January 1918, when sailor Zhelesnjak gave his famous explanation: "The guard is tired". There exists a deep-seated rejection and fear of revolution in Russia to-day, because revolution is associated with mass terror, liquidation of the elites and Gulag.

Fear of a revolutionary crack down is, of course, a positive feature of political culture. Yet it is used to prevent the necessary steps to overcome totalitarian structures and to build democratic institutions. Looking back to the period following August 1991, one comes to the conclusion that it was a time if missed opportunities and lost chances. The dividend of freedom was not adequately invested, in the way Poland and the Czech Republic used it, for example. \Although August 1991 marked the defeat of the old regime, the Yeltsin team proved unable to bring about the thoroughgoing changes that were necessary, to render Russia's road to democracy irreversible.

Two years after the putsch, Russia has no freely elected parliament, no democratic constitution; political parties are still in their infancy, no adequate legal framework exists for a market economy. Instead those political forces stemming the tide of changes were not only able to gather momentum, but also to push the victors of August 1991 more and more toward the right and to slow down the pace of democratization and westernization. It seems that victors and defeated alike were so overwhelmed by what had been changed and destroyed in Russia within a few years, that they agreed to a silent coalition for consolidation, preservation and restoration. The gap between East Central Europe and Russia widened. Also in this respect history Also in this respect history returned. Whereas in the mid-1980's the impulses for change in the socialist "bloc" often came from Russia, since 1991 Russia turned to its special or third road. Whereas East Central Europe rapidly proceeded toward westernization fighting for an early integration into EC and NATO, Russia discovers its "Eurasian" heritage, and makes clear thatit is not simply part of the West.

An important reason for the inability to overcome the communist legacy lies in the fact that there has been only a very limited elite turnover. A part of the old political institutions has been dissolved, but the nomenklatura was able to stay in power. Within the Soviets, the KGB, public administration, factories and last but not least, the humanities there may have been less elite turnover since the end of the 1980's than during Krushchev's de-Stalinization in the second half of the 1950's, let alone Stalin's purges. The most disquieting problem may be not the ex-communists but those leading cadres who are still communists in mentality and convictions, only slightly distancing themselves from parts of the old weltanschauung and Stalinism. There are many reasons for the almost untouched position of the old elite. To a certain extent, the old elite brought down the CPSU and its ideology itself, therefore claiming the fruits of the "revolution" for themselves. Also, there has been no alternative elite in Russia, which is a different situation from Prague or Warsaw, where a take over in the administration was possible.

Wheras the Czech parliament in July 1993 adopted a law branding the former Czechoslovak communist regime of 1948 to 1989, as "illegitimate" and "criminal", in Russia nobody has been convicted of high treason for taking part in the communist coup d'Etat in August 1991. A number of former communist states, including Poland, the

Czech Republic and the three Baltic countries, have introduced legislation to bar former high-ranking communist functionaries and leading officials of the KGB from holding certain public offices for the next few years. On the contrary, the Supreme Soviet adopted a number of laws protecting yesterday's and today's officials of the security services and their activities from public scrutiny. When Galina Starovoitova, a leader of Democratic Russia, in May 1993 proposed a screening (lustration) law for Russia, it caused an outcry in the media. Even the former political prisoner and chairman of the Supreme Soviet Committee for Human Rights, Sergey Kovalev came out against such a law.

The most radical event seems to be the least acceptable in Russia: the fall of the Russian Empire, since 1922 called the Soviet Union. The demise of the Soviet Union in 1991 may turn out to be one of the main events in Europe at the end of the 20th century. It marks not only the end of Soviet history but of many centuries of Russian history. The history of Moscovy since the 14th century was characterized by centralization inside the state and expansionism toward the outside world. Russian self-perception and national consciousness was and is intimately connected with Russia as a huge country, inhabited by many peoples, large and small, but dominated by Russian culture, language and political talent for building an empire. In contrast to European normalcy, Russian national consciousness was first of all attached to the territory, to the state and only in the second place to the nation, the Russian people. The attachment to soil (pochva) was more important than to blood. This constituted a first-rate condition for successful empire-building.

We are currently witnessing the second round of the break-up of the Russian Empire. The first occurred in 1917-1921. The time for multinational empires in Europe seems over for good. If one considers the reduction of the Russian Federation in comparison with the Soviet Union as a loss, the way large sections of the political class in Russia do, then a depressing picture of national disaster emerges. In large parts Russia's frontiers have been reduced to those of the middle of the 17th century, before the incorporation of left bank Ukraine into the tsardom of Moscow. It is true that Russia today, unlike what was the case in the 17th century, has direct access to the Baltic Sea, the Black Sea and the Sea of Japan. Nevertheless, nobody in Russia had ever considered that the administrative borders of the RSFSR inside the Soviet Union could become state borders, separating independent national states from each other. As a rule these borders are neither historical nor ethnic nor economic, in many instances they are Stalinist frontiers.

After the fall of the empire, Russian national consciousness finds itself in a completely different situation compared to the national consciousness of the other nations on the territory of the former Soviet Union. Whereas the Estonians, Ukrainians and Tatars were able to re-establish their independent state or are attempting to build a state, the Russians have lost their state. So far they first and formost have to pay the bill for 70 years on the wrong track of history. This is one of the reasons for the crisis of identity which is currently afflicting Russia. The Russians are not only confronted with the necessity to

144 PERESTROIKA

reconcile themselves with their considerably reduced geopolitical significance but they have to change their mentality, from an imperial to a national, normal European one. A comparison with the history of Germany during the 1920's illustrates how difficult a challenge this is. The losses of Germany after the treaty of Versailles were small, indeed, compared to the end of the empire in 1991. Nevertheless, revisionism united many political parties and groups in Weimar Germany. Resentment against Versailles was not confined to right-wing extremists. The revisionist consensus became an important element of the rise of the Nazis.

In Russia today the fall of the empire is widely considered as a loss and a disaster, not an opportunity. Among those who are convinced that the break-up of the Soviet Union was inevitable, many believe that the disadvantages far outweigh the advantages. Those who dominate the Soviets, the administration and the media today regret the end of the Soviet Union, not its beginning. This again is evidence of the inability of the elite to distance itself from the old regime. In my view the misfortune for Russia was the creation of the Soviet Union, not its break-up. Lenin and the bolsheviks prevented the establishment of a modern European order of national states on the territory of the Russian Empire. What was left undone at the beginning of our century has to be made up for at the end of it.

The voices of the empire-savers became much louder and harsher after the demise of the Soviet Union. A large spectrum of political groups from the communists and so-called national patriots, to the self-appointed "centrists" and to Yeltsin's crew, excluding only the most radical-democratic groups are today quite convinced that Russia is not a state like any other, but that it has to play a special role and must carry out a mission vis-a-vis its neighbours and even the world at large.

Political terminology is revealing. In 1992, a new term entered the Russian political dictionary: the "near abroad", encompassing the territory of the former Soviet Union. It means that, for example, Tajikistan - many thousand kilometers away from central Russia - is considered "near abroad", wheras Finland at the gates of St Petersburg belongs to the "far abroad".

This is not just a matter of terminology. Journalism, foreign policy doctrine and political actions made it clear, that Russia is not prepared to conduct political business with the former Soviet republics under the same conditions as with other neighbours, not to mention countries of Western Europe. "All of the geopolitical space of the former Soviet Union is considered a sphere of vital interests" for Russia, wrote Andronik Migranjan in August 1992 (Rossijskaja gazeta, August 4, 1993); he became a member of the Presidential Council in February 1993. From this axiom he drew two conclusions: The new states dispos only of a limited sovereignty, since Russia should prevent them from entering political-military alliances with each other or third parties. Secondly, Russia should be prepared to incorporate non-Russian peoples and Russians outside the Russian Federation and their territories into Russia if they so wish. In other words present-day borders should be considered as tentative ones.

Much of this reasoning found its way into a memorandum of the Supreme Soviet's commission on foreign affairs under its chairman Yevgeny Ambartsumov. Here law-makers claimed a Russian Monroe Doctrine: "The Russian Federation's foreign policy must be based on the doctrine that proclaims the entire geopolitical space of the former Soviet Union the sphere of its vital interests..." "Russia must also secure from the international community the role of political and military guarantor of stability throughout the former space of the USSR." (Izvestija, August 7, 1992).

Also President Yeltsin and Foreign Minister Kozyrev moved to the right since since the autumn of 1992. Yeltsin addressing the so-called centrist Civic Union forum in February 1993, spoke of "Russia's special responsibility" on the Euro-Asian space. "I believe the time has come for distinguished international organizations, including the UN, to grant Russia special powersas a guarantor of peace and stability in the former regions of the USSR." (Izvestija, March 4, 1993).

CIS is widely considered the apt institutional framework to re-establish Russian domination in what is called Russia's geopolitical space. Notwithstanding the fact that a number of new states never became members, (the three Baltic states, Georgia) others opted out (Azerbaidjan, Moldova), or are quite reluctant to co-operate (Ukraine, Turkmenistan) many politicians and journalists in Russia are convinced that CIS will finally lead to ever growing integration guaranteeing the leading role of Russia due to sheer size. Presidential adviser Sergei Stankevich told a journalist in July 1993 that he believes in a new union, with Russia at its centre, in the not too distant future. Russia's historical task is to stabilize itself and then conduct a gradual "economic and cultural expansion" into the near abroad (Novaja ezednevnaja gazeta, July 7, 1993).

Two events have deeply wounded the Russian national consciousness and national pride: the separation of Ukraine and the fact that suddenly 25 million Russians are living beyond the borders of the Russian state. Most Russians - interested in politics or not - never took Ukrainian claims of sovereignty and independence seriously. Until late in 1991, Russian politicians and the public at large were convinced that the Ukrainian question boils down to a handful of Ukrainian nationalists, most of them in Galicia, fighting for independence wheras the vast majority of the population was determined to remain with Russia in a common state. The independence of Ukraine came as a shock to most Russians threatening their perception of historical identity of of the three Eastern Slavic nations.

Most political groups in Russia today do not recognize the independence of Ukraine as something definite and claim that the tide of separation is already receding and some new form of confederation or federation between Russia and Ukraine will and must develop. De jure Russia did recognize the independence of Ukraine, but not de facto.

The Supreme Soviet in Moscow became an outspoken mouth-piece of Russia's unwillingness to accept the status quo after the dissolution of the Soviet Union. The Supreme Soviet supported a political movement in the Crimea aimed at severing the peninsula from Ukraine and establishing direct political relations between the Crimea and Moscow, bypassing Kiev. The Russian law-makers passed a resolution in May 1992, declaring the transfer of the Crimea from the RSFSR to the Ukrainian SSR in 1954 as "null and void from the outset". Possession of the Crimea means disposal over the former Soviet Black Sea Fleet, another point of dispute between Russia and Ukraine. In July 1993, the Russian Supreme Soviet went even further and asserted in a resolution, Sevastopol - headquarters of the Black Sea Fleet - was and remains part of the territory of the Russian Federation. This trepassing of domestic and international law was denounced by President Yeltsin who declared himself "ashamed of this decision".

The self-perceived centrist line has been aptly summed up in a memorandum of the Russian Academy of Sciences Institute of Europe in mid 1992: "Keep the Ukrainian problem within a definite framework... and maintain the basic elements of cooperation ... through a combination of policies of reconciliation, pressure, and wide-ranging use of international instruments, waiting until Kiev outgrows its period of striving for self-assertion." (Vechernii Kyiv, June 18, 1992, as quoted in: R. Solchanyk, Back to the USSR?, in : The Harriman Institute Forum, vol.VI, No.3, P.9). Such an integrationist approach, striving for a new political union between Russia and Ukraine represents the middle of the road political line. The chauvinist-communist "united" opposition, disposing of about 1/3 of the deputies in the Supreme Soviet, uses quite a different language. The "shadow foreign minister" from the right-wing National Salvation Front - whose name was not disclosed - argued "we should investigate possible scenarios for a sudden nuclear war with Kiev" (Den', February 7, 1993). To clarify the situation, Sergei Baburin, a leader of the National Salvation Front, told Ukraine's ambassador in Moscow: "Either Ukraine reunites with Russia or there will be war" (Izvestija, May 26, 1992).

Since 1992, suddenly 25 million Russians became residents of foreign states; 11,3 million of them are living in Ukraine. The Russians at the periphery of the empire had always been a factor of homogeneity and a guarantor of stability. Millions of Russians lived outside Russia proper already before 1917; this distinguished the Russian Empire from other European empires. The Soviets systematically used and enlarged the role of Russian elites and workers in the non-Russian republics. Russians and Russified elites became the transmission belts between the communist center and the non-Russian periphery. The majority of political groups today is not prepared to abandon this instrument. They are determined to use the Russian minorities in the "near abroad" as leverage to bring about new integration.

The Russians in the "near abroad" are "a powerful economic and political enclave, they will be the basis of our political influence" said Sergei Karaganov, deputy director of the Russian Academy of Sciences Institute of Europe and an adviser to the so-called centrist political organizations (Diplomaticeskij vestnik, November 15, 1992, p. 43-44). It is widely accepted in the political class that Russia should use economic levers and, if need be, military pressure to secure the rights of Russians and Russian-speaking compatriots in the "near abroad".

At the present stage this seems easy to realize since many of the new states, including Ukraine, as the largest one, heavily depend on Russia for economic reasons. If Russia suddenly charged world market prices for oil and gas or cut off the supply of energy resources this would cause a very serious crisis in many CIS-states. In addition to economic dependence Russia has another powerful instrument at its disposal: the Russian military. Two years after the end of the Soviet Union Russian troops are still stationed in all the new states. To be sure, no CIS or other troops are garrisoned within Russia. Only with one country - Lithuania - did the Russian government conclude an agreement in 1992 providing for a complete withdrawal of troops until August 1993. The pull-out of Russian troops from the three Baltic states has been marked by constant stop-and-go, reflecting the convulsions of the Moscow domestic scene. To many people in Moscow, the incapability of the "near abroad" to pay world prices and the moral right to have Russian troops stationed in these countries are clearly intertwined.

In some cases Russian troops were used for limited military actions to safeguard what is perceived as Russian interests by Russian revisionists. In Moldova, on the left bank of the Dniester, a self-styled socialist Dniester Republic claimed independence from Chisinau and was supported by the 14th Army stationed in Moldova. The Russian communist leaders of the Dniester Republic consider themselves bearers of Soviet and Russian values and strive for the final unification with Russia. The Dniester Republic, internationally not recognized, depends for its continued existence completely on the Russian army.

From August 1992 the Abkhazians fought a bloody war for independence from Georgia, which they were able to carry out only because they were heavily supported by the Russian military, at least with supplies and sophisticated weapons if not with instructors and other personnel. Minister of Defense Pavel Gratchev made it quite clear that Russia has the highest geopolitical interests in Abkhazia and Adzharia - both parts of Georgia - and Russian troops should therefore remain there. On the other hand, Yeltsin and Shevardnadze reached a general agreement on the withdrawal of Russian troops from Georgia in May 1993, without fixing a timetable.

The most extensive military involvement so far occurred in Tajikistan and particularly at the Tajik-Afghan border during the summer of 1993. The Russian army backed the pro-Moscow factions and regions in Tajikistan in the course of the civil war, which broke out shortly after independence, and by the same token supported the old communist elites. Anti-Russian Tajik volunteers retreated to Afghanistan and fought back in a mujahedinlike-manner. Russian soldiers defended the Tajik-Afghan border, widely seen as far advanced border of Russia in the public discourse. This time President Yeltsin and the Supreme Soviet were united in thinking that Russian soldiers should fight for the geopolitical interests of Russia in far away Tajikistan.

Nobody knows to what extent imperial mentality is rooted in the Russian nation at large. There have been no general elections since the end of the Soviet Union. (Since the writing of this paper a general election did take place in Russia in December 1993) The

Supreme Soviet, the political "pseudoparties" and blocs do not adequately reflect the political will of society. There are indications that the oeople (narod) may be much less interested in the restoration of the empire than politicians and journalists. From elections and referenda held since 1989 a picture emerges of a moderate, commonsense and reform-minded electorate. The idea of Russia as a superstate may appeal to voters less tha Russian media suggest today. Opinion polls show that neither the communists nor the right-wing nationalists are very popular, although the so-called centrists - also striving for a Russia more equal than others - command some backing from society. Two things seem clear:

1. The Russian people are not prepared for any large-scale military action outside the Russian Federation in order to return Ukraine or any other region back to the fold.

2. Russians outside Russia have not been mobilized as empire-savers to any extent, at least so far.

There are reasons to suggest that finally the empire-savers will have to accept the inevitable, the end of empire and the challenge to rebuild Russia as a nation-state, i.e. to bring Russia in line with European normalcy. In contrast to those who regard the demise of the Soviet Union as a misfortune and loss, there are minority voices urging to use the situation as a chance for a new and democratic Russia in the future.

The nation-builders belonging to the camp of the democrats and westernizers distance themselves from the empire-savers. The empire has been a liability for Russia - so runs the argument. The empire entailed constant overcommitment on the part of Russia. The country used all its resources - material, intellectual and spiritual - for expansion and outward glory to the detriment of development and prosperity at home. The end of the Soviet empire meant "salvation from evil also for Russia", in the words of Vjacheslav Dashichev, the democratic political scientist. The centuries-old development of Russia broke off, "during which democracy and citizens' freedom had been sacrificed to imperial interests". (Izvestija, March 10, 1993). Ljudmila Saraskina, a prominent national-democratic journalist, draws the conclusion: "Yes, we feel humiliated, but only because our earlier ambitions were false" (Moskovskie novosti, 1/1993). Russia should now concentrate its limited strength on development inside the country - runs the message of the nation-builders - and forget about superpowers ambitions.

Russia should not claim but rather refuse the role of gendarme on the territory of the former Soviet Union, wrote Yelena Bonner, widow of Andrei Sakharov and spokeswoman for the democratic movement. "First of all because of psychological reasons, the Russian army cannot act as peacemaker on the territory of the former Soviet Union. The army cannot be neutral" (Literaturnaja gazeta, July 28, 1993). Russian intervention - military or peaceful - is perceived as an attempt to reclaim Moscow's former role. Former colonial powers are ill-suited to make peace or prevent conflicts on the territories of former dependent countries.

Russia must now make a choice. It either becomes once again the hegemon of the Euro-Asian continent, dominating neighbours by economic pressure and military might and has an authoritarian-nationalistic political regime. Or Russia accepts its role as a normal state, albeit larger than Estonia but on the same level by international law. Then Russia gains the chance to devlop its own democratic system, civil society and government of law. It seems inconceivable that Russia should exercize authoritarian rule vis-a-vis its neighbours and develop democratic institutions within the country at the same time.

Much depends on the person at the helm. This holds true, although currently all institutions of power seem weak and only to a limited extent able to enforce decisions. It nevertheless makes an enormous difference whether Yeltsin or, for example, vice-President Rutskoi rules the country. It is true Yeltsin made advances to the centrist group in the second half of 1992 and simultaneously abandoned certain positions of the radical-democrats. et Yeltsin repeatedly contained incipient conflicts with Ukraine and the Baltic states. Rutskoi, on the other hand, belongs to a group of Russian politicians termed the "war party" by Foreign Minister Kozyrev. Rutskoi publicly admitted in July 1993 that he gave orders to kill Chechen President Dudaev and to bomb Georgia. Neither order was carried out. Rutskoi as well as the majority of the Supreme Soviet, supported by large numbers of the military, stir up conflicts all over the "near abroad", considering this to be the best way to re-establish Russian control and at the same time to secure power positions for the old elite.

What are the chances for imperial restoration? Can the clock be turned back in Russia? The period of transition means not only cohabitation of the old regime with certain features of a new democratic order. A loss of direction as well as a power- and value-vacuum seem even more characteristic. Communist values are exhausted and do not appeal to society nor the elites. It is hardly feasible that a Leninist party could return to power in Russia. But it is disquieting that the new values of democracy, government by law and market economy are equally discredited in the eyes of a large part of the population - before they have really been introduced. There is s risk that many people in Russia resent westernization of their country and reject a liberal-democratic order even before getting a chance of experiencing it. Since the old regime has outlived itself and new values have not taken root yet, Russia after Yeltsin may drift toward a revisionist authoritarian rule at the top combined with much chaotic counter-rule further down the line. This would entail permanent and growing conflicts with the "near abroad" and the economy would be heavily dominated and overwhelmingly run by the state. The west should be prepared to see Russia in a state of unrest, unpredictability and ungovernability for many years to come.

Perestroika and Czechoslovakia

Alexandr Ort

Before the 'Velvet' revolution, in November 1989, an overwhelming majority of the Czechs and Slovaks living under communist rule was much interested in the political development of the Soviet Union. They all knew perfectly well that any change in Czechoslovakia itself depended on the political situation there. Dissidents and former communits were especially keen to follow the evolution of the Soviet Communist party to anticipate evolution at home.

There was a marked difference between the situation in the Czech provinces and Slovakia, with a more repressive attitude on the part of the communist party in the former, where large-scale purges had taken place since 1971, while nothing of the sort had been carried out in the latter province. This was one of the reasons why the dissident movement was noticeably stronger in the Czech regions, where it exercised much greater influence on the population than in Slovakia. Soviet Perestroika, therefore, made a significant impact on the Czechoslovak people only in the Czech parts of the republic and its influence will only be assessed in this respect.

The Czech dissident circles and the former communists were comparatively well informed about the situation in the USSR, not only through the Soviet press and publications, but also through personal contacts between former Czech and present day Soviet communists, who in addition were linked with numerous family ties. Gorbachev's 'revisionist' speech at the end of 1984 was intensely scrutinized and subjected to endless discussions in the dissident circles that existed in many Bohemian and Moravian towns. It was clear that new forces were at work in the Soviet Communist party and the most striking feature of this development was that many of the ideas expressed by Gorbachev, who at the time was not yet secretary general, but undoubtedly one of the top Soviet leaders, were similar to those that had been aired in Czechoslovakia during the "Prague Spring".

By 1985 it was obvious that the 1968 set of reforms would have been a good basis for modernizing Czech society, and would probably be good for and applicable to Soviet society. However, Czechoslovak experience had also shown that economic reforms must sooner or later be followed by changes in the country's political system, since even a 'free socialist market' economy could not thrive in a totalitarian setup. It was widely expected that perestroika reforms in the USSR would undoubtedly have to follow the same course as in Czechoslovakia in 1968. This certainty aroused great expectations among the Czechs, though few people believed that the Czech 'normalized' CP leadership would allow similar changes to be effected in their country without a struggle.

Nonetheless, because of the bad economic situation Czechoslovakia, like the USSR, was also in urgent need of reforms. Soon after Goirbachev's launch of perestroika the Czechoslovak leadership was forced to follow suit. As in 1968, however, a successful continuation of economic reform in Czechoslovakia very much depended on changes in politics. However, the Husak leadership was determined that any steps in this direction had to be limited to minimum intra-party changes and minute internal affairs modifications. Both dissidents and presentday Czech reformers were weary of initiatives with repercussions in foreign affairs and adverse Soviet reactions. However, on the other hand and unlike in 1968 Czechoslovakia, in the USSR perestroika changes in foreign policy were a pre-condition of successful Soviet economic restructuring.

As was to be expected, the election of Mikhail Gorbachev as the head of CPSU was followed by the introduction of "new political thinking" in the field of foreign affairs. It was first aired in the context of his European tour and formulated as a wish for a "European common house" before his visit to France in September 1985. The idea was taken up again during Gorbachev's meeting with US President Reagan in Geneva in December of the same year. After these public manifestations of Gorbachev's new thinking Czech society was ready to believe that these Soviet new attitudes were being adopted not only as regarded European policy, but also vis-a-vis Czechoslovak internal development.

At first Gorbachev's offer of disarmament in January 1986 failed to strike an positive echo in the international community, as it smacked too much of the old methods of Soviet foreign policy and appeared like another propaganda campaign manouevre. Only later, did Western countries recognize that the new leadership of the Soviet communist party was genuinely trying to find new approaches to the solution of decades old problems of world politics and were willing to respond. By contrast the idea of "glasnost" was received with great enthusiasm by all peaceloving people in Europe and the whole world immediately. Both policy innovations turned out to be the first step, though an important one, on the road to democracy. However, Gorbachev's task of establishing democracy in a country like the Soviet Union, without a democratic tradition and without any experience of what real democracy meant, was by no means easy.

To Czech observers it was clear that Soviet reforms had to start with the economy and foreign policy. Economic growth was impossible without changes in the rigid central planning and cooperation with developed countries was urgently required for such modernization. It was therefore essential to press ahead with the policy of detente and improved relations between the superpowers. Czech democratic circles were not surprised by this development in the Soviet Union, since the ideas of it were already gleaned from Gorbachev's little publicised (perhaps secret?) speech of late 1984. Significantly Soviet changes were seen as hopeful signs for Czech society as well international detente. In any case they could only mean an improved future for CSSR.

The leaders of the Czechoslovak communist party had their misgivings as soon as they found out about Gorbachev's perestroika. They knew from bitter experience that any economic reform, if it is to succeed, must be followed by political changes. They were not unaware of the possible consequences for Czechoslovakia and tried to tighten relations with the leaders of 'orthodox' GDR, Poland, Hungary, Bulgaria and other communist countries. In addition Czech communist leaders knew that Gorbachev's reform policies had met with a strong opposition within the Soviet leadership and were prepared to exploit it. However, they dared not to initiate any action, but had to wait for further development in the USSR. As for the Czech opposition it welcomed all these new Soviet *points de depart*, such as the decision taken in Madrid at the Helsinki follow up meeting to organize a cultural forum in Budapest. It was the first time that a CSCE venture was due to take place in a communist country and it was ready to exploit it. Also for the first time not only diplomats were to participate in the discussions, but also representatives of non-governmental organizations were asked to join in. The forum was carefully prepared by the Hungarian organizers and found a vibrant response among the opposition in Czechoslovakia and other communist countries. By then Gorbachev's perestroika and 'new polical thinking' were already aiding Czech and Slovak opposition.

The Vienna follow up meeting, which started on November 4, 1986, also attracted much attention since the speech made by Eduard Shevardnadze, the Soviet Foreign Minister, on the role of culture in international politics was in clear contradiction with Czechoslovak official policy in the field of human rights. The invitation extended to all the participants in Vienna to attend a subsequent conference in Moscow on human rights problems was an unwelcome challenge to the Czechoslovak government and the Communist party leadership.

Soon afterwards the announcement of an official visit to be made by Gorbachev in Czechoslovakia brought fresh hopes to dissidents and former communists of impending changes in their country. Political development in the Soviet Union began to look more and more like the "Prague Spring of 1968" and the 'opposition' (those excluded from the CP in 1971) communists believed that the Soviet leader's visit would force the leadership of the Czechoslovak Communist party to suspend its policy of 'normalization' and to return to Alexander Dubcek's policy of "socialism with a human face".

The experience of the 1960s led the 'opposition' communists to believe that Gorbachev would try to bring the Czechoslovak Communist party policy into line with the 'new political thinking' of Soviet communists. Information leaked from CP organizations and officials confirmed that Czech leaders were ready for widespread changes not only in the orientation of party policy, but also as far as personnel of the central committee and CP praesidium were concerned.

Unfortunately Gorbachev's visit to Prague came as an anti-climax for dissident circles and the population at large, dashing their high expectations. The Soviet leader spent most of his time with President Husak, lavishing praises on him for his anti-nazi past, as well as for his past and present actions in the party and state administration. It looked as if the Soviet leadership firmly believed that Husak alone would change once again CP's political orientations and course on the strength of Gorbachev's public encouragement and Soviet overall support only.

On the other hand, in Czechoslovakia at least, it became clear that Gorbcachev's perestroika policy did not include democracy neither in the framework of the state nor within the communist party. Everybody could hear him on the television and local radio how he vigorously criticized the Prague Spring, 'remembering his walk about in the streets of the Czech capital', early in 1969. He declared himself deeply shocked when hearing of the existence of 19 youth organizations, at the time flourishing practically without official permission and outside party management. Little did he know that, a few months later, there would spring up in the USSR more than 30.000 non-governmental organizations completely out of party control.

Thus, Gorbachev's attitudes had proved to the Czechs that Soviet society was not ripe for democracy. The same impression was gained from his book on "Perestroika", published in Czech soon after it first appeared in the USSR. There was hardly any mention of democracy in it, and no significant element of democratization was included in the picture of the future Soviet society it was supposed to offer. However, Gorbachev's efforts to exploit his stay in Prague to present the whole of Europe with a hope for changes in the offing should not be underestimated. His declarations on the role of culture in European policy struck again a novel sound. He simply had two options in mind. He either envisaged the future of Europe as an atomic cemetery or as 'the dynamic growth of a great and multi-coloured culture, based on a thousand years old common tradition'. It was for the first time that a Soviet leader had spoken about culture as a basis for the future international order. In the past, only army divisions and strategic weapons came into the picture, as Soviet leaders based their foreign policy purely on the balance of power.

Despite a certain disillusionment Gorbachev's book on "Perestroika" was well received by the Czech population, though the dissidents pointed out loudly its lack of any mention of democracy. The Czechs continued to reason that deep changes in economics always bring about changes in politics. If Gorbachev's visit disappointed high expectations at home, the Czechs were hopeful that these fundamental changes would be realized at least in the Soviet Union.

Yet a bitter aftertaste remained in the wake of the Soviet leader's visit, since no changes whatsoever could be discerned neither in the party leadership nor party polical line.

Czechoslovakia remained one of the most rigid stalinist regime in the communist bloc. The Czech people could not understand the policy of 'non-intervention in the internal affairs of another party-state', applied here by the Soviets. After all the Husak regime was the product of their direct military intervention. Many of the people who had accepted the principle of non-intervention intellectually were adamant in their opinion that politically the new Soviet regime had to repair the 'distortions caused by the invasion of the Warsaw Pact armies', before starting to apply the new policy of non-intervention. However, Soviet reality was very different from this type of reasoning.

After finishing his book on "perestroika", Gorbachev convened a Central Committee meeting in February 1988, in order to discuss the democratization of the Soviet political system and Soviet society, as outlined in the book. It was a logical consequence of previous changes in the USSR, but it marked an important threshold and crystalized an opposition among leaders of the communist party and state official to the new policies.

The present regime in the USSR was an antithesis of democracy, and there was no doubt that all the privileges of the personnel at the top would be abolished in the next stage of Gorbachev's campaigns of modernisation and democratization. This is why intense internal fighting within the CP and the USSR went on at the time. It was not clear who would emerge as victor.

***

In the mid 1980s the Czechoslovak Communist party split into two factions. One centered round the Prime Minister, Strougal, attempted to carry out various limited economic reforms, which seemed absolutely unavoidable. The other faction, the hardliners, favoured neo-Stalinist policies. These party leaders feared that any economic changes, however modest, would bring about vast political innovations, as occurred in 1968. They were right, of course, but hoped to preserve their privileges by blocking in the CP preasidium any alteration of the existing situation.

It now appears that in the autumn of 1987, Premier Strougal who was appreciated in the USSR for his pragmatism and realistic attitude to economic problems, tried to forge an agreement with President Husak, whereby the latter would celebrate his 75th birthday in January 1988 with great pomp and circumstance, feast the 40th anniversary of February 25, 1948 (coup d'Etat de Prague), continue as president of CSSR, but hand over the post of secretary general to a younger member of the CP, probably meaning himself.

However, the neo-Stalinist members of the leadership around Bilak and Fojtik were opposed to such a smooth handover. They kept in close touch with Ligachev, one of Gorbachev's conservative opponents in the Soviet leadership, and with his assistance they overruled Strougal and prepared an alternative plan for changes in the Czechoslovak Communist party. Their counter-stroke followed Strougal's visit to Moscow, where to all outer appearances he was treated as the top leader of the Czechoslovak party. Czech journalists, accompanying the Premier, were told by a reliable Soviet source that Strougal was considered in the USSR as the future "gensek", Czechoslovak secretary general.

Strougal's photograph as he shook hands with Gorbachev appeared on all the front pages of Soviet newspapers, tending to corroborate the fact. Thus, it came as a surprise when the Central Committee of the Czechoslovak Communist party announced in November 1988 the stepping down of Husak and his replacement as secretary general Milos Jakes. Husak remained President of the republic and member of the party presidium. Rumours circulated in Prague at the time to the effect that Husak had accepted the decision of the party parliament with tears in his eyes. Confidential information emanating from Moscow made much of the fact that during the first ceremonial visit of secretary general Jakes to the Soviet leader, the fresh Czechoslovak leader was instructed to cooperate closely with Premier Strougal, ceeding to him perestroika-like reforms of the economic system and their execution at government level. He was supposed to concentrate on intra-party problems and political decision making.

However, it soon became clear that Jakes had not been appointed as a real "gensek", but a sort of stop gap, transitional leader. Thus, the neo-Stalinists found him weak and indecisive, the reformers unconvincing and confused, as if no 'agreement' existed. The former found it easy manoeuvre him to suit their interests, the latter could never obtain green lights for the implementation of reforms with which he agreed. Unfortunately for Jakes all his ambivalence quickly became public knowledge. A Czechoslovak TV crew interviewed him on his return to Prague from Moscow, where he had met Gorbachev for the first time as No. 1. The Czech public was convinced that the interview was 'sabotaged', designed to portray him as a selfish selfmade party hack hanging on to power from the start. In it Jakes appeared insufficiently briefed and his off the cuff remarks had sounded politically naive, if not outright silly, bordering on catastrophic. Later on both the reformers and hardliners took advantage of Jakes' mental incoherence to undermine his political position. Some of his impromptu speeches made at internal party meetings were taped and circulated in selected party circles, but also among dissidents, as entertainment. To all Jakes' reputation remained what it had always been, that of a pompous mediocrity. However, from the start, his reputation also reflected badly on the Czechoslovak government and its policies.

On the occasion of the 40th anniversary of the February coup d'Etat, Jakes floated his 'first perestroika idea' à la Tchécoslovaque. His plan for "a zone of confidence and cooperation in Central Europe", especially on the Czech and GDR frontiers with the Federal Republic of Germany was to reduce tensions and increase economic cooperation sounded as airy as any other past idea of his. Yet obviously the CP did not elaborate the idea properly and the Czechoslovak government was unable to offer the slightest suggestion for improving such relations and for increasing such cooperation. Similar questions raised by other West European countries how to improve relations and develop cooperation remained unanswered in concrete terms. The Czechoslovak side stuck to slogans only and empty, verbose proclamations which could be no solid basis for serious negotiations leading to the establishment of a zone of confidence in Central Europe.

Throughout 1988 all the communist, as well as Western observers could see that the Federal government was incapable of putting forward any new policies either at home, in the economic sphere, or abroad, in the field of foreign affairs. Since 1969 the position of Czechoslovakia had never been so dismal. A few governmental proposals to improve flagging economic performance were turned down by the party presidium fearful of their effect on political life. In more than one way the confusion was the result of a struggle within the hardliners camp, between neo-Stalinists and a more flexible group of communists. The latter were willing to let through purely economic adjustments, but the former succeeded in blocking any attempt at modernization of the economy and any move toward democratization in the political system. In the end the neo-Stalinist group blamed not Jakes, but Strougal for these failures. He was forced to resign as Federal Prime Minister. Nonetheless Adamec, Strougal's successor, just like his predecessor, searched invain for ways of modernizing the economic management, under the impact of a worsening economic situation. Though Adamec, just like Jakes, was an "apparatchik" without much imagination, he quickly realized the urgency of economic reform to avoid collapse. Inevitably the disputes between government and party leadership about reforms became as fierce as when Strougal was in charge with no solutions nor compromises in sight.

The new Soviet moves toward real detente in Europe were never fully accepted by the party leadership and government in Czechoslovakia. Yet the cold war tensions were rapidly diminishing as result of the new situation emerging in Europe after Gorbachev's initiatives. The new wind of detent was enough to sweep away any official attempts by Czechoslovak foreign policy executives to keep the country in the old cold war ways. Eventually, after some back pedalling in the party presidium, the German Chancellor, Helmut Kohl, and the French President, François Mitterand, were invited to pay official visits to Prague.

While Chancellor Kohl's visit went without a hitch, above all the first ever visit of a French President to communist Czechoslovakia was an event most unwelcome among party officials. It might have been possible to postpone the visit as suggested by the French government to mark the 70th anniversary of the founding of the Czechoslovak republic, for which France could claim some credit. However, Husak and Jakes would not have. However, in December, once the French President was in the country the communist leaders found it impossible not to allow the distinguished visitor to ask leading Czechoslovak dissidents to have breakfast at the French Embassy in Prague with him. In addition Mitterand's speech at an official meeting in the Prague castle gave a tremendous boost to the morale of every Czechoslovak democrat and dealt a deathblow to communist international prestige.

The similarity of Mitterand's and Gorbachev's views on and handling of European detente policy in their Prague speeches was strikingly evident and gave credence to the wrong impression, gained by both official and unofficial Czechoslovaks from the visit, of a coordination between France and the USSR on European problems. For the

Czechoslovak government the wrong impression made it increasingly difficult not to accept invitations from both sides of the European continent to cooperate in establishing a new pattern of relations between East and West. Moreover, at the end of 1988, after a document was agreed on in Vienna at the conclusion of another Helsinki follow-up meeting, during which not only disarmament was discussed, but also the human rights dimension of the CSCE, it became virtually impossible for a communist government signatory to prevent top foreign visitors from entering the country. This opened the floodgates of Western influence.

***

In time, however small, certain amelioration in the field of Human Rights did occur, largely as a result of the new situation in Europe and visits from prominent politicians. The creation of a "Committee of the Czechoslovak Public for Human Rights and Humanitarian Cooperation" was a response on the part of the CP leadership to the new orientation of European politics. Nonetheless it was hoped that nothing would come out of this formal gesture.

After the Czechoslovak government's acceptance in principle and formal signature of the Vienna document, hitherto unheard of concessions followed. Thus it had to permit a non-governmental meeting to take place, convened to celebrate the 40th anniversary of the signature of an Universal Declaration of Human Rights by an overwhelming majority of United Nations members on December 10, 1948. The meeting which for the first time gave a chance to top dissidents, formost among whom a playwright, Vaclav Havel, to speak in public without being disturbed by police. This event clearly demonstrated to the population at large all the weakness of the tough 'normalized' communist regime.

In an effort to give some international credibility to the "Committee of the Czechoslovak Public for Human Rights and Humanitarian Cooperation" the communist authorities were obliged to accept among its leading members several personalities who had been at times labelled as "enemies of socialism" such as Emil Zatopek and others. Instead of being another ploy manipulated by the federal government this committee became a source of support for people, largely dissidents, who found the communist authorities particularly unresponsive in the area of Human Rights, despite the positive development in Gorbachev's USSR.

The beginning of 1989 was marked by another anniversary event, the "Palach Week". A peaceful demonstration in the Wenceslas Square in Prague on a peaceful Sunday was dispersed by police using tear gas, dogs and water cannon. The next day, on January 16, Vaclav Havel was re-arrested together with other dissidents, because they had laid flowers on the spot where, exactly twenty years before, Jan Palach had set himself on fire in protest to Soviet occupation of the country. Throughout the 'Palach week' Wenceslas Square remained a theater of peaceful demonstrations and less peaceful rioting, in which only once did the police refrain from intervening. At the week-end the police stopped people entering Vsetaty, a small town in the vicinity of Prague, where they wanted to lay flowers on the grave of Jan Palach. The contrast between the USSR's and Czechoslovakia's implementation of perestroika was signficiant. While dissidents in the former country were released from prison, in Czechoslovakia they were repeatedly arrested. The decision of a court in Prague to send Vaclav Havel to jail for nine months, provoked a wave of protestations, not only in the Czechoslovak Republic but also abroad and even in other communist countries. The Czechoslovak authorities were surprised by the strength of the reaction everywhere and agreed to free Havel conditionally after serving half his sentence.

Czech dissidents and former communists knew well in advance about the contents of the Vienna document. They tried hard to exploit this foreknowledge by founding new human rights organizations in order to implement the principles and ideas expressed in the document 'legally', with official approval. However, official requests at the Interior Ministry for legalization of such an organization were repeatedly turned down. These officials argued that time provision for a legal recognition had to be allowed for the Ministry to arrive at a decision. In the meantime former communists tried to launch an political organization called "Obroda" (Revival) whose aims coincided with the ideas of 'Socialism with a Human Face'. It was a great improvement when compared to the past, since such organisations were neither 'legally' recognized nor banned.

Encouraged by this show of tolerance another organization, the Association for the European House, addressed itself to the problems of the Helsinki process within Europe. It based its action on the final document of the Vienna follow-up meeting. The name was taken from Gorbachev's figure of speech in one of his past policy statements. As such it was officially supported by the Czechoslovak government. Other similar organizations went even further and gained much less government support. One of them proclaimed openly as its philosophic basis ideas of democracy, whose reference to 'democratic socialism with reference to the Socialist Internationale' failed to provoke official ban.

The fading of the cold war and the rise of perestroika policy in both international politics and internal affairs led many party officials, though not top leaders, to establish contacts with these new organizations. Premier Adamec even appointed a special assistant, Dr Oskar Krejci, for the liaison with dissident movements because official party policy was still inflexibly orthodox, leading inevitably into a blind alley. Inside the CP differences between hardliners (Bilak) and progmatics (Prime Minister Adamec) trying to modernize the state, the economy, the environment and so on reached a climax. The spring of 1989 was marked by dithering on the part of the party leadership which may have been an indication of the changing balance of power between these two factions.

A campaign in June 1989 for signing of another petition, "Just a few sentences" calling for the establishment of democracy gave the neo-Stalinists a pretext for getting tough with troublemakers. However, their power to act was limited. Henceforth organizers of the new associations, who had been able to take part in discussions with party officials, were branded as dissidents in various party documents serving as a guidance for rank and file. Party members were warned against associating with them and special lists of such persons were distributed through lower party ranks. But no association was banned, nor any dissident arrested. However, the general public had no knowledge of such new directives and cared even less. The popularity of dissidents or former communists, invariably and unjustly criticised in the mass media, soared ever higher, so as to make them real leaders of the population. In contrast party leaders looked more and more like generals without soldiers.

By then events abroad, particularly in Hungary and the GDR, made sure that the influence of "perestroika" among the Czech public became predominant. In fact Czechs and Slovaks wanted to imitate such examples. In the summer of 1989 the Austro-Hungarian border was opened, allowing tourists from the GDR holidaying in Hungary to go safely through Austria to the Federal Republic of Germany. There followed a mass exodus of citizens, particularly the young ones, from the GDR to the FRG: "they all voted with their feet for the democratic system".

Many GDR citizens on holiday in Czechoslovakia were interested in the same type of vote. They decided to camp in the gardens of the FRG Embassy in Prague - on extra-territorial premises - waiting for permits to travel from there directly to the West. Something similar took place in Warsaw. It was all very exciting for the Czech population, but they could not do likewise, since there was no other Czech state to go to.

Another perestroika initiave was launched in Berlin at the time of the celebrations of the 40th anniversary of the GDR. In a walk-about among citizens of the city, broadcast on television throughout Czechoslovakia, Gorbachev expressed the view that, when a government is not able to create suitable conditions for normal life, the population is entitled to put pressure on it. Soon enough large demonstrations occurred in various East German towns and cities. With the slogan "We are the People" demonstrators were demanding far-reaching changes in the social and political life of the GDR. This is where perestroika, as paradoxically practised in 'orthodox' East Germany, proved most influential. Such examples of perestroika could easily be followed and imitated by the entire Czech population.

Another example imitated by the Czechs and Slovaks from East Germany proved destructive. Among the slogans scanded by the growing crowds of demonstrators in the GDR was "We are one nation". It proved to the whole of Europe the width and depth of national feeling existing among German citizens. If this mass sign of integral nationalism pointed the way to an eventual process of re-unification of the two German states, its appearance in Europe boded ill for the rest of Central and Eastern Europe. For Czechoslovakia it potentially meant the end of the unitary state; in Yugoslavia it meant civil war. However, at the time this consequence of resuscitated nationalism was not at all considered and the Czech and Slovak opposition forces, as well failed to appreciate it.

By the time of the fall of the "Berlin Wall" the Czechs finally saw clearly how push down the perestroika disrupted edifice of communism. Practically all the other communist states followed the same pattern with minor variations according to the conditions prevailing in each country. The time of instinctive mass imitation by entire populations had arrived. Just like everywhere else a student demonstration was permitted in Prague on the occasion of the 50th anniversary of November 17, 1939. On that day Czech university students in Prague demonstrated against German occupation of Bohemia. They were brutally dispersed by troops and one students died of wounds. Czech universities were closed down and thousands of students were sent to "Konzentrationslagern" and forced labour in Germany for the duration of war. This anniversary celebration also ended tragically, with a brutal charge by the communist police in which many students and other demonstrators were injured. Inevitably a rumour had it that one student had been killed, arousing violent widespread anger against not only the police but also the communist party and its unpopular regime.

This 'attack on innocent youths' was the Czech start of the "Velvet Revolution", a clear byproduct of a sequence of events triggered of by Soviet perestroika. The foundation of "Civic Forum", which embraced all the democratic forces in Czechoslovakia, made it possible for a group of representatives to open negotiations with the moderate members of the communist leadership under Prime Minister Adamec.

There followed a decision by workers of Prague factories to join forces with students, actors and artists in a general strike to support "Civic Forum". This demonstrated the total isolation of the old communist party leaders, but it was the mass participation in the wave of protests that brought down the communist regime. The neo-Stalinists had lost all influence and the 'moderates' accepted to cooperate with the nascent political force, Civic Forum, in the creation of a "government of national reconciliation". The CP's apparat collapsed and spontaneously new leaders were taking over. The 'election' of playwright Vaclav Havel as President of the Republic signified the smooth takeover by the emerging opposition. These two steps amounted to a full victory of the "Velvet Revolution" in Czechoslovakia.

There is no doubt that Soviet perestroika played a decisive role in the collapse of communism in Czechoslovakia. In international conditions in 1989 its repercussions proved fatal, while in 1968 they had combined to defeat the 'Prague Spring'. In 1968 the Soviet leadership had been able to throttle "Socialism with a Human Face", but since 1985 Gorbachev's "perestroika" had prepared the ground for the collapse of the communist regime in Czechoslovakia as elsewhere. Unexpectedly Soviet perestroika made possible the re-birth of democracy in this country.

Perestroika and Germany

Wilfried von Bredow

The first important story run by the weekly Der Spiegel about Mikhail Gorbachev as supreme leader was published in July 1985. Even its headlines expressed a certain mistrust of the new Soviet leader: "Stalin's heir - Soviet Tsar Gorbachev". In the same year, Der Spiegel published another story concerning the secretary general of the Soviet Communist Party. However, this time the attention was focused on Gorbachev's personal life: "Raissa Gorbachev - The Woman in the Kremlin" (11.11.1985). This was quite unprecedented. Never before did the weekly show the slightest interest in the family life of Soviet leaders. However, in this case Raissa Gorbachev appeared as a kind of a shooting star in the international league of at the same time serious and glamorous women worthy of investigative journalism.

In years that followed 1985 Gorbachev and his policies-perestroika had become a regular feature of Der Spiegel. Attention was centered on his personal characteristics and peculiar charisma that they inspired in the West in general and in Germany in particular. By then all German public media joined in. In December 1988 Der Spiegel proclaimed Gorbachev "Man of the Year - Man of the Hour" In June 1989, when Gorbachev visited the Federal German Republic he was greeted with open enthusiasm by politicians and the crowds alike. In December 1990, when he was given the Nobel Peace Prize, the popularity of Gorbachev in Germany reached its apogee: he could do nothing wrong. He was regarded by most Germans as the man really responsible for the unification of the two German states. However, even in 1993, Gorbachev as ex-President, has a special status in Germany. The public is interested in him as a person and in his political activity since the collapse of the USSR, which in particular helps with the promotion of his book of memoirs.

The "Gorbachev factor", his personal appearance and his ability to respond to Western media's 'show bus needs' have obscured to a certain degree Gorbachev's real political performance. As it happened he launched his reform programme with a slogan "back to

Lenin" and wanted glasnost and perestroika to make socialist society more flexible. When he was forced to resign, he did so because there was no more the USSR nor socialist society. THis article is not intended to analyze Gorbachev's policies, nor give judgements on his achievements or failures. Instead, it will be attempted to give an account of the West German perception of Gorbachev and his endeavors to reform the USSR. At the outset it should be said that the German perception was on the whole inadequate. This inadequacy on the part of the German political leaders (with only very few exceptions) and of the public was not speciafically German, for other Western countries experienced the same phenomenon. However, within the context of West Germany's foreign policy, especially her Ost- und Deutschlandpolitik, this misperception was mitigated. Usually, such misperceptions in politics lead to wrong decisions and therefore to political damage. In this case, the course of events- the end of the East-West conflict and subsequent unification of Germany and Europe- was not distorted by these misperceptions.

The Decline of the East-West Conflict

In the Federal German Republic in the first half of the 1980s, the public political discoruse was dominated by the issues of peace and disarmament. The NATO double-track missile decision of December 1979 and the Soviet reaction to it, namely the disruption of all arms control negotiations, created a general feeling of insecurity, Kriegsangst, and a growing Anti-Americanism in West Germany. The German peace movement began to organize demonstrations against the security policy of the government. The influence of the peace movement was rapidly increasing. For the time it had reached and influenced people of social status traditionally immune to anti-militarist propaganda.

As a consequence the social democratic-liberal coalition of Chancellor Helmut Schmidt had lost the support of the majority of the Bundestag, chiefly because of its continued support for the NATO-oriented security policy and the INF deployment on West German territory. Many social democratic Bundestag members refused to follow their political leader. By 1982, a conservative-liberal coalition took over and under the leadership of Helmut Kohl (and Hans-Dietrich Genscher as Foreign Minister), has stayed in power for more than a decade. The new German government proved strong enough to resist the charms and pressures of the peace movement. It found itself in a luckier position than the previous coalition. The International climate of East-West relations began to change in the middle of the 1980s. Though the first term of Reagan's presidency seemed to have renewed the Cold War conflict, his second term brought about a breakthrough in arms control between the USA and the USSR. Eventually not only the renewed cold war came to an end, but also the East-West conflict, the most important structural conflict of international relations in the 20th century.

In 1985 the West Germans felt relieved by this development. Many had thought that the very deployment of Pershing II missiles would bring about an immediate nuclear response of the USSR. Others were concerned about the further development in inter-German relations, built successfully over the previous decades and practically untouched by the icy climate between the East and the West between 1980-1985. Government and opposition, the media and captains of private industry had demonctrated their goodwill towards the socialist regimes of Eastern Europe by stressing as many common points of interest as possible, by channelling huge financial credits into Eastern Europe and by looking for a modus vivendi between the ideologies of marxist-leninist socialism (communism) and Western democratic socialism.

In 1985, most evidently such a political and discoursive constellation proved extremely favourable to the new Soviet leader, Mikhail Gorbachev. After the long years of stagnation under the zombie-like Brezhnev and his two successors, Gorbachev appeared as the man for new initiatives in Soviet domestic and foreign policy. He did not disappoint them. Almost immediately after his accession to power new initiatives began to be launched right and left.

Needless to say, Western politicians found it difficult to determine whether Gerbachev's vision of a complete and general nuclear disarmament and his other arms control proposals were meant seriously, or whether they were just a political charade as before. In the Federal Republic, with its background of Anti-Reaganism and its relief over the removal of the threat of nuclear war provoked by the West, Gorbachev became instantly very popular. Der Spiegel (18.11.1985) praised Gorbachev's 'noble dream' of a modernised, democratic USSR within a peaceful, international environment in no uncertain terms. However, the journalists who followed Gorbachev during his official visit in France, were even more impressed by the Soviet leader's knowledge of the rules of the Western public media game. Thus, in an interview on television Gorbachev was asked about the fate of political prisoners in the USSR. French commentators gave him a chance to refute convincingly their "their fanciful assertion that 4 millions of Soviet citizens were prisoners for political reasons". However, Gorbachev's proud answer to this 'insinuation' was "this is absurd, you know, it reminds me of the propaganda of Goebbels." The Spiegel journalist classified the answer rather weak, but was nevertheless impressed by the personality of the new leader.

This episode was repeated in a certain way in October 1986 in an interview of Chancellor Kohl with the American weekly Newsweek. At the time the West German government was not yet convinced of Gorbachev's good intentions. During the interview Kohl compared Gorbachev's knack for efficient propraganda with Goebbels' ability to dominate the propaganda apparat of German National Socialism. This clumsy comparison stirred up a storms of indignation, mainly in the Federal Republic, where Gorbachev was already considered the greatest reformer of the USSR and the world's 'greatest peace monger'.

Perestroika as the New Testament of Tired Left

It may appear an inappropriate penchant for political science to analyse fringe groups of the West German political system when considering its reception of perestroika ideas. Nonetheless it is not eccentric at all, but rather significant. It was exactly these fringe groups which issued first triumphant statements when it became known that the new Soviet number one was launching a sweeping reform of socialism within the only superpower to oppose world imperialism. The fringe groups of West German academic circles were well prepared for this volte de face. In the 1980s Soviet policies had gained a certain credibility in these circles, not so much for the actions they resulted in, but rather on account of Soviet peace propaganda and a certain anti-Americanism.

On the other hand Gorbachev and his proclamation of such slogans as "new thinking" or "Common European House" elicited a comparatively sober response from the leaders of the Moscow-affiliated German Communist Party (DKP). They were evidently politically attached to East Berlin and the ruling party of the German Democratic Republic and there Gorbachev's reform statements were regarded with instinctive distrust. However, soon afterwards the DKP leaders were forced to change their minds about Gorbachev when confronted with the enthusiasm of their rank and file. In any case the DKP's attitudes were representative of only a small fraction of the left. More important for such political attitudes on university campuses and among German intellectuals in general were the floating unorthodox left consciences, particularly among university social scientists.

A typical German academic response to Gorbachev's rather diffuse and vague public atterances was a book by Professor of Philosophy at Free University of West Berlin and editor of the influential left-wing journal 'Das Argument'. This was a clear product of the German intellectual tradition for systematisation of ideas, even if, as it was in Gorbachev's case, there were not enough ideas to construct a system with. Wolfgang Fritz Haug's book was called "Gorbachev - Essay on the Cohesion of his Ideas" and its 500 pages were divided into four parts: the coordinates of perestroika; destruction of an apparat which produces apathy; revolution from above?; and the discovery of civil society. The author, a prolific and sometimes original marxist philosopher without the blinkers of obedient party men, stated in the introduction his conviction that "perestroika is based on consistent thinking and a solid analysis of the current reality, its dangers, possiblities and necessities...(His) study wants to contribute to a theory of perestroika.." He then demonstrated the deep and by no means surmountable gap between the political development in the USSR and its philosophical observation by German marxism.

Haug published as extracts from his voluminous study a collection of articles with three other baffled marxists trying to come to terms with Gorbachev's renewal of leninism. Haug's own hope was expressed in the following statement: "The USSR has begun a radical reform of socialism, and this means that the idea of a rebirth of marxism is no longer a rumination of isolated intellectuals; post-marxism is thus loosing its last legitimisation." However, a more skeptical view of Gorbachev's efforts was voiced by Frank Deppe, another marxist and influential political scientist. He took Gorbachev for a new type of political leader struggling with the problems and contradictions of the socialist version of modern society. He is reluctant to attribute to him the signs of ideological renewal, but praises him for his anti-capitalist stand. Haug's wishful thinking is replaced by Deppe's vagueness and a certain resignation: "The future of socialism will mostly depend on the progressive forces in the East and the West and whether they can make of this new policy (of Gorbachev) a practical success."

Clearly such hopes and predictions were never realised. The existential crisis of Western marxism was one of the causes for the breakdown of the USSR and its power bloc. There was no such thing as 'a theory of perestroika' and the 'progressive forces' everywhere (with a few exceptions chiefly in Third World countries) instead of supporting perestroika became increasingly more confused. Perestroika and glasnost never became the messages of a new socialist bible.

Social Democratic Responses to Gorbachev

In 1982 the Social Democratic Party (SPD) was forced to hand over the responsibility for the government of the country to the Christian Democratic Party (CDU), largely because of its refusal to accept the security policy advocated by Chacellor Helmut Schmidt. Additional reasons for SPD's dissatisfaction with its own government were the liberal coalition partner's (FDP) influence on social and economic policies, but they were secondary to the security considerations.

Henceforth the SPD had to act on the federal level as an opposition to which role it found difficult to adjust. In the first years after the loss of power the party continued to proclaim its dissention from Western security policy as a priority. Gorbachev's new approach to re-structuring of domestic and foreign policies only strengthened their opposition. The SPD thought that Gorbachev's reforms would have a positive impact on international security and East-West detente.

In 1988, the former SPD minister for the developing countries, Erhard Eppler, published a book about the 'potentiality of peace' both in the East and the West. At the time Eppler represented an influential faction within the SPD which was interested in the elaboration of party programme and in ideological questions. In a sense he was the representative of the 'emotional, academic left' of the SPD. In this capacity he headed the Social Democratic delegation to a number of intra-party meetings with the East German SED, particularly in 1986-87. The aim of these meetings was to define a common statement of ideological differences and common values. Such a statement should launch a new era of peaceful relations between communists and social democrats. Naturally, this idea was much criticized by the liberal-conservative government, but also by many anti-communist social democrats. The statement was finally published in August 1987, but had no measureable effect on the relations of the two German states. After the fall of the Berlin wall in 1989 social democrats tried hard to forget this common statement.

In 1988 Eppler considered Gorbachev as a politician motivated by two ideas: to reform the inefficient economy of the USSR and to stop the ruinous arms race. Both ideas were intertwined as the arms race was a heavy financial burden for the USSR. For Eppler nuclear war had to be eliminated as a political option and this should become a common aim for both superpowers. Gorbachev was depicted as a sort of pacifist, in contrast to the American President, Reagan, whose SDI projects were vigorously criticized as warmongering. In Eppler's eyes Gorbachev had already scored an important ideological point by conceding that 'capitalism and imperialism could live side by side without falling victim to militarism'. "This particular communist (Gorbachev) does not speculate on the decline and fall of capitalism, though his ideology tells him that it is inevitable. Instead he presupposes common concepts of the world for all..." This conclusion Eppler considered as the basis of Gorbachev's 'new thinking'.

A comparable view of Gorbachev and of his policies is expressed in the same year by another prominent social democrat, Egon Bahr. In the early 19880s, as a member of the International Palme Commission, he propagated a new kind of approach to East-West security problems. His proposal was labelled "common security". It was based on the principle that in a world of nuclear bipolarity it was in the interest of both superpowers to avoid nuclear war rather than square their ideological differences. "Common security" was certainly not an original solution of the strategic problems, but it was a new approach. At this time, however, the American administration was more interested in confrontation with the USSR. Thus, Bahr's more cooperative approach fitted well with the policies of European social democrats who were opposed to what they perceived as "American hegemony". For Bahr it was a great victory when Gorbachev accepted 'formally and officially' the Palme Commission's concept of "common security". In a sense it was a significant change of Moscow's attitude towards security problems. Up to then Soviet military strategists had always avoided using Western terms and concepts in their formulations. In addition other social democrats, such as Willy Brandt, considered Gorbachev as an efficient and reform oriented polician and not a windpipe as of old. They greeted him with measured enthusiasm because they sensed behind his marxist-leninist terminology a real determination to disarm and a certain advance towards social democratic values. This analysis was confirmed increasingly frequently, especially after 1987. In the second half of 1988-89 Soviet conduct during the Vienna follow up CSCE conference was considered as a most promising development.

Genscherism

Perestroika and Soviet Foreign Policy

Michal Klima

Mikhail Gorbachev's accession to power in March 1985 marks a breakthrough as regards Soviet Foreign Policy (SFP) in the history of almost seventy years of Soviet power. This assertion reveals perhaps nothing new, but it makes it clear that under the "Troika" leadership of Gorbachev-Shevardnadze-Yakolev the SFP pursued different, "post-imperial" foreign policy targets. In fact this obvious discontinuity not only demonstrates a radical break with Brezhnev's foreign policy and its impasses, but also indicates a fundamental deviation from the communist and even Leninist ideological principles. It marks the policy end of expansion by the largest empire in the world, built over four centuries. At the same time it endorses the belated collapse of an industrial feudal empire, the USSR, and inducts the Russian national state and other independent succession republics into international affairs. Since the end of the 20th century is characterized by the processes of interdependence and globalisation this Soviet development is contrary, in many ways also a landmark in world politics.

Why should the term of "post-imperial" foreign policy be coined? This question will be answered in the course of this article, but first of all the views of Gorbachev and his allies of Soviet reality will have to be assessed. They are found in the emerging process of "counter-ideology", i.e. in the rejection of ideological parameters being applied to concrete situations and actual conditions, both internal and external. This type of assessment is contained in the so called "new political thinking" (NPT), formulated by Yakovliev and applied by Gorbachev and Shevardnadze. Furthermore, it will be necessary to examine the internal and external environments for SFP and by means of NPT establish the limits of national consensus in both.

What was the legacy Gorbachev's regime inherited? In the first instance the USSR was the last, and the largest empire in the world, a superpower consisting of an inner-empire, the USSR itself, which contained non-Russian nationalities, and an outer-empire in Eastern Europe, WPT, containing a safety belt of satellites. Furthermore, it was an extended-empire of self-proclaimed communist countries in the Third World. This nebulous, ideological and all-embracing superpower had a dual role: one was to lead and represent the communist world movement and the second was to be the other pole in a bipolar world.

Ideologically, the Soviet superpower continued to act in accordance with the concept of "correlation of forces", which postulated a permanent movement of the balance of world power in favour of socialism, an ideological label of bureaucratic Soviet communism. In Soviet terms this meant that economic, political and ideological forces were working in conjunction with military power to maintain this inbalance, to accelerate the movement and achieve the aim of world domination. According to this reasoning the world revolutionary movement would move closer and closer to a decisive victory of 'socialism over capitalism', which also signified a victory of "good over evil". In this same context, peaceful co-existence was perceived as a temporary respite in the implacable march toward the inevitable victory. Military power, therefore, played the most significant, if not the decisive role in realising this worldwide ideological blueprint.

If the Soviet leadership perceived the concept of detente as a possibility for peaceful expansion and military growth, then the USA sought to limit this disruptive force of the USSR in world politics. Any Soviet offensive, expansionist move naturally brought about US counter-measures and 'counter-attacks'. During the decade 1976-1985 SFP did in fact pursue a global expansion by means of a series of military interventions. The main front was situated in the Third World, whence it was expected to produce a decisive shift in the correlation of forces in favour of socialism would come. Thus, the USSR was engaged in the entire "gamut of crises" that extended from the Middle East to South-East Asia. Moreover, Soviet military presence was apparent in Nicaragua, Salvador, Angola, and Ethiopia (with Cuban assistance). The Soviet military supermachine sent its fleet into the Indian Ocean and the boundaries with China were beleaguered by Soviet troops. However, the key elements of Soviet offensive capabilities remained located in Central Europe.

Even before the Soviet invasion of Afghanistan in December 1979, the Chinese leader, Deng Xiaoping, called for an anti-Soviet united front consisting of the Sino-American-Japanese-West European coalition forces to combat Soviet expansionism. In any case Soviet expansion provoked, in particular, an effort in the USA to counterbalance the Soviet military power with its own military build-up. This buildup started in the late 1970s under the Carter administration and was extended still further by President Reagan. Thus, by the beginning of the 1980's it was clear that Soviet expansion could not continue 'peacefully', without a Soviet armament 'counter-buildup'. Therefore, SFP found itself in more than one way (political, military and economic) in an impasse.

Reagan's Strategic Defense Initiative (SDI) was in fact an intense technological arms race and coupled with the counter-deployment of cruise missiles and Pershing 2's in Western Europe, and Soviet setbacks in the Afghanistan war it demonstrated publicly the limitations of Soviet military power. Such deterioration in the "configuration of forces" even posed threats to the Soviet Union itself. Moreover, the proceedings of the

Conference on Security and Co-operation in Europe (CSCE) and other series of parallel negotiations such as Mutual and Balanced Force Reduction (MBFR), the Intermediate-Range Nuclear Force (IRF) and the Strategic Arms Reduction (START) talks were deadlocked because of Soviet intransingence. Clearly, the USSR was in trouble, possibly in danger of nuclear war, and SFP's expansionism and militarism were responsible for the impasse.

Thus, the main problem of the USSR was the militarization of the country, both external and internal. It was this militarization which on the one hand enabled the USSR to play the role of a superpower, but on the other hand exhausted its ability to develop in other spheres; in particular, it now restricted its economic growth. Moreover, the gap between military expansion and economic decline was widening. Gorbachev's problem was how to reverse this process, if widespread social unrest was to be avoided at home and the threat of a global war averted abroad, either nuclear or conventional, or both. It was necessary to inject new realism not only in SFP but into domestic politics as well. In reality the phenomenon of militarization represented inner attributes and functions of the totalitarian system camouflaged by the ideological notions of socialism-communism.

This was the reason why Gorbachev's arduous task of demilitarization, that is the removal of the military burden from the economy and foreign policy had to start with a radical reappraisal of the operative concepts of communism, the so-called "socialist ideology". He was convinced that only a radical transformation of the rigid and militaristic ideology could alter the tenets of strategy and tactics in the SFP and improve the Soviet international position and domestic economy. By 1985 this seemed the only way to do away with the militaristic notions of international class enemy, capitalist encirclement and economic isolation.

For Gorbachev an immediate re-evaluation of principles governing the relations between communism and imperialism, became a top priority, if he was to make any headway in international politics. In addition such global questions as "What is to-day's world characterized by" had to be asnwered urgently. If the answer was "de-ideologization" or a rejection of 'socialist and Leninist' concepts, then Gorbachev's USSR might still have a chance to resolve its crises peacefully. Obviously such an approach could trigger a rapprochement between 'socialism and imperialism', which would narrow the gap between the two systems of the bipolar world. Instead of ideological struggle between capitalism and socialism, whose actual manifestation was the conflict between the USA and the USSR, convergence might take its place. Gradually international tensions would decline and would ultimately be transformed into a real detente. But ideology as a guiding principle for relations between the capitalist system and the "world communist system" would have to disappear.

Gorbachev became convinced that only such an "ideological somersault" could remove the ideological blinkers from the new Soviet leadership and thus begin the process of de-militarization of Soviet society, and the political (hegemonic) and military withdrawal from the various parts of the world. At the same time to reverse Soviet economic decline and deal with domestic crises successfully, it was indispensible for the Soviet superpower to carry out global retrenchment.

The new political thinking (NPT) embodied all the miracle remedies and became the strongest argument of the reformists against status quo. The first task was to "abolish the situation of cold war". That is, everything linked with ideological notions of international class struggle and correlation of forces had to be rejected. In turn, Gorbachev's team accepted new perceptions of the world and its various parts. This involved the most fundamental systematic re-assessment of the nature of "socialism" and "capitalism" and their relationship in a new world environment, end of the 20th century.

If the strategy of the correlation of forces towards socialism led in fact to the "second cold war" and caused economic decline in the USSR, then it was necessary to free the SFP from imposing worldwide, at least on paper, the interests of the proletariat and socialism. Such interests could not be enforced at the expense of peace and other human values the world over. Thus, the core of NPT advocated the ideological thesis that human values take precedence over the interests of any particular class, including the proletariat. This assertion was unprecedented and was closely connected with another philosophic self-evident argument, namely that the world is increasingly interdependent. Thus, Gorbachev's NPT began to play down the concept of international class struggle, that is the ideological struggle between socialism and capitalism, in favour of humanitarianism (human rights), globalism and interdependence. Gorbachev's statement "Our world is united not only by internationalization of economic life and powerful information and communication media, but also faces the common danger of nuclear death, ecological catastrophe and global explosion of the poverty-wealth contradictions of its different regions" [1] became the cornerstone of NPT.

Numerous other proclamations were added to the new body of doctrines by other reformists such as Yakovlev. For example, he insisted that in the context of a nuclear world, peaceful co-existence could no longer be seen as a specific form of class struggle: "The struggle between two opposing systems is no longer a determining tendency of the present-day era." [2] Thus, the confrontational model of international relations based on a Leninist concept of peaceful co-existence, reflecting class conflict was stripped of its ideological antagonism. There was no further room left for fundamental conflicts with the West based on territorial, economic or social interest clash. NPT represented the removal of confrontational elements at all levels of the concept of correlation of forces. That is, it blunted and later broke off the "offensive edges" of all parts of the world revolutionary movement, namely the expansion of socialist countries and the communist bloc, the expansion in a sense of social and national liberation struggle, and the confrontation of workers' and communist movements in the West. The "world revolutionary process" was made redundant and marginalized.

Thus, the international co-operation in defense of universal values superseded the ideological conflict between socialism and capitalism so far at the heart of international relations. To gain a different picture of the world, and redefine the Soviet role in it,

Gorbachev and the reformers had to proceed even further. When human interests have taken precedence over the interests of the international working class and socialism, the concept of the "international class struggle" was de-ideologized only by half. Consequently, to free the other half from the ideological animus the picture of capitalism had to be removed from the world class struggle. Up to now capitalism has been characterized as imperialism which represented a growing threat to the very existence of the human race and tended to exacerbate its own general state of crisis. In contrast to this definition, Gorbachev authorized a change in the perception of capitalism as expressed in his speech on the occasion of the 70th anniversary of the October revolution, repeated in another statement in February 1988. In it he posed the following fundamental question: "Is it possible at the present stage, given the interdependence and unity of the world at the end of the 20th century, to exert the kind of influence on the nature of imperialism that would block its most dangerous manifestations?" In a former speech in November 1987 he had posed three other concrete questions. The first asked whether imperialism could cope with its own aggression. The second referred to the first: Can capitalism free itself from militarism and function without it in the economic sphere? The final question asked whether the capitalist system could do without neo-colonialism. [3] Since Gorbachev's answers to all three of them were affirmative, the spectre of imperialism as a class enemy and universal evil was abandoned and removed from the body of operative doctrines.

To reformers such ideological transformations meant that the NPT, when put in practice, would inevitably lead to the cuts in the arms race and enable de-militarization of international relations in general, and the Soviet Union, in particular. Gorbachev's new view of the world also necessitated a basic re-evauation of the nature of war and peace. The Leninist notion that there could be no peace until socialism was established on a global scale had to be discarded. There followed the rejection of the Clausewitz's dictum that "war is the continuation of politics only by different means" as a communist doctrine. It was argued that nuclear weapons as well as modern conventional arms had become so destructive that they could not be used as a means for achieving political, economic or any other goals. This meant that international security was increasingly seen as a political problem, which could only be resolved by political means. The NPT stressed that security should not be based on the accumulation of military power, but on such political measures as arms control and the peaceful settlement of regional conflicts.

Outdated views on and obsolecence in the usage of weapons of mass destruction were rectified by the reformers. Ideological modernization was closely connected with the globalization in the economy, communications and many other aspects of world affairs. The Leninist notion of national security was also altered by the realization that the security of the planet earth had become indivisible. This conclusion gave rise to the idea of a "comprehensive system of international security" (CSIC), first mooted at the 27th congress of the CPSU in 1986. [4] International security was no longer simply defined as a military problem, but had to be tackled as a complex and global problem. Security could no longer be seen as a matter for one country, but for the whole world at political, military, economic and ecological levels, influenced by humanitarian considerations, such as human rights. Thus, Gorbachev's NPT proclaimed the need for a different balance between political and military instruments in foreign policy. Quite logically this concept led to a revolutionary shift in Soviet military strategy and made possible a reduction of the military expenditure, in any case an excessive burdon imposed on Soviet economy, distorting the very development of Soviet civilization.

As for the Soviet military strategy, the NPT introduced a dramatic shift from offensive to defensive principles. This represented a novel formulation of Soviet military doctrine dictated by Soviet political leaders. The new 'doctrine' was couched in terms of the concepts of "reasonable sufficiency" and CSIS. This meant that the Soviet military leaders should not seek to build up both nuclear and conventional forces to win a major war, but should concentrate on 'defensive sufficiency'. This ideological bidding implied that nuclear war or a large-scale conventional war could not be won in Europe. Military strength all round was no longer the distinguishing mark of the superpower status but rather the reason for its decline, since the notions of imperialist enemy and international class struggle were no longer relevant. The world was so over-armed as a result of the current concepts of strategic deterrence and the balance of terror (MAD-Mutually Assured Destruction) in the past forty years, that both sides had to reduce their nuclear arsenals as well as weapons of mass destruction and conventional arms. Almost immediatly the Soviet superpower started cutting its military expenditure in order to reverse the process of its economic decline and to abandon its position of isolationism and to finally engage in the interdependence of today's civilization. This rapprochement was not merely associated with the phenomenon of disarmament in the Soviet Union itself. The process also referred to military forces located in most parts of the world (i.e. particularly the Third World regimes established by Soviet arms.)

At this point it should be noted that the NPT represented nothing new, neither surprising, nor original. In fact it adopted older concepts of the 1970's from Western social sciences, such as "transnationalism" and "globalogical" approaches or the "functionalist" views. For example, Western functionalists maintained that contemporary global problems in international politics could neither be eliminated nor even reduced, unless a greater social, economic and political co-operation was achieved on earth. Neither one country nor a whole region could insulate itself against the effect of global problems. The solution lay in inventing new ways for global political organizations to tackle such problems, possibly create new international bodies. All these 'innovations' were slightly out of date, even if accepted by practically the whole world community. No one showed any astonishment when Foreign Minister Shevardnadze at the United Nations General Assembly session in 1987 made his 'extraordinary' statement to the effect that the USSR sought a world in which peace was ensured "exclusively" by the UN and its Security Council and not by the two superpowers. [5] However, for the communist world the new political thinking was something revolutionary, in fact a new ideology contradicting the hitherto recognized Leninist tenets of "marxism-leninism". As it was, it, therefore, developed very gradually over years and took Gorbachev some considerable time before proclaiming it openly and fully as the official ideology. Additional complications arose once the new ideology began to be implemented.

The NPT as an ideology of the reformists consisted of "de-ideologized", "de-militarized" and "post-imperial" tenets that had to be pursued with utmost caution. It emerged "step by step", disturbing the long-set pattern of communist thinking and feeling, which were the outward expressions of considerable political, military and economic interests in Soviet society. In addition, to understand the transformation processes of SPT, they must be assessed in view of the NPT and in the context of the broader revolutionary streams of Soviet Perestroika. Perestroika itself pursued broad but gradual systemic changes, from the present monolithic toward a pluralistic society, from a party system towards a genuinely political one. Within the political system the NPT generated an almost permanent shift in the balance of power from the CP leadership towards all sorts of leaders, be they officials, academics or intellectuals. The decisive turning point came in 1988 with the transition from the blatantly party to the presidential system. This phase of development was the most dangerous for the Soviet Union: a transitional hybrid system with the still dominant Communist party in its centre, but with a strong and quickly emerging institutional basis of a pluralistic society. It served as an important transitional period when elements of dual power were put in place. This phase was characterized by structural instability and by increasing tensions in society.

The Communist party itself illustrated the processes of social differentiation and diversity of interests which made the appearance of new significant elements of competitive politics inevitable. The Communist party symbolised not a traditional political party in the Western sense, but a certain kind of corporation, a type of medieval structure. In one sense the Communist party was a scale model of Soviet society. Under Gorbachev's leadership the party was evolving and gradually came under the same process of differentiation as society as a whole. This development is best demonstrated by the fact that former Communists either created or played a more or less important parts in the establishment of the whole spectrum of newly emerging political parties, from the Right to the Left.

At the time of the 19th party conference in 1988 the Communist party was characterized by its Democratic, Centrist and Marxist platforms (with other factions on the fringes). In this guise it also paradoxically bore semblance to Sartori's 'polarized pluralism' of his CP typology. This polarized pluralism was at the time represented by three major political forces: revolutionary-democratic, centrist and conservative. Such a polarized party adopted practically all the major attributes of full pluralism, such as "bilateral opposition", "centre positioning", "centrifugal drives" and "ideological patterning". In this sense, Gorbachev and his allies consciously accepted their role in the centre of multipolar competitive mechanics. Such a centre-based system was rested on a tacitly acknowleged assumption that the central area-base is out of bounds for competition. That is why, such a political system, and in this case the Soviet Communist party, discouraged 'centripetal drives' leading to centre-fleeing, or centrigugal processes which in turn produced extremist politics.

Thus, Gorbachev in applying his perestroika policy at large had to respect the rules of such a balance of power within the CP. Nonetheless, such a permanent balancing caused waves of instability all round. From 1985 onward, Gorbachev had to move toward general democratization very cautiously so as to retain control of the transformation processes and avoid disrupting the entire system. In 1991 this gradual shifting of the power balance was broken by conservative forces. So that when consideration is given to Gorbachev and like-minded reformists, no real people with their own interests and reactions come under it. Such considerations merely describe statements, articles and decisions of politicians involved in a dangerous power game to which strict rules were applied and had to be observed. For these "unreal people" the foremost political commandment was not to be themselves, but to act in a pragmatic way. Why mention this aspect of domestic policy? Simply to point out the circumstances under which the SFP found itself and the limitations to wich it was subjected.

In this context it seems pertinent to point out that the SFP played a progressive role in foreign relations, but also intiated democratic changes in domestic area. In this respect SFP could be seen as a tendency in the Perestroika evolution somewhere ahead of the centre position of Gorbachev's official domestic reform policy. The following figure demonstrates the dynamic aspect of the power balance:

Revolutionary democrats

Totality   Conservatives centre   Plurality

Perestroika may have been one entity, but the term referred to both, domestic and foreign policies, with significant differences between them dictated by the different environments in which they had to be applied.

It follows that the centre, embodied by Gorbachev, had to use flexible and opportunistic tactics of compromise to pursue successfully its overall strategic aims. Sometimes its progression could be labelled "one step back - two steps forward", at other times exactly the reverse. From the autumn of 1990 the march of "two steps backward" leading to the unsuccessful coup d'Etat, was followed by "four steps forward" in the summer of 1991 after the coup. However, these tactics of compromise were in evidence throughout the whole period of perestroika strategy, particularly as applied to SFP. This was especially apparent in the strong pressures exerted against specific "measures" taken under SFP. The sustained opposition on the part of political and military hard-liners to the INF, CFE (Conventional Forces in Europe) and START treaties is the best example. Moreover, efforts were made by these 'backwoodsmen' to violate the most basic provisions of these treaties. For instance, the transfer of thousands of tanks behind the

Urals instead of their destruction disturbed the CFE treaty's application. In this context, Shevardnadze stated: "I lodged a protest against this violation with the President (Gorbachev)...Marshal Sergey Akhromeyev, however, submitted a memorandum completely justifying this move". [6] In 1989 the loss of Central and Eastern Europe together with the Soviet alignment with the USA in the Persian Gulf crisis gave rise to unprecedented assaults on reformers by conservatives, leading to Shevardnadze's resignation in December 1990, also connected with the evolution of domestic situation. Stephen White points out in his book how slowly and gradually did the NPT emerge in SFP. This contention, however, indicates that the basic notion and structure of the NPT existed within the CP system even before Gorbachev's accession to CP leadership in March 1985. He traces the necessary stages particular parts of this new "ideological construction" through which they had to pass to be "smuggled onto the Soviet political scene". Moreover, significant differences in Gorbachev's speeches could be detected according to whether they were intended for domestic or foreign consumption. Thus, Gorbachev, at the ideological conference in December 1984, violently accused capitalism-imperialism of resorting to wars and international terrorism. Yet later, in the same month, he had considerably altered the accusatory tone in a speech to British Members of Parliament. In it he expressed his wish for renewed international dialogue and cooperation. He emphasized "the new way of political thinking" used by the Soviet in the atomic age of an interconnected world with global problems. In February 1985, Gorbachev singled out European integration as of interest and expressed his hope of setting up "our common European house". Gorbachev's speech on his election as party leader addressed itself to the notion of a "peaceful, mutually advantageous cooperation" with the capitalist world, which could lead to a complete elimination of nuclear arms. In April 1985, he stressed again the importance of civilized inter-state relations based on a genuine respect for international law. He also and publicly re-iterated the idea that there was no "fatal inevitability in confrontations" and that "new progressive and democratic forces" had appeared in capitalist countries to make such confrontation avoidable. [7] It is surprising how many elements of the NPT were present in Gorbachev's speeches as early as 1985. Of course, these first realistic terms were counter-balanced by orthodox banalities, "wrapped up in the old goods official ideology" such as "aggressive imperialism" and so forth.

Another striking characteristic of this stealthy ideological development is worth pointing out. For legitimacy's sake Soviet political leaders had to follow the logic of political struggle dictated by Soviet history, namely to be in undisputed possession of the "deposit of truth". Just as Stalin usurped the ideological heritage of Lenin and proclaimed him and consequently himself infallible, so did Gorbachev and other reformists. They had to take up the ideological arms of Leninism to prove their fidelity to communism. Once again Lenin's views and generalizations were adjusted to fit the current interests of Soviet leaders in power. In October 1986, Gorbachev conformed to this logic as he declared that "Lenin in his time expressed an idea of collosal depth - concerning the priority of the interests of social development, of all human values, over the interests of one or another class". Similarly, Shevardnadze elaborated on this in July 1988 by stating that "peaceful co-existence was acquiring a new meaning in the light of this concept, and condemned as 'mistaken' and 'anti-Leninist' the views expounded during the Brezhnev years, namely that peaceful co-existence was a specific form of international class struggle." [8] Thus, the new axioms of the NPT were placed under Lenin's protective auspices. The paradox was that, at the time, it was not a simple matter of "removing from international politics deformations of Leninism", for which Gorbachev's predecessors and himself declared themselves more than ready. What was involved this time was a conscious and thorough liquidation of basic Leninist tenets: the role of class struggle in international relations was linked with the concept of peaceful co-existence as a "specific form of class struggle" and the notion that peace could be established until socialism has won over capitalism all over the world, was discarded. Thus, the NPT was gradually abandoning 'revolutionary Leninism' in favour of a form of evolutionary social democracy.

While retaining a dynamic social consensus at home proved very difficult, the application of SFP in the West appeared much easier. The reason why the new attitudes were welcomed and developed into "Gorbymania" is clear. It meant the removal of confrontation in international relations as the Soviet Union retreated from its empire and began to create a more stable and predictable international environment. The SFP was successful with the international community because it had become less demanding. In additional Gorbachev and his entourage were skillful enough to fend off all Western attempts to take advantage of temporary Soviet weaknesses. This was particularly evident during the 'velvet revolutions' in Central and Eastern Europe when Western leaders did not seek neither further weakening of the inner Soviet empire nor hasten the demise of the Warsaw Pact as a whole. This Western approach was best demonstrated in the Malta summit meeting in December 1989 between Gorbachev and Bush. Among the apocaliptic upheavals the two leaders put a diplomatic end to the cold war and indicated the ways to manage Europe and world relations in future.

Moreover, in the summer of 1991 Bush warned Gorbachev of the imminence of a coup against his power. Afterwards the West continued to support the Soviet leader even he had clearly lost. Territorial integrity of the inner empire was recognised almost to the last minute, when it dissolved itself of its own. It seems that, between Gorbachev and the Western leaders there existed a tacit agreement to retain the stabilized transformation of the USSR and Europe as a vital strategic target. This could be taken to represent some kind of alliance among world humanitarian forces against conservatism and militarism personified by the Soviet hard-liners and other cold war warriors. In this context Aspaturian wrote: "...The coup plotters maintain that they were repeatedly confronted with accomplished facts and giveaways made in the negotiations with representatives of foreign states without prior warning or discussion." [9] The West was solidly behind Gorbachev and reformers.

As was mentioned above, the process of de-ideologization, de-militarization and the shift in favour of humanitarianism, interdependence and globalism signified the existence of a different ideological framework and implementation of a new Soviet strategy of imperial retreat. The USSR as the other superpower was pursuing, without openly saying it, a smaller role in world affairs. Sestanovich gave two other examples of Soviet international diminution and retrenchment due to the increasing gap between extremely ambitious foreign policy and limited domestic resources. He cited the Egyptian President, Sadat, and the American leaders President Nixon and Secretary of State Kissinger, pointing out their ability not to produce a victory, but to orchestrate a successful retreat and likening their actions to those of Gorbachev and the reformers. In these comparative examples, Sestanovich's methodology can be questioned. Undoubtedly there existed important dissimilarities between the two periods, the 1970s and 1980s and above all between societies. Gorbachev and Soviet reformers inherited a society in deep economic, political and ideological crisis. Moreover, it was a society reflecting the distorted social development of the communist empire, in which the military cast predominated. They inherited a totalitarian system in control of at least one third of the planet, threatening by its excessive military power its very civilization. This is a substantially different situation from that of Egypt and the USA, whose military power, even if excessive, was firmly under civilian control. In view of Soviet circumstances it was indeed a miracle that the collapse of the Soviet empire did not bring about widespread human and material destruction.

This peaceful imperial dissolution was entirely due to Gorbachev's will to modernize and democratize the USSR in a completely different way. Those who merit the world's admiration for their brilliant strategy and tactics to bring about such tremendous changes are the communist reformers who gathered around the "Trojan Troika": Gorbachev, Yakovlev and Shevardnadze. They not only personified the Soviet cause of reform-perestroika, but also representated the worldwide intellectual revolution in an era of global civilization. Perestroika and its ideology - the NPT, thus represented the transitional phase, in which the USSR itself solved the problem of transforming society from a totalitarian to a democratic one. During this period SFP had to cope with excessive military and disproportioned imperial burdens. This was the reason why SFP appeared as a continuation of unilateral concessions without any clear "bottom line"-limit. The strategy of retrenchment was marked by such spoiling actions as unilateral and disproportional cuts in Soviet conventional weaponry, the IFN treaty (without counting British and French systems and without links with START), Afghanistan (troop withdrawal without conditions), China (with three conditions fulfilled), the reunification of Germany, the loss of Central and Eastern Europe, the withdrawal from many regional conflicts in the world and so forth. The process of retrenchment was consciously pursued to its bitter end leading from empire to democracy and bi-polar cold war to universal peace. The alternative interpretation is also on record: "The pace of decline can be slow and irregular, and clever politics can do a great deal to conceal its extent - from adversaries, from allies and clients, and from domestic audience alike." [10]

At this stage, the US academic analyst, Aspaturian, wondered whether Soviet policy was a purposive action or incompetence. His answer was yes on both counts. He also pointed out a kind of conspiracy theory underlying the process, as if a certain hidden agenda included Gorbachev's skilful, manipulated, gradual ouster of every member of Politburo and Secretariat, as well as the gradual elimination of the monopolistic role of the Communist party. He also drew attention to the fact that crucial decisions were not subject to public debate and were concealed even from the Politburo as a whole. "This inevitably reminds one of the very high-handed command-administrative system of decision-making criticized by Gorbachev and Shevardnadze, whereby a small handful of individuals had made the most critical decisions." [11]

It seems unclear whether the perestroika reforms went out of control. The well known speeches and articles of Yakovlev, who was the chief ideological architect of perestroika, exhorting the public spirited efforts in favour of fundamental changes as a necessary condition for the democratization of society, indicate that all was under control. On the other hand, the logic of perestroika and NPT seems in line with Shevardnadze's claims that his foreign policy was guided by a 'hidden agenda'. He indicated in his book how he told the German foreign minister, Gentscher, after the unification of Germany that he had come to that conclusion as early as 1986 and that such development was inevitable. He made similar comments concerning the loss of Eastern Europe, the collapse of the Warsaw Pact, and the erosion of Soviet military power in general. [12] What was the 'hidden agenda'?

If Lenin's political revolution in 1917 and Stalin's economic industrialization between 1927-34 represented the prolongation of the life of the Russian empire under a new ideological "label, then Gorbachev's perestroika meant undoubtedly the end of it all. This type of reasoning leads inescapably to the conclusion that the SFP during Gorbachev's perestroika period represented post-imperial foreign policy.

There remains another question to be answered, but one of vital importance. Were the processes of democratization really necessary prerequisites for a market economy and perestroika reforms as a whole? This leads to the following question: is not China's way out of the totalitarian state more appropriate that the USSR's? Can we compare China and the Soviet Union at all (insurmountable national and agricultural differences)? In this context it would be wrong not to stress a final consideration slightly tangential to the theme of the SFP.

In the USSR, as soon as the policy of perestroika was launched and the democratic element began playing a significant role, Soviet society received a formidable impetus with renewed dynamism. This phenomenon revealed a whole complex of hidden contradictions in the Soviet system, which started the inevitable erosion of the Soviet empire. The logical conclusion was inexorable. Such developments plunged the USSR headlong and led unavoidably to a configuration of interests that brought about the final collapse. As early as the autumn of 1990 the signs of the end were there. It was not only the loss of Eastern Europe as the outer part of the Soviet empire, but the domestic repercussions of this loss. It began to appear that the continuation of perestroika meant the end of the Soviet Union itself, particularly in regard of the Baltic states.

From then on Gorbachev became a "captive" of the conservative counter-offensive, which attempted to stem the decline. He wanted to break from the conservative grip to carry out the ultimate reform of the Communist party, consolidate economic changes and sign the new all-union treaty in the summer of 1991. This in turn precipitated the coup d'Etat and the break-up of the Soviet Union as a unitary state and a superpower in international relations.

Thus, from the very beginning the innermost nucleus of perestroika there was encoded with a logic of potential disruption. To sum up Gorbachev's leadership we could award him four medals of excellence: one for his courage in launching the process of reforms-perestroika; the second for his brilliant power game; the third for opting for humanism and the fourth for ending the cold war, allowing Eastern Europe to be free and so on. However, only the future will show the real consequences of the collapse of the Soviet empire and into what type of "post-Gorbachev" chaos the formerly communist one sixth of the world will turn into.

Bibliography

R. Sakwa, Gorbachev and His Reforms, Cambridge, 1990

S. White, Gorbachev and After, Cambridge, 1991

M. Light, The Soviet Theory of International Relations, London, 1989

M. Gorbachev, Perestroika, London, 1987

Materialy XXVII syezda KPSS, Moscow, 1986

August Coup d'Etat
End of Perestroika

Nicholas Bradley

I.

In 1985 M. S. Gorbachev's launch of perestroika was approved unanimously by the communist party leadership, but not by the apparat nor the nomenklatura. This disapproval increased with years that followed, especially when it became evident that Gorbachev, the supreme leader, really wanted to loosen the totalitarian structures of the Soviet system by means of glasnost and democratisation to make it more efficient. He came to this conclusion when he became convinced that without it the communist system simply could not be reformed. However, the supreme leader was a consumate party tactician, who until 1991 invariably anticipated all the internal moves against him and his perestroika by the apparat, preempting them in time. Thus, he had rid himself smoothly of the old guard, who elected him, before they could in turn dismiss him. Moreover, he manipulated their successors so skilfully that neither the radical nor the conservative factions, whom he balanced against each other, could ever be sure of whom Gorbachev really preferred. Nonetheless, the struggle for perestroika became essentially political, largely within the communist party. However, by 1989 a point of no return was reached after several quasi-democratic elections, when the party apparat as a whole considered itself definitely threatened and on the way of being gradually eliminated from power. Only a few hardliners survived these elections with power unimpaired. By then the uncoordinated conservative groups began to formulate in secret emergency plans for a political come back without Gorbachev.

It is generally agreed that the year 1989 was an important turning point of perestroika. By then all the chief components of Gorbachev's policies, glasnost, demokratizatsia and economic restructering had reached their apogee. The communication media were reasonably free, the political system was sufficiently reformed (or disrupted enough) to make a return to totalitarianism impossible and new economic laws were in force to convince everyone at home and abroad, including the USA, that this overall process of restructering was irreversible and that the USSR was on its way of becomimg a 'socialist democracy' with a 'socialist free market'. Despite the ambiguities and imperfections the totalitarian party systems ceased to function. All this was possible because the secretary general Gorbachev wanted it and because he had negotiated with the USA the abolition of the cold war, which since 1945 has always been the excuse and the principal hindrance to peaceful restructuring in the USSR. On the other hand this was also the time that the conservative forces finally mobilised themselves and decided on perestroika's reversal by means of a series of power coups culminating in a coup d'Etat.

On paper the conservatives still had an upper hand in all the organs of totalitarian power. Within the party the secretary general and his faction were increasingly isolated and conservatives were 'elected' to important new offices within the Central Committee (secretary Sheinin) or the vital 1st republican secretary of Russia, Polozkov. The elected bodies, the various soviets on regional, republican and union levels, were still controlled by a crashing communist majority opposed to perestroika. The central governments consisted of the same 'experts' almost exclusively drawn from the higher echelons of the communist party, who sabotaged the application of perestroika measures. Foreign affairs were under a tight communist control and the armed forces, too. The KGB remained an exclusive party domaine, though ostensibly under parliamentary control. Only public opinion was partially decontrolled, while the civil society, after a spate of 'unplanned, improvised and uncontrolled' elections, became an unknown quantity in reality rejecting Gorbachev's leadership, which according to it, incerased their difficulties rather than solved them. In such fluid circumstances it is now evident that no formal meetings could be convoked with a view of ousting Gorbachev and reverse the 'perestroika' development, but now doubt every conservative leader actively thought of it. Nonetheless, with hindsight it seems certain that the 'conservatives' began to act in a conserted way to achieve a reversal as early as 1987, when Gorbachev began to take steps to eliminate them one by one. In that year he finally selected the timid reformer, Marshal Yazov as his defence minister- though Lukianov determined this choice. To counterbalance this 'conservative' appointment still further he got rid of the radical 1st secretary of Moscow City, Boris Yeltsin, again on Lukianov's bidding. During the following year, after an extraordinary conference, which endorsed his 'socialist democracy' plans, Gorbachev was finally able to relegate from key offices, four arch-conservative rivals Talyzin, Ligachev, Vorotnikov and Cherbrikov and isolate Ryzhkov as the head of the federal government. Henceforth an ambiguous Kryuchkov headed the KGB, the plotting Lukyanov, his alter ego within the party and soon in parliament, were counterbalanced by Shevardnadze and Yakovliev within the supreme power circles. However, such tactical moves eliminating or balancing the most radical and the most conservative elements in the Soviet Union without democratic restructing solved nothing, except that both extremes now began to plot actively against each other or anticipate plots.

However, at this stage Gorbachev could not proceed with further restructuring without the aid of the army, the KGB and the military-industrial complex and preserve the Soviet Union as a unitary state. Moreover he mistakenly thought that he had Yazov as his client, Kryuchkov as his ally and Oleg Baklanov as his close collaborator in the party secretariat, all three key factors for moving forward to democracy or stopping the process of perestroika altogether. Cautiously Gorbachev confined Lukyanov and Boldin, both conservatives but personal friends of his of very long standing, with the task of gaining over the totalitarian institutions to his views and also making doubly sure of his control of these vital three power apparats. They were charged to swing these powerful 'corporations' as a whole behind Gorbachev and his perestroika. With hindsight this seems to have been the only serious tactical mistake that Gorbachev had made. Far from performing the tasks assigned to them Lukyanov began to prepare rather subtly a coup d'Etat against his own master, while Boldin covered up for him feeding Gorbachev with all sorts of misinformation. They both retained Gorbachev's confidence to the bitter end, but their appointments and rise in power made quite sure of a coup sometime in the troubled future.

The close cooperation of Lukianov and Boldin enabled the coup preparations to continue even after Lukianov had left the party secretariat to become Speaker of the newly elected Supreme Soviet by the National Congress. Throughout 1989 Lukianov went on building up his own 'structures' by means of appointing his clients and allies to vital positions for an eventual takeover. He had a failed and corrupt hack politician, Genady Yanayev, appointed as his deputy, after rejecting Shevardnadze and Nazarbayev for the post. He had the 1st Latvian secretary, Pugo, placed as chairman of the party control commission, before having him appointed as Minister of the Interior. As Ryzhkov would not be his client, not even an ally, Lukianov took a chance with the undistinguished finance minister, Pavlov, to enroll him as an ally in the central government. Late in 1990 he finally succeeded in having him appointed as Federal Premier. By that time he forced on Gorbachev to sanction either the dismissals or resignations of practically all the radical protagonists of perestroika, who remained in power after Yeltsin's ouster.

It became clearly visible that in the economy Gorbachev's perestroika was not working at all. Yeltsin's assertation that this was so because of Ligachev's sabotage was rejected even by Gorbachev himself. He was persuaded by Lukianov that Yeltsin was wrong and had to be kept out of power because of his unpredictibility and mischief making. However, in foreign affairs the cold war came to an end and the relations with the USA, thanks largely to Shevardnadze, improved beyond initial hope. This became the primary factor for further change and development of perestroika. It enabled Gorbachev to expect economic aid from the US and the West in general, to prop up his failing perestroika reforms at home and neutralise conservative opposition to them. However, by the end of 1990, Shevardnadze resigned unexpectedly because of the threat of 'a coup d'Etat'. Though Gorbachev disengaged in the Third World, signed a series of disarmament agreements and above all permitted Eastern Europe to go free, at home private enterprise, private farming and political plurality were not on the statute book. Ironically Lukianov and Kryuchkov were both involved in the international disengagement of the USSR, undoubtedly much against their will. Nonetheless the real credit for the 'loss' of Eastern Europe went to Shevardnadze, particularly as far as the conservatives were concerned. Ostensibly the Soviet Union was being reintegrated into the world system only gradually, whose full economic and political admittance would occur after the enacting of reforms establishing a really free market and liberal democracy, not before.

A. Yakovliev, the 'ideologist of perestroika' and since 1985 responsible for both political and economic democratisation, the most decisive aspect of Gorbachev's re-structuring, had suffered as years went by several setbacks. By the end of 1990 he was isolated by the conservatives within the top leadership, held responsible for the mischief caused by the 'pluralistic' suffrage of the National Congress and Supreme Soviet elections and particularly the republican elections in which the communist parties suffered an irreversible loss of power and decline in several of the 15 republics. He also persuaded Gorbachev that economic failures of perestroika should be counterbalanced by further democratisation. Without Gorbachev, however, Yakovliev was incapable of political action. He was easily outmanoeuvered within the party, lost his seat in the preasidium in July 1990 and was to be excluded from the party altogether on 15 August, even before the coup. On the other hand by remaining in Gorbachev's entourage-presidential council, he was able to infuse increasingly greater doses of democratic suffrage. This electoral democratisation became the features of subsequent elections, particularly the presidential ones. As a result, in March 1991, Yeltsin was finally elected Russian President with universal suffrage against multiple party and non-party candidates. Yakovliev also cried wolf, just like Shevardnadze in December 1990, about a coup. In fact Le Monde published his warning on the very eve of the August coup d'Etat.

By the summer 1991 all the personnes du drame were in positions to attempt to make fall Gorbachev and reverse the perestroika process. Though they all agreed that 'something should be done', it took them several months to overcome mutual distrust and form two loosely bound groups. All of them were waiting for something concrete to happen to serve as a pretext for launching a coup or counter it. The pretext was finally found in the two events scheduled for the summer of 1991. The summit meeting between Gorbachev and President Bush and subsequent economic aid to the USSR confirmed the ones in defending the status quo; and the signature of a new union treaty giving the republics genuine sovereignity and most of the powers that far detained by the Union was the final straw, for the others.

At the same time with this bipolar struggle the ousted Yeltsin was preparing his political comeback. Though it still depended on Gorbachev's benevolence he was now determined to stage it, if need be, outside the communist hierarchy. In March 1989 he was elected to the National Congress by an 87% majority and by a last minute gesture of a Siberian deputy even to the new Supreme Soviet, where neither Gorbachev nor Lukianov particularly wanted him. However, his election results were such that he could not be ignored. After the election of the Russian Supreme Soviet he was elected its president against the express wish of Gorbachev. Once in power in Russia Yeltsin began to build up parallel power structures to Gorbachev's union ones. In the summer of 1990 he left the communist party after telling its congress publicly and walking out in full view of the communication media. By March 1991 he was the only directly elected executive President in the USSR psychologically fully prepared parry off any coup directed against his power from whatever quarter it came.

II.

On the eve of the summit meeting Gorbachev had another warning driven home to him by the central committee session. Though ostensibly his proposed organisational changes of the party were endorsed by the central committee fiercer opposition to them was expected to them from the extra-ordinary congress to be convoked at the end of 1991. Full of confidence Gorbachev ignored Yakovliev's resignation as his senior presidential advisor in protest against the same session which renewed the President's self-confidence. However, the Union leader, whose falling popularity was not to be halted by the summit meeting with Bush in Moscow, as he had hoped, was still determined to bulldoze his way out of his political impasse by means of the communist party. Neither was it to restore his popularity with the economic aid coming from the USA. The meeting did, however, earn him an invitation to the G7 London meeting. Most disappointingly, as the US before them, the seven most industrialised countries were not prepared to grant Gorbachev's USSR massive economic aid before the establishment of a free market and full liberal democracy. The rejection of the much desired aid in a sense sealed Gorbachev's fate. Since he could not meet many of the aid conditions (Japan for example wanted the return of the two Kurille islands before granting the USSR a development loan), he finally alienated both the radicals and conservatives from himself. He had no choice but to put all his hope in the new union treaty, to convince the G7 countries that by it he transformed the USSR in a free confederation thereby more or less abolishing totalitarian communism. If the West remained unconvinced Lukyanov persuaded himself that Gorbachev reached the political limits and was on the way of committing suicide. He was determined to speak publicly against the treaty, before it was signed. The other plotters finally had a pretext for acting. Moreover, they had found out from Kryuchkov of a secret meeting between Gorbachev, Yeltsin and Nazarbayev, in the last days of July, at which the three agreed that the new confederation would require new leaders: Nazarbayev was to be Premier and Yazov and Kryuchkov were to be replaced. Thus, full of hopes in another political rebound and 'inevitable' Western aid Gorbachev left the Kremlin to take a vacation in the Crimea on 4 August 1991.

All went smoothly with the Gorbachev family. The Ilyushin 62 aircraft carried, apart from Raissa and Mikhail, also his daughter with her husband and the two granddaughters to the luxurious villa at Foros. The presidential aircraft was kept under surveillance at the military air base at Belbek near Sevastopol, while the rest of the journey was by limousine. All the security measures were executed by the 9th Department of the KGB which was in charge of transport to Foros, within the residential perimetre as well as the beaches and sea next to the presidential villa. Gorbachev brought with him two secretaries and both Chernyayev and Shakhnazarov were lodged nearby to be called to the villa whenever Gorbachev required them. The former was currently on duty looking after routine telegrams and preparing Gorbachev's new union speech. All other personnel, above all his presidential chancellor, Boldin, were left behind in the Kremlin to look after the exercise of power in Gorbachev's absence.

It is still a bone of contention whether Gorbachev dealt with any one else while in the Crimea. He claims in his memoirs of the coup that he remained put at Foros and that no one paid him a visit during this period. It is true that he had a whole battery of telephones on his desk which enabled him to dictate letters, send off telegramms and speak every day with Boldin. Apart from this administrative routine Gorbachev was drafting the mentioned report on current political situation with Chernyayev, listened to music and walked around in the immediate neighbourhood of the villa. However, it seems now most probable that he did more than what he claims to have done. It is probable that he spent the day of 13 August in Moscow. The reason for this top secret journey is obscure. According to certain witnesses he attended a full-scale meeting in the Kremlin with all the future plotters in attendance. It may be that the final details of the new union treaty had been discussed and approved. Unwittingly Gorbachev must have confirmed the plotters of his resolve to have a new union treaty they all feared. He returned to Foros the same day in the same military aircraft, not in the presidential plane. If this visit did indeed take place it was probably to reassure himself that all was right in the nerve centre of power. For the plotters it was a chance to make up finally their mind to launch the coup d'Etat. If Gorbachev seemed assured, the plotters failed to make up their mind once and for all. On the 18th, in the morning, before he was cut off from the world, Gorbachev seems to have received what can be considered the last chance visit from Marshal Yazov, whether he would do something to stem chaos and dissolution. It was only after this visit that the putchists finally went into action, without the President. Perhaps we shall know more about this visit in autumn 1992, when Yazov's indictement is ready. What is certain is that both antagonists misjudged each other. The putchists thought that Gorbachev would somehow sanction their coup, if not participate in it. Gorbachev remained convinced that he was all the time one step ahead of every one, able to outmanouevre all and sundry.

Curiously what finally helped to resolve the plotters' hesitations vis-a-vis Gorbachev was his slight accident. During a walk, on 14 August 1991, in the nearby hills Gorbachev had slipped and dislocated a vertebral disc which in turn trapped a nerve. Since he was in pain Gorbachev decided to call Dr. Anatoly Liyev, a lumbago specialist on 15 August. From Moscow Liyev asked for written orders so that he could clear his urgent visit his illustrious patient with the KGB. He was told that written orders were sent to the KGB already and he should have his permit in a few hours. Instead it took another day before the KGB gave him permission to attend to Gorbachev at Foros. He arrived on the 17th, relieved his pains and was firmly told that he would have to 'cure' the president by the 19th, as he had to return to Moscow on that day- to sign the new union treaty. Liyev was therefore asked to return next day to make sure that the president could undertake that important journey without pain. It now is certain that Kryuchkov, who was coordinating the plotters' moves exploited the fact of Gorbachev's disablement to give the coup a constitutional cover. If Gorbachev refused to back the plotters, they would use his 'ill health' as a excuse to power takeover.

At the time of Dr. Liyev's arrival at Foros the NSA and CIA had observed, just like the good doctor himself, an unusual multiplication of customary security measures in the area. These observations were passed on to the top administration members, but were met with incredulity: Gorbachev's fall was predicted several times in April 1991. The CIA's final warning was issued at the same time as Yakovliev's: he announced on 16 August 1991 that he was resigning from the CP and warned the Soviet public against a coup d'Etat allegedly prepared by a group of Stalinists. In an article published subsequently by Yakovliev together with Shevardnadze, Shatalin and Yavlinsky were asking themselves the same question: what would exactly be the role of Gorbachev in a 'legal' coup? However, no one in power at home or abroad paid the slightest attention to these warnings: the cries of wolf were too frequent.

The chief organiser of the coup, Kryuchkov, took first steps towards a coup as early as April 1991 when he circulated a top secret document on the possibility of a civil war in the USSR to all the principal agents at home and abroad. On 16 August, knowing of Gorbachev's injury, he signed another top secret document which put the services on a state of alert, ordering the destruction of 'sensitive' documents and doubling the wages of all the top personnel. The CIA was in possession of this document on the same day from the same agent who had been reporting also on the frequent meetings of Kryuchkov, Pugo, Pavlov and Baklanov. He also reported that Kryuchkov met Yanayev in the Kremlin on 15th August and that Lukyanov and Yazov took part in several meetings of this 'group'. On 5 August all the plotters finally met in KGB's cover place 'ABC' and all put in hand prepartions for the coup. However, there was never a 'general plan', only individual initiatives of KGB, MVD and the army, which were the power instruments of the coup. Nothing was done about these serious leaks originating from the KGB itself, when they finally reached Washington on the 18th. Surely Gorbachev had to know about such activity of his collaborators, it was reasoned.

However, the 18th August became a decisive day for both Gorbachev and the plotters on account of the former's 'state of health'. It was unplanned, but had to be politically exploited. Almost certainly Marshal Yazov was with Gorbachev at the villa at Foros before Dr. Liyev's visit. Yazov was undoubtedly there to appraise Gorbachev's attitude towards the proclamation of the state of emergency in certain regions of Russia and the postponement of the signature of the new Union Treaty. Since Gorbachev had flatly refused even to consider these two measures Yazov must have given the plotters green light to go ahead with the 'legal and constitutional' coup without Gorbachev. Yazov must have deceived his master with consumate skill, for Gorbachev calmly saw his doctor afterwards, worked normally with Chernyayev on his Union speech and even fixed a rendez-vous with Shakhnazarov in the presidential aircraft at 8 pm the following day. He was the last to speak to Gorbachev around 4 pm that afternoon. At 4.32pm   telephone lines at Foros were cut by the KGB.

At 4.45 Chernayev was alerted by Gorbachev's secretary that an important delegation arrived at the villa to see the supreme leader. Five minutes later General Medvedev, chief of his personal guard, told Gorbachev that Boldin, Baklanov, Sheinin, General Varennikov and General Plekhanov of the KGB arrived to see him. Medvedev was given a dressing down for allowing them entry, but excused himself by pointing out that he had to obey Plekhanov's orders: he was his superior officer. Before receiving the 'delegates' Gorbachev dashed to his office, where he found that all the lines of communication were dead. He then spoke to his wife and daughter who confirmed the same. At this critical moment Gorbachev said clearly: 'I shall never cede to any blackmail, threat or pressure. You must realise that anything can happen (to me).' Then he left to face the plotters.

The 'delegates' received the supreme leader with a mixture of cheek and menace. If he would sign the decree establishing 'legally' the Committee for the State of Emergency he could stay freely at Foros. If not, Yanayev would do it instead of him. Baklanov spoke to Gorbachev quite cynically; Boldin tried to make fun of him, while Varennikov acted like a bully-soldier. No one however issued an open ultimatum, all went on pussyfooting. Later they claimed that all problems were freely discussed and rejected firmly by Gorbachev, who apparently quite calmly   spoke of measures that the plotters were proposing to take. According to Varennikov Gorbachev even shook hands with them. Since Gorbachev refused to install the Committee to 'save democracy' he was placed under arrest--General Medvedev was also arrested and replaced by General Generalov, but the bodyguards were not even disarmed. Generalov then ordered quantities of vodka and wine, though it was rumoured that Gorbachev did it. The delegation's visit seemed pointless and surrealistic: the plotters were obviously incapable of real plotting, as they distrusted each other. It was Colonel General I. Maltsev who had previously ordered the presidential plane back to Moscow so that   the missing nuclear control key could come under the plotters' control-- the other two keys of this complicated system were already in the hands of Yazov and Moyseyev, the CoS. However, after this last chance visit Gorbachev lost power for ever without as much realising it.

III.

The transfer of power should have been effected in the afternoon of this 18th August in the Kremlin. Kryuchkov, who prepared all the relevant documents convoked in there, to Yanayev's office, all the committed plotters and the potential ones for 5 pm. The delegates whom he sent to Foros arrived there directly from the airport at about 9pm, together with another independent plotter, Lukyanov. The first lot of 'opportunist' plotters, which included Yanayev and Pavlov, had a four hours discussion on the formation of a committee to proclaim and administer the state of emergency in the capital Moscow, Leningrad (soon to become St. Petersburgh) and in the Baltic states. On that Sunday afternoon all seemed calm in Moscow and particularly in the Kremlin. Foreign minister Bessmertnykh thought on arrival that the meeting to which he was summoned by Kryuchkov and physically brought to by KGB agents from Byelorussia was postponed. However, Kryuchkov, the moving force of the coup, quickly filled him in: an insurrection was about to be staged in Moscow. The insurgents were to occupy the TV HQ, several railway stations, TASS agency and hotels Rossiya and Ukraina. Two lists of persons to be arrested and even executed had been seized by his agents. Thus a committee for the administration of the state of emergency had to be set up, else they could all perish. After long discussions, but without any concrete proofs of the alleged insurrection being furnished by Kryuchkov, Yanayev and Pavlov were willing to sign decrees creating such a committee and issuing a declaration to the Soviet people and the world that the plotters were saving themselves, the country and the world from chaos and civil war. However, Bessmertnykh himself refused to sign such a declaration , since he had his doubts about the real reasons for Gorbachev's absence. Nonetheless, he did agree to distributing the committee's solemn proclaration to Soviet representatives abroad so that they could act on the committee's behalf. However, it was clear that at this assembly were not the most important plotters. The real signing of documents necessary for a 'constitutional' launch of the coup occurred only after the delegates' had returned from Foros. Kryuchkov asked by then inebriated Yanayev to sign a decree making himself the constitutional head of the USSR, since Gorbachev 'for health reasons' could not sign it. Yanayev, Baklanov and Pavlov then signed another decree proclaiming the state of emergency and setting up a committee of eight to administer it. They were listed in Russian alphabetical order : O. Baklanov, the chief of the militaro-industrial complex, Kryuchkov himself, Premier Pavlov, Interior Minister Pugo, Starodubtsev, leader of the collective farmers, Tiziakov, head of national enterprises and Defence Minister Yazov with Yanayev the acting President last. Collectively all the eight members signed an appeal to the peoples of the USSR on the reasons for the state of emergency as well as a resolution on measures to be taken. Yanayev alone sent a message to all the heads of foreign states and the UNO secretary general explaining the changes in the USSR. Discussions continued until the early hours in the morning accompanied by heavy drinking. On his way home Yazov passed through the ministry of defence and sent out telegrammes cancelling troops' leave and placing them on alert. He also convoked a ministerial college session for 6 am. Shortly afterwards TASS was the first communication agency to distribute Yanayev's decree and the two declarations of the committee of the state of emergency. Kravchenko insured that they all were read on the TV and broadcast on state radio the same morning. Afterwards both TV and radio programmes were interrupted: a film of the ballet Swan Lake was showed on the TV and classical music was played on all the state radios giving the impression that someone allpowerful had died. The party newspaper, Pravda, printed on its front page Lukyanov's article rejecting the new union treaty. Everything so far went off smoothly without a hitch. Politically, however, the coup was launched at 5pm, in the afternoon of the 19th, when Yanayev and the most important members of the committee appeared on the TV to explain themselves to the public. In the absence of Boldin, Kryuchkov and Yazov, who were otherwise engaged, they put up a most unconvincing political show. Yanayev's trembling hands impressed Western observers more than his promises to preserve democracy and honour all international engagements negotiated by Gorbachev. Two hour later Pavlov's federal government, with two exception, N. Vorontsov and S. Khadzhiyev, declared itself for the coup. However, there all political initiative ended and the plotters passively waited for the entire USSR to rally to their coup.

Two active measures were taken the same early morning. At 5 am the KGB Kantemir armoured division was alerted, men and officers put on combat readiness. At 6am its T-54 tanks and personnel carriers set out in the direction of the capital. Simultaneous Kryuchkov ordered General Karpukhin and his elite Alpha commandos reinforced by special KGB troops to arrest the Russian President, and closely survey Mme Bonner and A. Yakovliev. The head of Moscow Regional KGB told his subordinates to 'forget democracy and perestroika. What in 1985 was perestroika has turned into a counter-revolution.' Action would be in old style: arrests, interrogations, executions. While Kryuchkov dealt personally,by telephone, with the future Ukrainian President Kravchuk. However, his subordinates whose moves were betrayed well in advance to Yeltsin, Rutskoy or Kobets, never executed fully his orders. After all they had their careers to worry about in these uncertain times. Nor were Kryuchkov's orders explicit. He also waited for the army and MVD special troops to move. In the end no one was arrested, except V. Urazhtsev, organiser of an army trade union. However, when the KGB agents tried to detain him, the jailers refused to take charge of Urazhtsev in the absence of 'legal documents'. Thus even he went free, not to mention Madame Bonner, Yakovliev or Yeltsin. In reality even the KGB found it difficult to plan anything. Kryuchkov was given the task of storming the Russian Supreme Soviet, the White House, at 9am of the 20th August. It was to be a joint operation codenamed Storm. Russian parliament should be taken by force during the night. The operation was postponed, first for 1am, then to 3am, and then abondoned. There were large crowds around the building and no one wanted to take the responsibility for civilian casualties. The army waited for the KGB and MVD to move and so on.

Marshal Yazov met all the military establishment at the same time. He explained succintly, without enthusiasm, that Gorbachev was ill, would not sign tomorrow the new union treaty. He was replaced by Yanayev who proclaimed a state of emergency to calm things down. Only the future Marshal Shaposhnikov and the deputy chief of the Navy expressed openly grave doubts. All the other military leaders remained silent and ready to carry out orders of the aging Marshal. The latter then ordered Generals Kalinin and Zolotov, CO and CoS of the Moscow Military District respectively, to send into the city two armoured divisions on patrol. Parts of the Taman division were ordered to surround the Russian Parliament and other civil objectives. Officers and men were not told the reasons for such actions; in fact most of them were sent to the city without ammunition. Again all these moves and orders were betrayed to the 'counter-revolutionary' leaders, such as Yakovliev, Shevardnadze and Yeltsin. General Grachev even declared that he would disobey orders to storm the Russian Parliament. Thus from the beginning in the armed forces vagueness and half measures led almost inevitably to confusion and eventually to chaos. After Grachev and Shaposhnikov had found real reasons, they proposed as countermeasures the bombing of the Kremlin. However, in practical terms the execution of the coup de force went off most unevenly.

During that day the world became quickly aware of the change of regime in the USSR. The British Premier was alerted first, because his secret agents stumbled on the KGB deployment in Moscow. However, it was President Bush who began to organise a Western coaliton against the recognition of the new regime as soon as he was told of Gorbachev's ouster. Only President Mitterrand publicly announced his acceptance of the new leaders to regret it shortly afterwards. Lech Walesa was alarmed by the coup, while President Havel appeared 'philosophically optimistic' after he had amassed his troops on the borders neighbouring the USSR. This quixotic gesture advised by communist generals who could not defend the country against the 1968 invasion, produced panic particularly in Prague. Everywhere else in Europe the coup enduced jitters and caused a degree of panic. Chancellor Kohl left precipitously Austria for Bonn. However, Bessmertnykh's ambassadors, particularly those in Washington, Paris and London tried in vain to stem international disquiet and persuade the West to recognise the new leadership. Only in Prague did the Soviet ambassador, B.D. Pankin, protest against the 'illegal removal' of Gorbachev with the result that he took Bessmertnykh's place a few days later. At the same time all the Western statesmen continued their efforts to join Gorbachev by telephone, refusing to speak to Yanayev. However, the most worried set of people were in Moscow in the Kremlin attending Mass on the 18th, when the plotters were putting final touches to their coup. They were there at a congress of emigres convoked by General Volkogonov and presided by Count Tolstoy to 'aid the new democratic Russia'. Despite anxiety they refused to abondon their congress and as the day progressed they appeared far from being distressed by the coup. In the evening their president spoke rather defiantly vis-a-vis the putchists. Once again as always in the times of confusion (smuta) the situation in the USSR bordered on surrealistic, smacking of the old Slavonic anarchy.

On the other hand as the day 1 of the coup went on, after the complete initial surprise, political initiative was slowly passing over to those against whom the coup was directed. Though President Gorbachev was impregnably sealed off by the Sevastopol KGB special troops, even he managed to make a video taperecording of his rejection of the coup. It took several days before the tape could be smuggled out from Foros and made no difference as far as the coup was concerned, but it demonstrated the utter inefficiency of the plotters' measures. It was, necertheless, an important political gesture which in a sense saved Gorbachev's political career, even if it be in short terms. However, Yeltsin's initiatives, the other top leader against whose political rise the coup was really aimed, made a decisive difference for the coup and his political career. Yeltsin arrived back from Kazakhstan on the 18th and went directly from the airport to his country dacha. In the morning he and his team heard of the coup on the radio. They all noticed the presence of the Alpha commando in the neighbourhood of their dachas at Arkhangelskoe. As general Kobets dashed to Yeltsin's villa he found there all the team: Ruslan Khasbulatov, Ivan Silayev, Genadyi Burbulis, Yuryi Luzhkov and also Anatolyi Sobchak as if to make the sweep of the Alpha thugs the easiest operation in the world. They all wondered aloud why they had not been arrested, but immediately took improvised steps to get out of this ideal trap. First of all, on the spot, they drafted an anti-coup declaration signed constitutionally by all the present leaders. By 8.30 they were in the White House (Russian Supreme Soviet) in Moscow facing journalists, while Sobchak was heading for St. Petersburgh.

Yeltsin immediately appealed to the population to demonstrate at the Manege Square and publicised their declaration to the citizens of Russia condemning the coup. Despite being gradually surrounded by the tanks all the Russian administrative centres, the Supreme Soviet, the Russian Government and the City Municipality continued to function and organise opposition to the coup. As crowds began to fill up the Manege Square shouting for the arrest of Yazov, Pugo and Kryuchkov Yeltsin left the White House and mounting a tank of the Taman division appealed to the citizens of Moscow and Russia to 'answer the coup with dignity and return the country to normal constitutional development.' With hindsight this intervention was the real turning point of the coup. While the plotters waited passively for the people and organisations to rally to them, their opponents were on the offensive. In Moscow, St. Petersburgh and the Baltic states public demonstrations against the coup were in progress all day, despite the deployment of armoured troops or paratroopers as happened at Kaunas in Lithuania, or at the MVD building in Riga, Latvia. Only the satellite Baltic communist parties, Nina Andreyeva and the Union parliamentary group dared to support the coup publicly, though four out 73 territorial administrations also did so. Yeltsin in the meantime charged General Kobets with the defence of the White House and took formally over the Soviet power institutions, such as the ministry of the interior, defence and the KGB and appealed to the policemen, soldiers and KGB agents to obey his orders. By the evening many soldiers of the Taman division and KGB agents responded positively, the first being Major Evdokimov who ordered his armoured detachment to deploy in order to protect the White House. However, throughout that night to Yeltsin and his allies the issue seemed unresolved: would at least some of the MVD, KGB or army troops obey their commanders, rallied to the putchists, and storm the White House? Spontaneous barricades were all over the city, but that failed to reassure the opposition. With Alpha commandos loose and OMON and army units milling around no one thought that they had won. In fact they were getting ready for a final stand. Ironically the first and only bloody clash occurred at during the following night, when all was lost. Tragically the crews of army tanks halted by a barricade panicked and fired at demonstrators surrounding them. Three men were killed, symbollically, a Russian, an Ukrainian and a Jew, by 'mistake', with Yeltsin winning the 'battle'. Nonetheless throughout the 20th the confusion continued in the city, in the Union and the World. False alarms continued to agitate the city, with the army going over to Yeltsin, with OMON troops ready to storm Yeltsin's centres of resistance, or Alpha commandos capturing the Russian President in person. Perhaps significantly the congress of Russian emigre congress continued its sessions uninterrupted and issuing more and more defiant declarations. Ukraine, Kazakhstan and Moldavia definitely refusing to join the coup, though Byelorussian, Adzeri and Uzbeki positions remained ambiguious. While Kryuchkov began to feel that the coup was collapsing and ordered the destruction of documents showing that he was its prime mover , Scheinin committed the communist party as a whole to the coup by sending out a circular telegram urging all local secretariats to report on the acceptance or the rejection of the commitee for the state of emergency. The central committee refused to meet at an extraordinary plenum and discuss the coup this was another indication of party complicity. However, the communist party was deeply divided as the overwhelming majority of people in power. They were all playing the usual game of wait and see who wins. The caution did not prevent Yeltsin to dissolve it and confiscate its property. Only in the Baltic states were the troops obedient to the committee on the offensive. By this time the entire world was responding to the events and with the exception of France openly rejected the coup.

It still is not quite clear who started talking to Yeltsin, after the 'official' telephone contact with President Gorbachev had failed. President Bush spoke throughout the 19th August to practically every leader, including the most tiny ones who had remotest interests in Russia lining them up behind himself. Only Lybia, Iraq and Cuba recognised the new regime outright sending greetings to the new leader, Yanayev. On this afternoon 20 August Bush finally managed to have a word with Yeltsin in person on an ordinary telephone line. He told him that all the world supported Gorbachev and Yeltsin and the USA would not even discuss the recognition of Yanayev. The European Community subsequently announced that it froze its financial and technical aid to the USSR until the situation clarified and there was return to constitutionality. Komplektov, Zamiatin and Dubinin failed to influence the three permanent members of the Security Council, though the last did managed to confuse the French more efficiently than the others.

By now Yeltsin and general Kobets knew that the Kantemir and Taman divisions were on their side, and the ministry of defence practically lost control of the army. Though Kryuchkov still appeared in control of the KGB it became evident that his operations could easily be deflected as was the case of the Pskov KGB division. The Dzezhinsky division flopped decisively together with the overestimated Alpha commandoes. The plotters began to doubt about the success of their coup. Pavlov fell oficially ill and Kryuchkov and Yazov were rumoured to have resigned from the committee. Clearly perestroika transformed both the KGB and the army , both key power institutions of any regime, beyond their leaders' recognition making them worthless instruments in any internecine political struggle. Notwithstanding Yeltsin was still worried that the White House would be stormed, though by now even Yanayev had vehemently denied to him that such possibility existed. Late that night KGB generals Kryuchkov and Glushko went round Moscow on an unofficial inspection tour and became persuaded that the coup had failed. Kryuchkov reacted in a typical secret policeman way: he ordered the destruction of documents implicating him and the KGB in the coup d'Etat. Then he took 'political' initiative by ringing Yeltsin whom he reassured about the White House security and proposed a joint journey to Foros to see Gorbachev.

Henceforth it became clear to all that the end of the attempted coup was at hand. The plotters panicked. Everyone of them wanted to go to Foros to see Gorbachev. In the end Vice President Rutskoy and Premier Silayev went there with Kryuchkov, Yazov and Lukianov to tell Gorbachev that the coup was over and that he could return to Moscow. Kryuchkov and Yazov were placed under arrest there and then, while the rest of the plotters were arrested on 22 August, with Pugo committing suicide. Lukianov's arrest followed a few days later. Though Gorbachev pretended to resume power by nominating new heads of the Soviet power bodies, including the KGB as if nothing happened, it was obvious that these were abstract gestures. The Soviet Union ceased to exist though its agony continued until December 1991. The Baltic states declared their independence immediately, while the other republics followed suit three months later. Russia took over virtually all the central organs of power including the KGB. However, this time it was clearly Yeltsin who became guarantor of Russian security and democracy. Perestroika phase was over. What was initially a communist party's effort to get out of a deep social and economic crisis became a movement towards national independence and a sort of democracy, resembling strikingly the ageold Slavic anarchy. If perestroika was to most foreigners Churchill's riddle of an enigma democracy can be likened to Gogol's troika in which each horse is pulling in his own direction.

Perestroika And The Warsaw Pact

Zdenek Matejka

The effects of perestroika began to be felt soon after the spring of 1985 in some aspects of life in the Soviet Union and the countries of Eastern Europe. But it took much more time for its first effects to be felt within the Warsaw Pact itself. This was true not only because the armed forces are traditionally - under any regime - more conservative than other institutions, but also because it is inherently difficult to push through change in an international organization that acts on the basis of consensus.

Furthermore, the Soviets were afraid to start an uncontrolled avalanche of change within the Pact, an institution which they considered vital to their interests. The Soviet Union's military and political leadership did not want to further deepen the substantial differences that already existed among the seven Warsaw Pact member countries. Any attempt to introduce ideas of perestroika would mean decreasing the Soviet influence and would lead to the spreading - as the Soviet generals saw it - of the disease of revisionism.

Romania had already been playing the role of main dissident in the Pact for years. It, for example, had refused to take part in the invasion of Czechoslovakia by five Warsaw Pact countries in August 1968. And later, in the mid-1980s, there had been mild attempts to change some minor aspects of the Pact. Czechoslovakia, for instance, attempted to lower its 13% contribution to common expenditures, which had been set in the early 1950s but which it considered too high.

The delay in the clear manifestation of restructuring in the Pact does not mean, of course, that one is unable to trace the language of perestroika in documents that were adopted by the Pact's organs rather soon after Gorbachev came to power. Evidence of a new language is certainly perceptible in communiques of the Pact's highest body - the Political Consultative Committee. This was a body that met once a year and that brought together the secretaries general of the member countries' Communist Parties, the Prime Ministers, Foreign Ministers and Defence Ministers. New thinking had also gradually been introduced into documents of the Committee of Foreign Ministers that met twice a year. To a much lesser extent, new ideas also found their way into documents of the Committee of Defence Ministers, which also met every six months.

First shy attempts to reform the Pact

One of the most visible signs of the fresh wind was the publication - for the first time - of the Pact's military doctrine in 1987. Of course, it did not reflect real thinking. It was a "purely defensive" document, one that included the notion of a "no first nuclear strike policy." But its publication was nevertheless a clear indication of the new times brought on by perestroika.

The most remarkable aspect of Soviet attempts to "reconstruct" the Pact was the growing pressure to strengthen political aspects of its activities. The main aim was to de-emphasize the military side and bring its public image more in line with what was generally known about NATO. In 1988 this trend found its expression in the creation of several new working groups of informative and consultative character.

Of all these groups, one designed to "improve the mechanisms of political and military cooperation" was especially important and specifically oriented towards perestroika. Through this forum the Soviets tried very hard to sell the idea of the creation of a permanent political body and of a Secretariat of the Pact. Warsaw and Moscow were most often mentioned as sites for these permanent bodies. This concept included a proposal to create the new post of "Secretary General of the Warsaw Treaty Organization," replacing the existing post of "Secretary General of the Political Consultative Committee of the Warsaw Treaty Organization." There was to be a tremendous difference between the two posts, though to outsiders the deletion of the three words "Political Consultative Committee" might seem meaningless.

The responsibilities and authority of the "Secretary General of the Political Consultative Committee" were formal in nature and only of an organizational character. I know this perfectly well, as I had held the post for the last year of the existence of the Pact. Despite the bombastic title, the official in this post actually only organized the work of the so-called United Secretariat during the summits and in between coordinated the activities of the working bodies, groups and commissions. He did not act as a spokesman for the Pact and was not supposed to be a political figure at all. The post was rotated every year. It was held by one of the deputy foreign ministers of the country hosting the next summit. The Secretary General's official responsibilities could not be compared in scope to those of the NATO Secretary General, who in fact became a model for a proposal to create a new, similar post in the Warsaw Pact. But it never materialized.

During early sessions of the working group on improving the functioning of the Pact, only Romania opposed notions aimed at creating permanent and meaningful political structures and posts. But after the political earthquakes in Eastern Europe in late 1989, the Romanians were joined in their opposition by others. During a session in February

1990 in Budapest, Czechoslovakia also rejected the concept. Up to then, the conservative Prague regime had supported the Soviet approach.

A lot of other ideas for "democratization" of the Pact had been presented at the group sessions. Romania and Hungary suggested that the post of Supreme Commander of the Pact's Joint Armed Forces and the deputy positions under him for the Air Force and Navy be made rotating posts. Until then, these had always been held by Soviet officers. The proposal found so much support that even the Soviets were willing to accept it.

Hungary suggested the abolition of the "Military Council of the Joint Armed Forces" in its previous form. The tasks of the Military Council would be taken over by the Committee of Defence Ministers and the Joint Staff. The Soviets refused to abolish the Military Council, but they were ready "to improve its activities." Hungary further proposed the review of the permanent presence of so-called representatives of the Pact's Supreme Commander at the Defence Ministries of member countries. Those representatives, of course, had almost always been Soviet officers.

Another working organ created in 1988 was devoted to disarmament. The duty of the "Special Commission for Disarmament" was mainly to coordinate the positions of individual countries at disarmament talks. It met whenever necessary - usually once every three months - in the capital of the country where the next summit was to be held.

The so-called "Multilateral Group for Topical Mutual Information" was also created in 1988, on the initiative of the Poles. The member countries were to exchange information on current issues and on intended foreign policy steps. During the first year of its existence, it held meetings in Moscow almost every month. But in early 1990, the participants lost interest in the exchange because the information on offer was mostly useless.

Until 1989, attempts to restructure the Pact had been coming both from Moscow and from some Eastern European capitals, but the goals were not the same. The Soviets did not want to change the substance of their dominance in the Pact, though they did recognize the need for some adjustments. They tried to create a political counterpart to NATO that would serve as a bargaining chip in future negotiations. The Soviets expected that such talks would be necessary for moving from the two-bloc arrangement to one of a pan-European security system.

Czechoslovak initiatives since early 1990

By late 1989 and early 1990 pressure for change within the Pact was coming from only non-Soviet members. The Soviets were being put under constant pressure and were going on the defensive. They resisted the most radical ideas but made one concession after another. This was true not only with regard to the West, NATO and Germany, but also with regard to the Warsaw Pact.

Since early 1990, of Eastern European countries, Czecho-slovakia had become most active. This was logical, for the election of a former dissident, Vaclav Havel, as President in late December 1989 pushed the country further away from Communism than Poland and Hungary. Up to then, Poland and Hungary had been the most reform-minded members of the Pact. Czechoslovakia's avant garde position found its expression in the priorities of its foreign policy, which were set by the new Foreign Minister, Jiri Dienstbier. He was also an active dissident who spent several years in the same prison as Havel.

Czechoslovakia's top priority was the withdrawal of Soviet troops that had been stationed there "temporarily" since the five Warsaw Pact countries' 1968 invasion. Though the talks on withdrawal were extremely sensitive for both sides, they were concluded in a relatively short time. The agreement was signed as early as February 26, 1990, during President Havel's visit to Moscow. Hungary seized the opportunity to get rid of uninvited guests and negotiated a similar agreement soon thereafter. Poland missed the first boat, so to speak, because it was not sure if it wanted the Soviet troops to leave abruptly, while Germany was still being united.

During the Czechoslovak delegation's visit to Moscow in February 1990, Minister J. Dienstbier agreed with his Soviet counterpart, E. Shevardnadze, that the Warsaw Pact Foreign Ministers should be invited to Prague. They met on March 19, 1990, and discussed primarily the German question. The differences among the participants remained deep. Shevardnadze did not insist any more on German neutrality, but together with East Germany (GDR) and Poland he expressed strong reservations about a united Germany's possible membership in NATO. The Czechoslovak host, Minister Dienstbier, was actually the only one who explicitly said that he would not mind united Germany's opting for NATO.

It was typical for the participants of the March 1990 Pact's Foreign Ministers informal meeting in Prague that practically all expressed the feeling that the existence of the two blocs should give way to a new pan-European security structure based on the CSCE. It was formulated most emphatically by the then Hungarian Foreign Minister Guyla Horn. He spoke of "convergence of the two blocs" as a way to overcome division of Europe and to bridge East and West.

Preparations for the June 1990 Pact summit

One of the important reasons why Czechoslovakia became most active during the spring of 1990 was that after the forthcoming summit it was to take over as coordinator of the Pact's activities. The summit was to be held on June 7 in Moscow. Preparations for it started in a quite routine way. A couple of weeks before the gathering, the hosts sent out its first draft of the final document. What struck us most, however, was that the Soviet approach to the session was full of complacency. Radical fundamental changes of the last several months in Europe had been dutifully but formally taken note of, but no specific conclusions had been drawn.

The Czechoslovak leadership decided to propose the adoption of a meaningful Declaration instead of a mere communique, as suggested by the Soviets. After prolonged domestic consultation and discussion on the working level, a special meeting was convened in Prague where our counterproposal to adopt a Declaration at the summit was to be finalized. The meeting was attended by the President, Prime Minister, Foreign and Defence Ministers and leading officials of both Ministries.

The thinking of the Czechoslovak leadership at that time was based on the assumption that a political and security vacuum in Central and Eastern Europe should be avoided. Everybody in his right senses realized at that time that the Pact was doomed to oblivion. The only question was when and how exactly to bury it. We anticipated that the Warsaw Pact could still be useful for a year or so. This applied, though, only to political aspects of its activities.

We clearly realized there were two distinct stages of disbanding the Pact - first of its military structures and then of the Pact itself. As for the military machinery, we did not see any role for it at all. It was only a matter of courtesy and pragmatic political judgement how long the military machinery would be tolerated. It should, perhaps, be added that there had never been any "grand design", a plan of action or even some kind of a "plot". Specific steps were taken mostly spontaneously.

As for the political role of the Pact, we expected that it could temporarily fulfil certain tasks on the way to a pan-European security system and that it could contribute to coordinating efforts in arms control and disarmament. I should remind the reader that all those discussions took place in the summer of 1990, when the talks in Vienna on conventional arms reductions were far from finished. The necessary prerequisite for prolonging our participation in the Pact activities, however, was that it had to be principally restructured, both politically and organizationally.

We wanted the Declaration to mention that the national armed forces could be used only for defence of their own territory, that units of national armed forces should not be a part of the Pact's Joint Armed Forces under the Joint Command. We suggested several specific steps. Among them were:

- To change the Staff of the Joint Armed Forces into a "Coordinating Group" with only a small number of civilian and military personnel. It would be an administrative and non-political body for preparing sessions of the Political Consultative Committee and the Committee of Foreign Ministers.

- To abolish the Committee of Defence Ministers and to create the "Military Committee" composed of Chiefs-of-Staff or Deputy Defence Ministers. The new body would be subordinated to the Committee of Foreign Ministers.

- To create an ad hoc group of senior goverment officials for basic transformation of the Pact. Its first session should be held before July 15, and by the end of October it should present its recommendations to an emergency summit meeting in November. The idea was to hold this summit before the Paris CSCE Conference.

The final Czechoslovak counterproposal was not ready until just a few days before a meeting of experts preparing documents for the summit was to start in Moscow. We sent copies of the draft Declaration through the Prague Embassies of the six other members of the Pact (Bulgaria, East Germany, Hungary, Poland, Romania and the USSR). Unfortunately, there was a weekend in between. It therefore came as no surprise that when our delegation at the first session of experts presented its draft for consideration, nobody knew what they were talking about.

When the Soviets and some other delegations saw the text, they resorted to a procedural rule whereby only the host's draft can serve as the basis for discussion. Other delegations were able to suggest amendments to this basic text sentence-by- sentence, word-by-word. Even with that handicap, during the three days of discussions of experts and Deputy Ministers the Czechoslovak delegation succeeded in pushing through much of its own original draft. But, of course, not all of the points were accepted. The hottest discussion concentrated on the character of the transformation of the Pact and on the attitude towards NATO. The Soviets tried to put both alliances on the same level but most delegations rejected it.

In the late afternoon of the summit eve on June 6, 1990, all members of the Czechoslovak delegation assembled in President Havel's apartment to evaluate the course of the hitherto discussion on the draft Declaration. As the head of our delegation at the Deputy Ministers' meeting, I tried to explain that some of the formulations had been considered with our partners for hours. I stressed that much of the approved language and even the disputed text in brackets was the result of tough bargaining and compromise. But the President, the Prime Minister, Foreign and Defense Ministers as well as a few other advisers and officials offered new amendments or wanted the delegation to insist on the original Czechoslovak draft. In spite of my desperate protestations, a new text was approved by the session and I was instructed to try to push through as much as possible.

I knew perfectly well that this was impossible. Time pressure saved me from an even worse situation. I had to leave for the last drafting session at about 10 p.m. Otherwise, I suppose, I would have been given the text with even more suggested changes. All the delegations expected that the night session would be rather short. They presumed that the previous text would be reviewed, some brackets removed and the remaining problems that the Deputy Ministers were unable to solve would simply be left to the Ministers for their final decision.

When I informed the participants of my instructions and intentions, they must have thought I had gone mad. Nobody can blame them, for it was really preposterous to open new discussions on almost every sentence of preliminarily agreed and relatively balanced text. Not only the Soviets but also others, especially the Romanians, refused to discuss the Czechoslovak draft, and we had to present individual amendments. The session lasted until 4 a.m. of June 7 - the day the summit was supposed to start. I admired the patience of my colleagues. I presume that it was the tremendous prestige enjoyed by President Havel that prevented them from flatly refusing our unconventional approach.

Needless to say, during the remaining hours of the night I did not sleep well, if at all. I was afraid that somebody from our leadership would reproach the delegation for not doing enough at the night session. I was relieved when in the morning a still sleepy President Havel, after a quick look through the latest text of the draft Declaration, said:" It's O.K. I understand that you could not do miracles."

It was not only I and our delegation who were nervous. There was a general uncertainty during the whole night about the ability of the summit to adopt any Declaration at all. Everyone was aware that a failure to agree on a final document would be disastrous. Shevardnadze came back to Moscow from his foreign trip only late on the eve of the summit and forbade anybody to bother him with anything while he was sleeping. The Soviet delegation was thus unable not only to get instructions from him on unresolved problems but even to brief him about basic developments.

In the morning of June 7 the Foreign Ministers met - though with much delay - to consider the text of the Declaration. They had actually only about half an hour to discuss remaining differences before the start of the summit itself. The outcome depended mostly on Shevardnadze. And he proved to be very flexible. The funniest situation occurred when he listened carefully to two options of the key sentence of the whole Declaration about the character of the transformation of the Pact. After pondering a while, he chose the wording "reappraisal of functions and activities" instead of "cardinal change" of the Pact. He suggested that the Ministers should prefer "the milder term reappraisal" (in Russian "peresmotr").

The text was finally adopted by the Ministers and the meeting of the heads of delegations could start more or less on time. While Ministers were leaving the room, one angry member of the Soviet delegation - who had been arguing for hours against the word "reappraisal" because he considered it too strong - said in total disgust: "It is a tragedy to have a foreign minister who cannot properly speak the Russian language!" He was, of course, referring to the fact that Shevardnadze is Georgian.

Key decision to transform the Pact

The result of long discussions, a two-page Declaration, reflected the radically changed situation in Europe. Its main conclusion was that the Pact should be "transformed into a Treaty of sovereign states with equal rights, formed on a democratic basis."

The preparatory meetings before the Moscow summit and the summit itself proved that there were wide differences in understanding the process of transformation. The hitherto dominant power - the Soviets - seemed totally confused. They felt they were being double crossed and even betrayed by their former allies. They did not know how to react to so many radical proposals for which they were not prepared. They suggested some concrete steps in non-military activities, but they clearly did not see any necessity to change much. The Soviet military were very adamant in resisting any radical changes at all. At the meetings the Soviets could count on only one staunch supporter -the Bulgarians. They had been advocating the preservation of the existing military structures and tried to justify it by the alleged threat from neighbouring Turkey.

It was the famous "Central European troika", later known as the "Visegrád troika" - Czechoslovakia, Hungary and Poland - that pushed through the most radical ideas. The three countries coordinated their activities very closely. Their officials met frequently on different working and vice-ministerial levels. On some issues the troika was supported by the Romanians, whose love for the Pact had dissipated a long time before. All of the meetings were attended by East German diplomats and military but the closer was the unification of Germany, the less active they became. Later in the summer they did not take the floor at all.

Hungarian representatives were most outspoken on the need of urgent dismantling of military structures of the Pact. They often referred to a mandate of the Hungarian Parliament that had asked the Government to get the country out of the Pact as soon as possible. It may seem rather surprising today but it is a fact that in June 1990 and for some months later, the Polish delegations expressed much interest in preserving at least some military functions of the Pact, though in a much-changed form. The reason was evidently their uncertainty about German reunification.

The main concrete result of the summit was the creation of the "Commission of Government representatives for Transformation". Its tasks were laid out in some detail in a protocol (actually the journal of the session), signed by seven Deputy Ministers - members of the so-called United Secretariat. These protocols have never been published. The Commission was to "reappraise all aspects of the activities of the Warsaw Treaty Organization, including gradual limiting of activities of organs for military cooperation. The reappraisal should take into account the development of the Helsinki process and formation of pan-European security and cooperation structures."

The Commission was to meet for the first time in Prague not later than July 15 and then monthly by rotation in other capitals. It was to present its recommendations in October. The emergency summit was to be held in Budapest by the end of November to consider the recommendations of the Commission. It really met in Prague on July 15 and then held its September and October sessions in Sofia and Warsaw. Its recommendations were discussed by the Pact's Foreign Ministers, who met for a working session at the Czechoslovak Permanent Mission in New York on September 30, 1990, on the margin of the CSCE ministerial meeting.

Though the tasks of the Transformation Commission were extremely difficult, it fulfilled them successfully. It recommended, inter alia, to start dismantling all military structures beginning January 1, 1991, and to finish the process by July 1, 1991. During the transitional period the Pact was to continue its activities only as a consultative organization for problems of security and disarmament. Merely three organs of the Pact were to remain:

- The Political Consultative Committee (which was to meet once   a year at   the summit level and also once a year at the level   of Foreign Ministers),

- The Special Commission for Disarmament (it was to be the main   working body of the Pact) and

- The Military Consultative Group.

The only problem left open was the contents of the Military Consultative Group's activities. The Soviets wanted it to fulfil some substantive functions, whereas the Hungarians - supported with various degrees of intensity by others - insisted that the group should concentrate only on dismantling military structures. The problem was to be discussed at another Commission meeting, but it never happened.

Central role of disarmament

Of all the working bodies that formally existed at that time, the only one really useful - and actually used in the fall of 1990 - was the Special Commission for Disarmament. The unusual emphasis on arms control and disarmament within the Pact, which today may seem strange, could be well understood if we take into consideration the situation in Europe just before the Paris summit.

The task of utmost political significance was to prepare the Treaty on Conventional Armed Forces in Europe (CFE Treaty). The talks in Vienna were difficult but there was steady progress, and they needed to be successfully finished. By fall of 1990 the blocs' ceilings for five categories of heavy weapons (tanks, artillery, armoured personnel carriers, helicopters and combat aircraft) were already agreed upon. It was relatively easy to define a rule for distributing the bloc ceilings in respective weapons categories among individual countries. Their percentages after the reductions were to be the same as those in 1989 reflecting their actual possessions.

Unforseen complications arose when it became clear that the GDR would cease to exist and that other Warsaw Pact countries were supposed to distribute the original East German share in all five weapons categories among themselves. President Havel and the Czechoslovak leadership had no doubts that our small country would not need more heavy weapons than it was supposed to have after the reductions. It was not difficult to convince the High Command of the Czechoslovak armed forces of this approach, for the former "frontline state" was oversaturated with weapons. We were too naive, however, in expecting that other countries would follow the same logic. In fact all of them tried to get as much East German "heritage" as possible.

To our utter astonishment the requirements of the remaining members of the Pact were much higher than the original East German share. I personally did not believe my ears when I was listening to Soviet, Bulgarian, Polish, Romanian and Hungarian generals and officers arguing about how many additional heavy weapons they would need to defend their countries. Against whom? I never got a satisfactory answer. Their language resembled that of the Cold War period.

Four long meetings of the Disarmament Commission in Prague and Bratislava (September 10-11, September 22-23, October 9-10 and October 26-27, 1990), with the Chiefs-of-Staff of member countries participating, discussed the matter. After the first two sessions, intervention on the part of the Foreign Ministers during the New York meeting on September 30, 1990, was helpful in calming some hot military heads. At the end of October, on the fourth attempt to find a consensus the agreement on the shares of conventional arms was reached after all. It cleared the way for signing the CFE Treaty in Paris next month.

The new percentage share of individual countries represented a problem not only for the Warsaw Pact but also for the West, as it insisted on a so-called "sufficiency rule." This stipulated that no single member of the two groups (actually USA and the USSR) should exceed a ceiling of 30%. As in many similar cases, this problem, too, was finally resolved bilaterally between Moscow and Washington. During his stay in New York for the CSCE Ministerial meeting at the end of September, Shevardnadze made a deal with his American counterparts. He had, though, a substantial handicap: he had no military big shot in his delegation. I remember Shevardnadze openly telling his Warsaw Pact colleagues that he hoped the Politburo would accept the deal but that he expected tough resistance from the military, especially from the Defence Minister, Marshal Yazov.

The deliberations of the Disarmament Commission on the setting of weapons' national ceilings were extremely important. They were a necessary prerequisite for a successful Paris summit. As coordinators of the Pact and the Commission's activities, the Czechoslovaks felt a special responsibility. We were afraid that without the agreement within the Warsaw Pact, the signing of the Treaty on Conventional Armed Forces in Europe would be in jeopardy. That was one of the reasons why we so vehemently insisted on an early solution. Our position was credible and convincing, because we did not ask for a single additional tank or any other heavy weapon from the East German share.

The result of the Disarmament Commission deliberations - the Agreement on maximum national levels of conventional weapons of individual Warsaw Treaty members - was signed by the six Foreign Ministers or their first deputies on November 3, 1990, in Budapest.

The Hungarian hosts originally proposed exactly the same day as the date for the emergency summit meeting. But Gorbachev asked to postpone it until after the CSCE Paris conference. He explained his request by his busy schedule due to domestic problems. As it was generally considered to be only a pretext, President Havel wrote a personal letter to Gorbachev on October 23. He insisted on holding the summit as soon as possible but not later than by the end of 1990. Hungary set a new date in December but the Soviets asked for postponement again.

As a part of coordination efforts of the "Central European troika" within the Pact, Deputy Foreign Ministers of Czechoslovakia, Hungary and Poland met urgently in Prague on December 28, 1990, to consider the situation. They reiterated the position that they would prefer to dismantle the military structures and the Pact itself with the agreement of all its members. They insisted that the Budapest summit should meet not later than in February 1991. They made it clear that if there were further delays they would have to resort to unilateral action coordinated at least within the troika. In plain language, they threatened to leave military structures of the Pact and the Pact itself without any summits.

Dismantling military structures

During informal talks with the Soviets we got a hint that one of the reasons for delays was in fact the reluctance of Gorbachev to participate personally in the Pact's funeral. We then suggested that the Political Consultative Committee could be held on the level of Foreign and Defence Ministers. The Soviets promptly agreed and even proposed to push the deadline for dismantling military structures from July 1 (a key recommendation of the Transformation Commission) to April 1. Given that day is known as Fool's Day in most European countries and actions taken during this day are not considered serious, we suggested to change the date to March 31. It was accepted.

The Soviets capitulated partly because the military structures of the Pact had been disintegrating anyway since the beginning of 1990. By January 1991 only a few officers from member countries had still been left at the Moscow Staff of the Joint Armed Forces. Out of 40-50 Czechoslovak officers during the late 80's, only four remained there at the beginning of 1991. And they had only one task - to end our participation in the Pact. Dissolving the military structures was especially easy for the Romanians because for many years there had been only one their representative in the Moscow Joint Staff - a general. Even he did not have much to do, for the Romanian leader Nicolae Ceaucescu had been refusing to participate in any common Pact activities.

The emergency meeting of the Political Consultative Committee on the level of Foreign and Defence Ministers was held in Budapest on February 25, 1991. The Ministers signed the "Protocol on ending the validity of military agreements concluded within the Warsaw Treaty and on dismantling its military organs and structures." The Protocol came into effect immediately after the signing.

The participants also adopted a short political statement. It referred to the Paris Charter and a new epoch in which former enemies had become partners. The statement stressed that dismantling the Pact's military structures would contribute to transition from the two-bloc system to pan-European security structures.

In his statement to the Budapest plenary session the Czechoslovak Foreign Minister bluntly said that "the Warsaw Pact is becoming more and more an anachronism and that it has lost its raison d'etre". After the Treaty on conventional armed forces in Europe was signed and dismantling of military structures secured there was nothing constructive the Pact was able to perform. It was clear that the Pact was outdated and lost not only its military but also its political role. In fact the Pact had been at that time in a state of clinical death. The main problem remained how to dissolve it in a civilized way.

With that in mind and having experienced delaying tactics previously, the Czechoslovak delegation in Budapest insisted that an exact date of the regular summit be set. We argued that we needed the exact date so that we could plan a successful session around the demands of the hectic tourist season in Prague. We also suggested that the only aim of this last summit - dissolution of the Pact - be stated in the protocol explicitly.

We were pushing for the date July 1, 1991, because only a day before that, on June 30, the very last Soviet soldier was to leave Czechoslovakia and also Hungary. The proposal was supported by four other member countries but the Soviets did not agree. The unpublished protocol of the session only mentioned that the next summit "was to be held not later than at the beginning of July 1991" and that "the date would be set through diplomatic channels". According to the protocol the host country was to "convene a working group for preparation of the session and corresponding documents".

It goes without saying that Czechoslovakia as the host of the summit was eager to start preparations as soon as possible. It is not surprising that the Soviets were not too helpful. We understood the feelings of some of them and were prepared to find a smooth and dignified way to bury the Pact. We wanted to avoid any excess bitterness or hurting superpower feelings. To put pressure on the reluctant Soviets and to push preparations forward we used a tested means: coordination by the Central European troika countries on different levels including that of Deputy Ministers.

In May 1991 the hosts got consent from all six partners with the date. The top leaders of five countries promised to come, only the level of Soviet participation remained open to the last moment. Gorbachev was as reluctant to come to Prague as to Budapest and avoided both sessions. Czechoslovak drafts of final documents did not evoke much resistance. The Soviets suggested, though, a lot of additional text to the draft Protocol on ending the validity of the Pact. But the five delegations succeeded in convincing the Soviets to put most of the ideas in the communique or statement. The Protocol was to be ratified by the parliaments, and controversial text could create some difficulties.

Unexpected hurdles, however, appeared. Soviet generals, for instance, came up with the notion that dismantling the Pact would fundamentally change the bloc basis on which the CFE Treaty had been built to such an extent that a new treaty would have to be negotiated. It was an extremely dangerous proposition but fortunately the Soviet military did not find enough support for it even among its own political leadership. It would contradict Gorbachev's and Soviet diplomats' efforts to create an impression that they had not been interested in prolonging the Pact's life indefinitely.

Funeral of the Pact

On July 1, 1991, top leaders of the six countries came to Prague for the final Warsaw Pact summit. Four presidents - Zhelyu Zhelev of Bulgaria, Vaclav Havel of Czechoslovakia, Lech Walesa of Poland and Ion Iliescu of Romania, Prime Minister of Hungary Jószef Antall and Vice-President Gennadi Yanayev of the Soviet Union participated.

It was only Yanayev's second trip abroad in his new capacity as the Soviet Vice-President after he had taken part in Indian Prime Minister Rajiv Gándhí's funeral. Yanayev joked about it in Prague expressing his hope that attending funerals would not be his only foreign activity. It is ironical that only six weeks after the Prague Warsaw Pact funeral Yanayev headed a plot to avoid another one - that of the Soviet Union - only to hasten it.

The historic document signed in Prague has a very complicated title: "The Protocol on terminating the validity of the Treaty of Friendship, Cooperation and Mutual Assistance, signed in Warsaw on May 14, 1955, and of the Protocol extending the validity of the mentioned Treaty of April 26, 1985". But its four paragraphs are very simple. The validity of the Warsaw Treaty ends after the Protocol comes into effect. The Parties declare that they have no property claims in connection with the Treaty. The Protocol is subject to ratification and will come into effect the day when the last ratification paper is deposited in Prague.

At the time of the summit, we expected that the parliaments of the six countries would ratify the Protocol before the end of 1991 or at the very beginning of 1992. The idea was to come to the Helsinki CSCE summer summit freed of one of the cold war relics. Actually it took a little bit longer, especially because of the problems in Moscow, mainly in connection with the Soviet Union's dissolution. The last ratification papers were deposited in Prague by the Russian Federation on February 18, 1993, and the Warsaw Pact officially and formally ceased to exist.

What was interesting and characteristic about the Pact funeral was its quiet, even serene atmosphere. One of the Prague papers carried its article on the summit under the headline: "Merry Funeral - Happy Survivors." The end of a military pact in such an atmosphere without much recrimination was a great historic innovation. Military blocs and empires in the past had always disappeared only after they had been defeated militarily.

It would be naive to believe, though, that all the nostalgic generals, officers and apparatchiks in the Soviet Union were as happy as the common people of the six countries and the rest of the world. Yanayev in Prague bluntly said he hoped that NATO would not last much longer than the Warsaw Pact. The Moscow Communist Party newspaper Pravda asked a typical question: "Why does only the Warsaw Pact have to disappear; why not also NATO?" Such an argument had been repeatedly used all the time during the discussions on the transformation of the Pact. The Soviet military always referred to a paragraph in the Warsaw Treaty about simultaneous dissolution of both pacts.

The end of the Pact formally cut the last of the ties that linked the Eastern European satellites to the Soviet Union. By coincidence only a week before the Prague Warsaw Pact summit another grouping of Communist countries - the Council for Mutual Economic Assistance, known as Comecon, had been disbanded in Budapest. Those two events are undoubtedly a watershed in postwar developments. It was a period of rightful satisfaction and joy over what had been accomplished. But it was also a time of visions later turned into illusions or at least of dreams that can be realized only in the distant future. One of them was the vision of a united, democratic, safe and peaceful Europe.

Dismantling the Warsaw Pact in Prague was symbolic because Czechoslovakia was the victim of the only massive military operation on the part of the Pact - the invasion in August 1968. Typical was also the fate of "restructuring" of the Warsaw Pact. What started as perestroika ended with a complete dismantling. The same happened with the Soviet Union and with Communism itself. Such an outcome was inevitable, and it perhaps would be the same if some new Gorbachev tried to start reforming something unreformable. He could be reasonably sure it would also end with the total destruction of what he had set out to reform.

Historians trying to find traces and reflections of those historic moments in the European press of the time would be surprised how unimportant the journalists considered the events. Though the Eastern European press carried much material on the dismantling both the Warsaw Pact and Comecon, there was almost nothing in the Western European press. The International Herald Tribune of July 1, 1991, for instance, did not mention any summit. Not until the next day, on July 2, did the IHT publish a rather short report from Prague with a few quotations from speeches. No commentary was made on that day or, for that matter, even later.

June 1994